# Early Missouri Ancestors

## Vol. 2: From Newspapers, 1823-1832

*by*
*Lois Stanley*
*George F. Wilson*
*Maryhelen Wilson*

Please Direct All Correspondence and Book Orders to:

**Southern Historical Press, Inc.**
**PO Box 1267**
**375 West Broad Street**
**Greenville, S.C. 29602**


ISBN # 0-89308-433-6


*Printed in the United States of America*

# CONTENTS

The Intelligencer was first published in Howard County; in Franklin until 1826, from there to Fayette until 1830. At that point it moved to Columbia, in Boone County.

The Monitor was published in Fayette; it had a short life.

The Jeffersonian Republican was published in Jefferson City, the earliest surviving Cole County newspaper.

The Independent Patriot was published in Jackson, Cape Girardeau County; Jackson in the early days was the county's main center.

The Enquirer, the Beacon, and the Missouri Republican were all published in St. Louis.

While coverage varied, all of these newspapers reached well beyond their immediate areas. . . the St. Louis press, for example, noted events not only in immediately adjacent counties but in Lincoln, Marion, Callaway, Madison, Crawford, and others farther south.

Note: the abbreviation "JP" which appears frequently refers to the Justice of the Peace who signed the "stray" notice.

Newspapers may not always have been quite accurate, but they've
always provided a picture of the contemporary world that might not
otherwise be known.  Equally important, they have always focused on
one important item: __names__.  Names make news now; names made news in
Missouri more than 150 years ago.

So here, as in Volume I, we find our ancestors as the newspapers
found them.  A long-ago Benjamin who had been accused of burglary,
broke jail, was sought; he was "surly and fond of drink."  The
well-bred young ladies of the St. Louis Female Academy and the country
girls, unlettered but agile, who were catching stray horses in the
outlying counties.  Doctors and midwives, hatters and milliners.
Prosperous business men, runaway apprentices.  The careless who had
lost valuables, the honest who found and described them.

There are more than 2000 family names here, and about 4500 individuals.
We hope that some of yours are among them.

ABBAY, Jonathan - appraised a stray taken up by Nathaniel Riggs.   26 Mar 1831
     - "              by David Onstott.   13 Aug 1831
ABERNATHY, James R. - JP, Rocky Fork Twp Boone Co., stray taken up
                 by Reuben Riggs.   21 Jan 1823
ACRES, William - licensed to sell wine and spirits, Howard Co.   31 May 1827
ADAMS, David - JP, Boonville Twp Cooper Co., stray taken up by
                 Leven Cropper.   16 May 1828
   John - appraised a stray taken up by John Bybee.   12 Apr 1825
ADKINS, Jesse & Mary (Yercum) - divorce petition in the State Legislature.   15 Jan 1831
   Owen - licensed to sell wine and spirits, Clay Co.   20 May 1823
   Robert - appraised a stray taken up by James Kertley.   29 Mar 1825
AGEE, Matthew - Vause (Aux Vasse) Twp Callaway Co., took up a roan horse
     appraised at $18 by A. Lomax & John Coats. Bethel Allen JP.   16 Sep 1825
ALEXANDER, Samuel - defendant, suit for debt by William B. Means,
              Howard Co. Circuit Court.   7 Dec 1827
   Willis - appraised a stray taken up by Wm. McLaughlin.   29 Feb 1828
ALLCORN, James - JP, Franklin Twp Howard Co., stray taken up by
               Zachariah Benson.   16 Dec 1825
     - "       by Francis Whitlock.   20 Feb 1829
     - guardian of James Snoddy, petitions to sell real estate.   6 Sep 1827
ALLEN, Archibald - JP, Nine-Mile-Prairie Twp Callaway Co., stray taken
               up by Thomas Harrison.  -   19 Jun 1830
     - "       by Andrew Hamilton.   23 Jul 1831
     - "       by Willis W. Snell.   17 Mar 1832
   Bethel - JP, Elizabeth Twp Callaway Co., stray taken up by
               Samuel T. Moore.   5 Aug 1825
     - ", stray taken up by Matthew Agee in Aux Vasse Twp.   16 Sep 1825
     - " by Henry Brite in Elizabeth Twp.   6 Jul 1826
   Elijah and his mother, Jane, of Boone Co.; see Jesse T. Wood.   26 Apr 1825
   Isaac - appraised a stray taken up by Zebediah Baker.   6 Feb 1829
ALLISON, Hugh - appraised a stray taken up by John Rice.   25 Sep 1824
   John - appraised a stray taken up by Benjamin Johnson.   16 Nov 1826
ALORTON, Joseph - appraised a stray taken up by Jonathan Gum.   25 Jan 1826
ALSOP, Jefferson - will pay cash for a mulatto boy.   15 Jan 1824
   Thomas - advertises a "sporting sweepstakes" on Welch's track
               in October.   16 Sep 1823
     - licensed to operate a tavern, Howard Co.   16 Dec 1823
AMBRESS, William - appraised a stray taken up by James Harris.   24 Sep 1831
AMICK, George - Boon's Lick Twp Howard Co., took up a bay mare ae 4y
     appraised at $30 by David & Philip Amick. Geo. Chapman JP.   12 Apr 1825
ANDERSON, John - JP, PerceTwp Boone Co., stray taken up by John Grayum.   10 Aug 1826
   Elijah - appraised a stray taken up by Stephen Rogers.   3 Jul 1829
ANDREWS, John and Elizabeth (nee Slater) - petition for divorce in the
               State Legislature.   15 Jan 1831
   Thomas and William - offer copper and tinware on the south
               side of the Public Square, Boonville.   13 Feb 1824
     - dissolve partnership, Thomas to continue
               the business.   14 Sep 1826
ANGELL, William and Willis A. - appraised a stray taken up by
               Elijah Winn.   25 Jan 1828
ANTHONY, William K. - offers a farm for sale 4m sw of Columbia; 160 a.,
       30 cultivated; two "never-failing" springs.   9 Oct 1830
ARMSTRONG, William - JP, Fulton Twp Callaway Co., stray taken up
               by James Moore.   31 Jul 1830
     - "     by Lewis Day.   17 Mar 1832
ARNOLD, Price - licensed as a merchant, Howard Co.   15 May 1824
ATTEBERRY, Edward - Richmond Twp Howard Co., took up a sorrel colt ae 3y
     appraised by Crenshaw White & John D. Sandford.
               William Taylor JP.   15 Feb 1826
   James - notifies "Mrs. Mary" that he intends to petition for a
     divorce in the State Legislature.   14 Aug 1824
   William - Union Twp Ralls Co., took up an iron gray mare ae 2y
     appraised at $25 by John M. Burton & Thomas Kelly.
               John Burton JP.   27 Feb 1829
AUSTIN, Isaiah - Cedar Twp Boone Co., took up a bay mare ae 11y appraised
     at $20 by Jonathan Pace & Wilton Rucker. James Harris JP.   8 Dec 1832

MIN

AUSTIN, John - appraised a stray taken up by Anthony Owsley.                7 Jan 1832
        Joseph - appraised a stray taken up by Gilpin Tuttle.              23 Jul 1831
AVERETT, James J. - appraised a stray taken up by Thomas Patten.           26 Apr 1827
BADGER, J. B. - a dentist in Franklin, "in the white house on the
                                        bank of the river."               24 Apr 1824
BAKER, Henry - appraised a stray taken up by Napoleon B. Ferguson.          7 Apr 1832
       John - appraised a stray taken up by Philip Prather.                11 Dec 1829
       Moses - JP, Rocky Fork Twp Boone Co., stray taken up by
                                        Daniel Hurter.                      6 Aug 1831
       R. - Jackson Twp Monroe Co., took up a bright sorrel mare ae 2-3 y
            appraised at $20 by John Godman & Anderson Willis.
                                        Edward M. Holden JP               24 Mar 1832
       Samuel - paid $1 fine, Callaway Co. Circuit Court.                 14 Jan 1823
       Thomas - JP, Auxvasse Twp Callaway Co., stray taken up by
                                        Wm. McLaughlin.                   29 Feb 1828
       William - advertises a fulling mill 2m south of Columbia on         3 May 1827
                 the state road. Later: William M., Columbia.              7 Apr 1832
       Zebediah - Fort Osage Twp, Jackson Co., took up a sorrel mare
                  ae 9-10 y appraised at $20 by James Baxter & Isaac Allen. 6 Feb 1829
BALLINGER, G. L. - appraised a stray taken up by Thomas Harrison Sr.      29 Sep 1832
BANCROFT, Timothy - Collector, Clay Co.                                   20 May 1823
BANKS, William L. - Chariton Twp Chariton Co., took up a white mare ae 9y
                    appraised at $20 by Lewis White & Joshua Potter.
                                        Henry T. Williams JP.             14 Dec 1826
BANKSON, Rev. James - will preach at the Courthouse in Fayette.           19 Oct 1826
BARCLAY, Robert - offers a 160-acre farm for sale in Boone Co., 50 acres
                  in cultivation and fenced.                              19 June 1830
         William - of Union, Franklin Co., lost two trunks and a box,
                   aboard the Cumberland en route from St. Louis to
                   Chariton, supposed to land at Boonville.               14 Apr 1832
BARKWELL, Major - Rocky Fork Twp Boone Co., took up a sorrel horse ae 3y
                  appraised at $25 by Thomas Owens & George Varner.        7 Jul 1832
                                        Esom Hannon JP
BARNES, Abraham & Shadrach - received licenses to operate a ferry,
                                        Howard Co.                        16 Dec 1823
        Abraham - advertises "fall races" for owners of fine horses,
                  will race his "Tecumseh" on the Franklin course.        14 Aug 1829
        Benjamin - Cedar Twp Boone Co., took up a mule ae 4y, appraised
                   at $20 by Absalom McDaniel & Isaac Johnston.            8 Mar 1827
                                        William Shields JP.
        Brimsley - appraised a stray taken up by Edward Snow.              3 Nov 1832
        James - JP, Columbia Twp Boone Co., stray taken up by
                                        Daniel Mourning.                  25 Jun 1831
              - JP, Rocky Fork Twp Boone Co., stray taken up by Geo. Titus. 1 Oct 1831
        Thomas - licensed to operate a ferry, Howard Co.                  11 Dec 1829
        William - appraised a stray taken up by Mark Reavis.               5 Feb 1831
BARNS, Aquilla - Persia (sic) Twp Boone Co., took up a gray mare ae 6y
                 and an iron gray colt ae 1y, appraised at $32 total by
                 Robert Corlew & James Martin. John Slack JP.              8 Mar 1826
BARR, Robert S. -dissolved partnership with James I. Tilton and
                                        Joseph B. Howard.                  8 Mar 1826
BARRETT, Thomas L., partner of Shelton Jones, Columbia, jewelry and
                                        watch materials.                  28 May 1831
             - dissolves partnership with Jones, Barrett will
               continue the business.                                      8 Dec 1832
BARTEE, Asa - appraised a stray taken up by Daniel Lay.                   16 Jan 1829
BARTLEY, George - JP, Callaway Co., stray taken up by James Toney.        23 Jul 1831
              - "   by Peter Mason.                                        7 Jan 1832
        John - appraised a stray taken up by James Toney.                 23 Jul 1831
BASKET, James - Bourbon Twp Callaway Co., took up a sorrel horse ae 5y
                appraised at $45 by Austin White & Thomas Ferree.         18 Jun 1831
                                        Isaac Black JP.
BATES, William A. - Rocky Fork Twp Boone Co., took up a bay mare ae 13y
                    appraised at $22.50 by Zadock Riggs & Wm. Woodrough.
                                        James Fenton JP                    3 Aug 1826
BATTERTON, Moses - bankrupt, Boone Co.                                     1 Jan 1825
              - allowed money for the care of Alford Batterton, a
                person of unsound mind, Boone Co.                          1 Jan 1825

MIN                                     2

BAUGH, Michael - a watchmaker in Columbia.                                                    22 May 1830
BAWGH, William - Rocky Fork Twp Boone Co. took up a bright bay mare ae 3y.
           Appraisal not shown. Jesse Turner JP.                                              23 Sep 1825
BAXTER, James - appraised a stray taken up by Zebediah Baker.                                  6 Feb 1829
BEATY, Samuel - Tete Saline Twp Cooper Co., took up a bay horse ae 10-11y
           appraised at $40, appraisers not shown. James Collins JP.                          31 Jul 1824
BEAVIN, Theodore - appraised a stray taken up by Joseph Robnett.                               5 Jun 1830
BEISTRUP, Herman E. - Cold Neck Twp Cooper Co., took up a dapple gray
                      gelding ae 4y, appraised at $40 by George Cathey                         2 Jun 1826
                      & Samuel Gibbs. William Briant JP.
BELL, Mordecai - appraised a stray taken up by Peter Mason; signed "x."                        7 Jan 1832
BELT, Mrs. S. - milliner and mantua-maker in Fayette.                                         16 May 1828
BENSON, J. H. & Co. - in Franklin; medicines, drugs, paints, oils, etc.                       12 Dec 1828
       Dr. James H. - "now located in Franklin."                                              11 Jun 1825
                    - partner in drug store in Columbia with James C.
                      Boggs & Alexander M. Robinson.                                           17 Jul 1829
                    - dissolved partnership with Boggs.                                        12 Mar 1830
       Zachariah - Franklin Twp Howard Co., took up a brown mare ae 4y
                   appraised at $20 by Lewis Scott & Daniel Recter.                            16 Dec 1825
                                                          James Allcorn JP.
                 - offered a farm for sale 7m from Fayette, 400 acres,
                   60 acres cleared, a two-room dwelling house with                            12 Dec 1828
                   and two chimneys; also a horse mill.   /passage
BERRY, Caleb - appraised a stray taken up by George W. Burt.                                   27 Aug 1831
       John K. - JP, Nine-Mile-Prairie Twp Callaway Co., stray taken up
                                                          by Thomas Moxley.  _                 19 Jun 1830
               - " by John Lorton.                                                            10 Mar 1832
       Milton - appraised a stray taken up by Mark Reavis.                                      5 Feb 1831
       Thomas G. - testified in favor of Jesse T. Wood.                                       26 Apr 1825
                 - dissolved partnership with Oliver Parker, Columbia.                        10 Apr 1829
                 - asks his debtors to pay.                                                     5 Feb 1831
                 - again dissolves partnership with Parker.                                    1 Oct 1831
       Tyre - appraised a stray taken up by Josiah Short.                                     19 Feb 1831
BIBB, R. - offers four houses and lots in Columbia for sale.                                  18 Dec 1830
BILLET, Jacob - appraised a stray taken up by Walter Maxey.                                    26 Apr 1825
BINGHAM, Wyatt - a blacksmith in Franklin, occuping the shop formerly                         24 Jul 1824
                 occupied by M. Johnston.
BIRD, Greenup - representing James Scott, asks debtors to pay.                                 29 Jun 1826
      John - JP, Franklin Twp Howard Co., stray taken up by Jonathan Gum.                      25 Jan 1826
           - JP, Boons Lick Twp, stray taken up by Henry Raines.                               24 May 1827
BLACK, Isaac - JP, Bourbon Twp Callaway Co., stray taken up by John Duncan.                     9 Dec 1825
             - also by John Willingham (6 Mar 1829), Ninian Ridgway                            9 Oct 1830
             - also by James Basket (18 June 1831) and Joel Haynes                            29 Sep 1832
BLANSET, Peter - Sugar Creek Twp Randolph Co., took up a bright bay
                 filly ae 2y appraised at $28 by A. G. & Wm. S. Cochran.                       5 Feb 1831
                                                          Joseph Goodding JP.
BLOY, John - licensed to operate a tavern in Howard Co.                                        16 Dec 1823
           - offers a house for rent.                                                         "
BOGGS, David P. - alleged to have fraudulently obtained a note from
                                                          Robert Y. Fowler.                    2 Oct 182m
       James C. - partner of James H. Benson & Dr. Alexander Robinson
                  in a drug store in Columbia.                                                 17 Jul 1829
                - dissolves partnership with Benson.                                           12 Mar 1830
                - advertises as a druggist and chemist in Franklin.                            18 Sep 1830
       Thomas J. - a lawyer in Franklin, opposite the Intelligencer office.                   12 Jun 1824
BOONE, Edward - Nine-Mile-Prairie Twp Callaway Co., took up an iron gray
                horse appraised at $37.50 by James Fowler & Jeremiah                           4 Dec 1830
                Davis. Enoch Fruit JP.
       J. M. - paid a $15 fine in the Callaway Co. Circuit Court.                             14 Jan 1823
BOOZER, Henry - moves his tailoring business to New Franklin.                                 25 Sep 1829
BOSS, James - in Chariton; offers "new goods" from Philadelphia,                               8 May 1824
              Pittsburgh, & New Orleans.
BOSTICK, John - dissolves partnership with George Harrison.                                   23 Jul 1831
         Taliaferro - offers a "likely Negro woman" and her male child,                       23 Jul 1831
                      ae 2y, for sale.
BOUNDS, Obadiah - appraised a stray taken by John Smelser; signed "x."                         4 Sep 1829
        James - Sheriff of Lafayette Co., advertises for escaped                              11 Apr 1828
                prisoners Reed and Smith.

        MIN                3

```
BOUSFIELD, Henry - wants to buy " a likely Negro girl."                    13 Jan 1826
BOWAR, George - appraised a stray taken up by Thomas Harrison Jr.          20 Oct 1832
BOWLES, Benjamin - defendant in a mortgage foreclosure suit brought
               by Taylor Berry & Thomas Smith.                             8 Jul 1823
          - Chariton Twp Howard Co., took up a sorrel mare ae 5y
               appraised at $30 by James Douglass & Pleasant Ford.        20 Jul 1826
                                             E.V. Warren JP.
BOYES, William - appraised a stray taken up by John Lorton.                10 Mar 1832
BOZARTH, J. S. - appraised a stray taken up by Benj. Cornelius.            16 Jul 1825
     Joseph - Richmond Twp Howard Co., took up a sorrel horse ae 15y
               appraised at $12 by David Mead & A. M. Johnson.            28 Mar 1828
                                             Wm. B. Means JP.
     J. H. - Randolph Co.; testifies as to recent disturbances
               by Indians in the area.                                    18 Sep 1829
BRADFORD, Hervey H. - his land was sold for debt.                          18 Jan 1827
BRADLEY, James - appraised a stray taken up by Walter Maxey.               26 Apr 1825
BRANNIN, Richard - bankrupt, Howard Co.                                    18 Dec 1824
BRASHEAR, Joseph - appointed to sell seminary lands in Moniteau Twp,
                                             with Wm. Brown.                8 Apr 1823
BRAY, William - St. Louis; found guilty of murdering J. Griffin,
               sentenced to two years in prison.                          11 Sep 1829
BROANT, William - JP, Cold Neck Twp Cooper Co., stray taken up by
                                             Herman Bedstrup.               2 Jun 1826
BRIDGES, James - a pauper, Howard Co.                                      16 Dec 1823
     P. S. - New Franklin; wants two or three journeymen carpenters.       25 Sep 1829
     Rev. Samuel - will preach in Fayette Tuesday.                          2 Nov 1826
BRISCOE, John - JP, Clear Creek Twp Cooper Co, stray taken up by
                                             Andrew Wallace.                4 Mar 1823
          - " by John Rice.                                                25 Sep 1824
     Ralph D. - SP, Spencer Twp Ralls Co., stray taken up by
                                             Robert Gary.                  18 Jun 1831
BRITE, Henry - courthouse & jail commissioner, Callaway Co.                14 Jan 1823
          - Elizabeth Twp, Callaway Co., took up a bay mare ae 12-15 y
               appraised at $15 by Irvine Hockaday & John Coats.            6 Jul 1826
                                             Bethel Allen JP.
BROADHURST, John - appraised a stray taken up by Daniel Munro.             25 Mar 1823
BROOKS, William - Union Twp Ralls Co., took up a bright sorrel mare
               appraised at $30 by Joseph Davis & Elijah Shanklin.        12 Aug 1825
                                             John Burton JP.
BROWN, Francis - Franklin Twp Howard Co., took up a brown colt appraised
               at $15 by B. C. Fugett & Elias Ware. N.S. Burckhartt JP    27 Feb 1829
     Joseph - appraised a stray taken up by Wm. Wright.                    14 Dec 1827
     William - appointed to sell seminary lands in Moniteau Twp,
                                             with Joseph Brashear.          8 Apr 1823
BROWNEJOHN, Samuel - wants to hire a Negro man or boy.                      6 Mar 1829
          - testifies that Potter's Vegetable Catholicon
                                             cured his scrofula.          29 May 1829
          - John Ringo warns the public not to accept a note given
               him by Brownejohn.                                          4 Sep 1829
     William - a suicide (shot himself) in Franklin.                        1 May 1830
BRUFFEE, James - defendant in a mortgage foreclosure suit by James Bryton. 13 May 1823
BRUNT, John - appraised a stray taken up by Lovell Snowden.                18 Mar 1823
BRYAN, Littleton - Columbia, offers a reward for a strayed bay mare.       23 Jun 1832
BRYANT, Richard - appraised a stray taken up by William Patrick.          26 Mar 1831
     William - Cote sans Dessein Twp Callaway Co., on Cedar Creek,
               took up a bay horse appraised at $30 by Jeremiah King       7 Jan 1823
               & John Stokes. Adam Hope JP.
          - fined $10 in the Callaway Co. Court.                           6 Jan 1824
BRYTON, James - plaintiff, mortgage foreclosure suit against James Bruffee. 13 May 1823
BUCKLAR, Martin G. - appraised a stray taken up by John Lewis.            17 Mar 1832
BUIE, Daniel - a pauper, Howard Co.                                        16 Dec 1823
BUMGARDNER, J. & L. - "new goods" in Fayette. . .dry goods, groceries,
               china, Queensware, etc.                                    11 Dec 1829
BUNTON, Elijah - Jackson Twp Monroe Co., took up a sorrel horse ae 20y
               appraised at $4 by John Curry & James B. Mathis.           11 Jun 1831
                                             John S. McGee JP.
BURCH, Jonathan - Clerk and treasurer of the Ray County Court.            25 Feb 1823
          MIN
                                   4
```

BURCH, William S. - appraised a stray taken up by Elijah Foley.                    12 Aug 1825
BURCKHARTT, J. R. - appraised a stray taken up by Wm. Sibert.                       5 Dec 1828
      N. S. - JP, Franklin Twp Howard Co., stray taken up by                        5 Dec 1828
                                                        Wm. Sibert.
BURNHAM, Henry - Dr. Oliver Rice had his office in                                 29 Apr 1823
                                        Burnam's home near Fayette.
              - licensed to operate a tavern in Howard Co.                         16 Dec 1823
BURRES, Thomas - advertises for his lost work steers, 6m north of Franklin.        17 Jun 1823
BURT, George - appraised a stray taken up by Wm. McCormack.                         6 Nov 1830
            - Nine-Mile-Prairie Twp Callaway Co., took up an iron gray
                mare appraised at $15 by John G. Galbreath & Caleb Berry.          27 Aug 1831
      John A. - JP, Nine-Mile-Prairie Twp Callaway Co., stray taken up            27 Aug 1831
                                                by George W. Burt.
BURTON, John M. - appraised a stray taken up by Wm. Atteberry.                     27 Feb 1829
      John - JP, Union Twp Ralls Co., stray taken up by Wm. Brooks.                12 Aug 1825
      " by Jordan Sizemore (23 Aug 1827), Jacob Whittenburgh                       15 Aug 1828
      " by Wm. Atteberry (27 Feb 1829), and David E. Sloan                          5 Feb 1830
BYBEE, John - Bonne Femme Twp Howard Co., took up an iron gray horse               12 Apr 1825
                ae 4y appraised at $22 by John Adams & Isaac D. Hargus.
                                                John Myers JP.
      William - Salt Fork Twp Ralls Co., JP, stray taken up by                    11 Dec 1830
                                                James B. Reavis.
BYLER, Joseph - offers $25 reward for runaway Negro Frederick, 7 miles             5 May 1826
                north of Boonville.
CALLAHAN, Thomas - Columbia Twp Boone Co., took up an iron gray filly              17 Mar 1832
                appraised at $6.50 by Samuel Campbell & Joshua Sweeney.
                                                James Kirtley JP.
CALLAWAY, Charles - appraised a stray taken up by Henry Raines.                    24 May 1827
      James - JP, Cedar Twp Boone Co., stray taken up by Walter Maxey.             26 Apr 1825
            - " by Thornton Hames (2 June 1826), Gilpin Tuttle                      1 May 1829
                and by Tuttle again                                                23 Jul 1831
CALVERT, John - appraised a stray taken up by Leven Cropper.                       16 May 1825
CAMPBELL, Amelia P. - sues David H. for divorce by next friend Nelson             15 Mar 1826
                Pepper, Howard Co. Circuit Court.
      Jesse M. - fined $5, Callaway Co. Court.                                      6 Jan 1824
      Samuel - appraised a stray taken up by Thomas Callahan.                      17 Mar 1832
      Thomas M. & Co. - "new goods" in Old Franklin.                                9 Oct 1829
                - dissolved partnership with John D. Stothart.                     25 Dec 1829
CARPENTER, William - JP, Tabbe Two Lafayette Co., stray taken up by               26 Jun 1829
                                                Moses Johnson.
            - " by John Smelser.                                                    4 Sep 1829
CARTER, Edward - appraised a stray taken up by Wm. Newman.                         29 Jul 1825
CARY, Armenius - appraised a stray taken up by Elbert Linch.                       21 Apr 1826
      Jefferson - Lexington Twp Lafayette Co., took up a yellow bay mare           29 Feb 1828
                ae 3y appraised at $16 by Isaac Wiley & Michael
                Turnage. James Fletcher JP.
      John - appraised a stray taken up by Robert Hinkston.                         4 Sep 1824
CASEY, Christopher & Hardin - appraised a stray taken up by Jonathan Ramsey.       15 Feb 1826
CATHEY, George - appraised a stray taken up by Herman Bedstrup.                     2 Jun 1826
CAVE, Catherine - appointed guardian for Reuben Cave, Boone Co.                     5 Apr 1825
      Henry Jr. - appraised a stray taken up by Macam Purcel.                       4 Aug 1832
      Richard - JP, Boone Co., stray taken up by James Kertley.                    ;5 Apr 1825
      William - Appraised a stray taken up by James Kertley.                         "
CHAMBERLAIN, Rev. H. - will preach in Fayette the second Sunday in July.           19 Jun 1819
CHAMBERS, Benjamin - clerk of the Saline County Court.                             25 Sep 1824
      Joseph - appraised a stray taken up by John M. Savage.                        3 Nov 1832
CHANDLER, Isaac - appraised a stray taken up by John Duncan.                        9 Dec 1825
CHAPMAN, George - JP, Franklin Twp Howard Co., stray taken up by                   25 Mar 1823
                                                Daniel Munro.
            - ", Boon's Lick Twp, stray by George Amick.                           12 Apr 1825
            - " by Jonathan Gum.                                                   24 Mar 1826
CHARLTON, Silas - appraised a stray taken up by John J. Clark.                     18 Nov 1823
CHICK, William - see Ann PULLIAM.
CHILCOAT, John - appraised a stray taken up by Reuben Smith; signed "x."           15 Jan 1824
CHITWOOD, James - Ralls Co., took up a black horse ae 10-12 appraised at           30 Apr 1831
                $50 by Wm. Greathouse & Elizure D. Webster.
                                                Wm. Forman JP.
CLARK, E. L. & Co. - new book store on N. Main St., St. Louis.                     14 Apr 1832

        MIN
                                        5

CLARK, Isaac & Reuben - appraised a stray taken up by Christian Hoozer.          17 Apr 1824
John B. - attorney and counselor-at-law, Fayette.                               24 Apr 1824
John J. - Moreau Twp Cole Co., took up a brown mare ae 6y
    appraised at $8 by James Claybrook & Silas Charlton.        18 Nov 1823
                     Drury Davis JP.
Robert P. - wants his lost books returned.                                       23 Sep 1825
       - his house and lot in Boonville are for sale.                22 May 1830
Susan S. - offers reward for a bay mare strayed or stolen from
    John B. Clark's stable in Fayette.                           27 Jun 1828
CLARKE, John G. - appraised a stray taken up by Robert Gary.                     18 Jun 1831
CLAYBROOK, James - appraised a stray taken up by John J. Clark.                  18 Nov 1823
CLENDENNON, Daniel - found a skiff near the mouth of the Osage River &
    Moreau Creek containing clothing, mostly old, and            11 Jun 1825
    a gourd of whiskey.
CLEVELAND, J. T. - appraised a stray taken up by Wm. Patrick.                     3 May 1827
       - took charge of the Fayette Academy.                       11 Apr 1828
       - proudly displayed two enormous beets he had grown.         3 Apr 1829
CLOPTON, F. S. - "handsome assortment of dry goods," also hardware,
    glassware, etc. in Fayette.                                    1 Mar 1827
Fleet S. - licensed as an auctioneer, Howard Co.                                 31 May 1827
COATS, Allen - Perce Twp Boone Co., took up a dark bay mare ae 3y appraised
    at $20 by Henry Coats & Thomas Ginnins. John Corlew JP.     16 Apr 1831
John - appraised a stray by Matthew Agee.                                        16 Sep 1825
" by Henry Brite.                                                                 6 Jul 1826
COCHRAN, A. G. & William S. - appraised a stray taken up by Peter Blanset.        5 Feb 1831
James - appraised a stray taken up by John Wheldon.                              11 Jan 1825
Rev. William - will preach at Fayette.                                           20 Jun 1828
William P. - Secretary of the Boone Co. Temperance Association.                   9 Apr 1831
COLGAN, Daniel - appraised a stray taken up by James Steward.                     3 Jul 1824
COLIER, David - runaway apprentice of Charles Hardin, tanner, Columbia.          14 Aug 1824
COLLIER - ", this time described as about 19, small, red-haired,
    freckled; Hardin offers 12½¢ reward.                        19 Jun 1830
Michael - licensed to operate a tavern, Howard Co.                               16 Dec 1823
Peyton - appraised a stray taken up by Wm. McDow; signed "x."                    17 Mar 1832
COLLINS, James - JP, Tete Saline Twp Cooper Co., stray taken up by
    Samuel Beaty.                                               31 Jul 1824
James L. - among a group entering the Santa Fe trade, leaving
    Blue Spring 1 June.                                          8 May 1829
Lewis - appraised a stray taken up by David Gordon.                              27 Mar 1829
COLMAN, Henry - advertises tinware, sheet iron, etc., in Franklin.               19 June 1829
    - moves to New Franklin.                                    25 Sep 1829
COMFORT, Dr. S. W. - "dental surgery" in Columbia.                               21 May 1831
COOK, Grove - took up a bright bay horse ae 3y appraised at $25 by
    Wm. Pennington & Wm. Douglass. (Boone Co.)                   1 Feb 1827
               John Henderson JP.
COOLEY, James - appraised a stray taken up by Charles Hatfield.                  17 Apr 1829
COOPER, Dr. L. - located on the ne corner of the Public Square, Franklin.         3 Apr 1824
COPPAGE, Simeon - Missouri Twp Boone Co., took up a black horse ae 10y
    appraised at $25 by Richard Jones & Landon Snell.            7 Apr 1832
               J. W. Hickam JP
CORLEW, James and Robert - among a group entering the Santa Fe trade,
    leaving Blue Spring 1 June.                                  8 May 1829
John P. - Perce Twp Boone Co., JP, stray taken up by Allen Coats.                16 Apr 1831
" by Tyre March.                                                                  3 Dec 1831
Robert - appraised a stray taken up by Aquilla Barnes.                            8 Mar 1826
CORNELIUS, Benjamin - Moniteau Twp Howard Co., took up a sorrel mare
    ae 12-13 appraised at $23 by John Bozarth &                  16 Jul 1825
    David Mead. Wm. B. Means JP.
Jesse - next friend of Alzada Pharis in her divorce suit.                         5 Apr 1827
William - partner of William H. White in a new dry goods
    store in Columbia.                                           6 Nov 1830
COTTEE, Susannah - plaintiff in a mortgage foreclosure suit against
    George Tennelle, Saline Co.                                  4 Sep 1824
COX, George - appraised a stray taken up by John Willingham.                      6 Aug 1831
CRAIG, Hiram - JP, Prairie Twp Chariton Co., stray taken up by John Fowler.      14 Dec 1827
Nat - appraised a stray taken up by Andrew Hamilton.                             23 Jul 1831
CRAVENS, Charles M. - one of a group entering the Santa Fe trade,
    leaving Blue Spring on 1 June.                               8 May 1829

MIN

6

CRAWFORD, George - JP, Boonville Twp Cooper Co., stray taken up     3 Nov 1832
                 by John M. Savage.
CRAWLEY, Major Jonathan - suicide by hanging, Howard Co.      7 Apr 1832
CREED, Augustine - Ralls Co., south fork of the Salt River near
           Benjamin Young, $20 reward for stolen bay stud horse.    14 Aug 1830
CREWS, Dr. S. T. - opens office in Fayette.           6 Jul 1826
        Samuel T. - $10 reward for bay roan horse, strayed or stolen.   20 Feb 1829
CRISP, Redden - Sni-a-Bar Twp Lillard Co., took up a gray horse ae 15y
      and a sorrel mare ae 5y, total appraisal $25 by William     21 Jan 1823
      Renick & Jonathan Hicklin. Henry Renick JP.
CRISWELL, Robert - appraised a stray taken up by Samuel T. Guthrie.   29 May 1824
CROLEY, William - Chariton Twp Howard Co., took up a brown mare ae 3y
      appraised at $40 by Obed Swearingen & Sarshel Woods.    29 Feb 1828
                      A. C. Woods JP.
CROPPER, Leven - Saline Twp Cooper Co., JP, stray taken up by Wm. Gibson.   21 Dec 1827
            - Boonville Twp Cooper Co., took up two mares appraised
      at $55 by John Calvert & James Farris. David Adams JP.   16 May 1828
CROWE, James - a typesetter; notice to public to prevent him (and
      James S. Linn) from "imposing himself on honest people."   23 May 1828
CROWLEY, Jeremiah - Ray Co., asks to be released as security for Meddows
      Vanderpool, who has left the United States.    22 Aug 1828
CROWSON, Thomas - Columbia Twp Boone Co., took up a sorrel mare ae 6y
      appraised at $25 by A. W. Turner & James Sutton.    24 Mar 1832
                  Warren Woodson JP.
CROYSDALE, Abraham - partnership with Samuel Moore and Edward M. Samuel
      (in Liberty) dissolved; Moore & Samuel to continue.    5 Feb 1831
CRUMP, Daniel - appraised a stray taken up by James Weldon.   16 Jul 1825
CUNNINGHAM, Mark - appraised a stray taken up by Daniel Vinston.   11 Nov 1823
        Wright - road reviewer, Ray Co.    25 Feb 1823
CURD, J. - JP, Callaway Co., stray taken up by Willis W. Snell.   14 Jul 1832
      - " by Thomas Harrison Sr. in Salt River Twp.    29 Sep 1832
CURL, Richmond - advertises the horse "Georgian" at stud (with Miner
      Neale & George W. Osborne).    19 Mar 1831
CURRIN, Waddy T. - moved to his new brick store.   25 Jan 1827
CURRY, John - appraised a stray taken up by Elijah Bunton.   11 Jun 1831
CURTIS, Elijah - appraised a stray taken up by John McGaugh.   30 Jul 1831
CUSTUER, John - JP, Montgomery Co., stray taken up by Edward Ford.   10 Mar 1832
DADE, John - selling the school lands in Franklin Twp, Howard Co.,
             with Samuel Teter.    25 Feb 1823
      - JP, Coleneck Twp Cooper Co., stray taken up by Henry Hatfield.   19 Dec 1828
DALY, James - opens a school in Franklin, will take 60-80 students.   5 Jun 1824
      John - licensed to sell wines and spirits, Howard Co.   31 May 1827
      Laurence J. - school superintendent, Franklin.    7 Jan 1823
DAVIS, Benjamin - appraised a stray taken up by James B. Reavis.   11 Dec 1830
      Drury - JP, Moreau Twp Cole Co., stray taken up by John J. Clark.   18 Nov 1823
      Henry C. - appraised a stray taken up by Eli Glascock.   22 Mar 1827
      James - appraised a stray taken up by Ezra Fox.    9 Jul 1831
      Jonathan - appraised a stray taken up by Edward Boone.    4 Dec 1830
      Joseph - appraised a stray taken up by Wm. Brooks.   12 Aug 1825
      - attorney in Fayette.    19 Jun 1829
      Josiah - appraised a stray taken up by Samuel Hardin.   25 Dec 1829
      Lawrence E. - opens Concord School, 8 miles from Columbia
           on the road to Fulton.    26 May 1832
      Reese - JP, Union Twp Monroe Co., stray taken up
           by Rumsey Saling.    23 Jul 1831
      Robert - JP, Cote sans Dessein Twp Callaway Co., stray taken
          up by Thomas Davis.    29 Sep 1832
      Rev. Samuel - will preach at Fayette "this evening by
          early candlelight."    16 Aug 1827
      Thomas - Cote sans Dessein Twp, Callaway Co., took up a bright
          sorrel mare ae 10-11 y appraised at $30 by Hugh H.    29 Sep 1832
          McGary & Henry Harper. Robert Davis JP.
DAY, Achley - appraised a stray taken up by Thomas Harrison Jr.   20 Oct 1832
      Lewis - Nine-Mile-Prairie Twp Callaway Co., took up a bay colt ae 2y
      appraised at $20 by Daniel Nolley & James D. Fisher.   17 Mar 1832
                 Wm. Armstrong JP.
      - JP, Salt River Twp, stray taken up by Thomas Harrison Jr.   20 Oct 1832

MIN        7

DENNIS, John B. - Missouri Twp Boone Co., took up a bay horse ae 5y
    appraised at $50 by James Hopper & John Williamson.      23 Jun 1832
                          Dabney Pettis JP
DENNY, James - Prairie Twp Howard Co., took up a bay mare ae 3y
    appraised at $12 by Thomas Patterson & Henry Serichfield.    17 Apr 1824
                          George Jackson JP.
    - took up a bay colt appraised at $20 by W. B. McLean
    & Wm. Adams. John Harvey JP.                  11 Jan 1828
DENSMAN, Thomas - Rocky Fork Twp Boone Co., took up a bay horse ae 4-5y
    appraised at $25 by Ammon Hicks & Wm. Dun.         25 Feb 1823
DEWALL, Daniel - road reviewer, Ray Co.                25 Feb 1823
DILLON, Dr. Hugh - opens an office in Franklin.           10 Aug 1826
DODSON, John - appraised a stray taken up by Lovell Snowden.     18 Mar 1823
DONAGHE, H. M. - a Negro man for sale, Columbia.           26 Feb 1831
DONALDSON, Robert - took up a dark roan horse ae 8y, Jefferson Twp,
    Monroe Co.; appraised at $45 by Daniel M. Swain &      11 Jun 1831
    Wm. Tally. Asaph E. Hubbard JP.
    - with others, offers lots for sale in Florida, Mo.      16 Apr 1831
DORRIS, Stephen Co. - County Court Justice, Callaway Co.      14 Jan 1823
DOUGLASS, Isham - appraised a stray taken up by Samuel Dyer.    12 Aug 1825
    James - appraised a stray taken up by Benjamin Bowles.    20 Jul 1826
    William - appraised a stray taken up by Grove Cook.     1 Feb 1827
DOW, James - advertises for a journeyman tailor.         12 Jun 1824
    - will pay cash for a likely mulatto boy, age 10-12.    12 Oct 1827
    - moved to Fayette.                      1 May 1829
    - moved to Boonville.                 5 Feb 1830
DRINKAIRD, William - lost a land certificate (Twp 52, Range 16).   22 Feb 1825
DUESON, Thomas - appraised a stray taken up by Jonathan Gum.     15 Feb 1826
DULE, Abraham - appraised a stray taken up by Robert Sconce.    18 Jan 1827
DUNBAR, Alexander - Tabo Grove, Lafayette Co., offers a $10 reward for
    a chestnut sorrel horse, strayed or stolen.       4 Jan 1828
DUNCAN, James - offers $25 reward for runaway Negro, Jim, Franklin.   11 Nov 1825
    John - Bourbon Twp Callaway Co., took up a yellow bay horse
    appraised at $30 by Wm. Edwards & Isaac Chandler.      9 Dec 1825
                          Isaac Black JP.
DUNKIN, David H. - appraised a stray taken up by Thomas Harrison.   19 Jun 1830
DUNN, James - appraised a stray taken up by Gilpin Tuttle.     1 May 1829
    - " by James Harris.                     24 Sep 1831
DYER, Samuel - Nine-Mile-Prairie Twp Callaway Co., took up a small black
    mare ae 8-9y appraised at $27 by Daniel Henderson &    12 Aug 1825
    Isham Douglass. Thomas Harrison JP.
    William H. - will buy tobacco, Callaway Co.        29 Feb 1828
    - wants "12 to 15 likely Negroes," Fulton.      13 Nov 1829
    - Miss Wales resumes her school at his house, near Fulton.
    He will board 6 to 8 young ladies, $40 for five months.   3 Nov 1832
EADS, Jesse - Moniteau Twp Cole Co., took up a black mare 2y past,
    appraised at $26.50 by John Miller & Thomas Murray.    7 Jan 1823
                         Joseph Inglish JP.
EARLS see Sam SAMUEL.
EARICKSON, Richard - Chariton Twp Howard Co., took up a dark roan mare
    ae 3y appraised at $25 by Wm. Wright & Thomas Perry.    9 Jan 1829
                         Wm. B. Warren JP.
ECKERY, William - of St. Charles, testified in favor of Jesse T. Wood.   26 Apr 1825
EDWARDS, William - appraised a stray taken up by John Duncan.    9 Dec 1825
    - a journeyman tailor in St. Charles, in jail for
    allegedly stealing a letter containing $348.65.     5 Feb 1831
ELLINGTON, Alexander - Missouri Twp Boone Co., took up a bright bay mare
    ae 4y appraised at $30 by R. M. Hatton &         30 Jun 1832
    Stephen G. Evans. John Henderson JP.
ELLIOTT, David - appraised a stray taken up by Joseph Montgomery.   19 Apr 1825
    Eppy - appraised a stray taken up by Josiah Short.    19 Feb 1831
    Harrison S. - runaway apprentice of Nathan Glasgow. Age about 17,
    dark hair and eyes, stout, lisps, is "very bold."    3 Dec 1831
    J. W. - appraised a stray taken up by Henry Raines.    24 May 1827
    Reuben - appraised a stray taken up by George Sexton.   16 Jun 1832
    Reuben and Elizabeth - their land sold for debt.     7 Apr 1832
ELLIS, Benjamin Jr. - Loutre Twp Montgomery Co., took up an iron gray mare
    ae 2y appraised at $15 by Jacob L. Sharp &      16 Dec 1825
    Daniel Graham. Amos (Amor?) Kibbe JP.

    MIN           8

ELLIS, James Jr - appraised a stray taken up by Cornelius Howard;  6 Jan 1826
                              signed "x."
ELMORE, C. - found a red morocco pocketbook between Franklin & Chariton.  2 Aug 1827
ENDECOTT, Albert - runaway apprentice of Lewis Scott & Jeremiah Magnor,  16 Jan 1830
    Liberty. Age 18, 5'5" tall, dark hair and eyes.
ENYART, David - Richmond Twp Howard Co., took up a gray horse ae 3y  12 Jul 1827
    appraised at $18 by John H. Mobley & Wm. Roberts.
                         Wm. Taylor JP.
ESTES, Ambrose C. - appraised a stray taken up by Samuel Pace.  3 Dec 1831
EVANS, Andrew - offers "a likely Negro girl about 12," for sale, Fayette.
    John - appraised a stray taken up by Benjamin Johnson.  10 Aug 1826
    Loverance - appraised a stray taken up by Jonathan Finnell.  20 Feb 1829
    Stephen C. - appraised a stray taken up by Alexander Ellington.  30 Jun 1832
EWENS, John - appraised a stray taken up by Abraham Winscott.  5 Feb 1831
EWING, Chatham Sr. - Lafayette Co., took up a bright sorrel mare ae 4y  9 Dec 1825
    appraised at $35 by Burton L. Renick & Wm. H.
    Galbraith. Henry Renick JP.
    Rev. Finis - to preach at Cooper Co. Branch Bible Society.  12 Apr 1825
    Patrick - road overseer, Callaway Co.  14 Jan 1823
    W. Y. C. - JP, Clay Twp Lafayette Co., stray taken up by  10 Aug 1826
                       John McGlothlin.
          - " by James Murray.  23 Jun 1832
FARIS, James - appraised a stray taken up by Leven Cropper.  16 May 1828
FENTON, James E. - JP, Boone Co., stray taken up by Hugh French.  12 May 1826
    - alleged to have "fraudulently obtained" bonds from  23 Dec 1830
                        Berry G. Griffin.
    - JP, Rocky Fork Twp Boone Co., stray taken up by Wm. Bates. 3 Aug 1826
FERGUSON, John - fined $5 in the Callaway Co. Court.  6 Jan 1824
    Moses - fined $5 in the Callaway Co. Court.  18 Dec 1824
    Napoleon B. - Cote sans Dessein Twp Callaway Co., took up a  7 Apr 1832
    dark brown mare ae 9-10y appraised at $15 by
    Isaac Langley & Henry Baker. Henry Neill JP.
FERREE, Thomas - appraised a stray taken up by Ninian Ridgway.  9 Oct 1830
    - " by James Basket.  18 Jun 1831
FERRY, Calvin L. - attorney, partner of Jesse T. Wood.  8 Jan 1831
FERRIER, Nathaniel - appraised a stray taken up by Wm. McLaughlin.  29 Feb 1828
FEWELL, Rhodias - appraised a stray taken up by Talton Turner.  27 Feb 1828
FIELDER, John - appraised a stray taken up by James Murray.  23 Jun 1832
FINDLEY, Jona. S. - school superintendent in Franklin, brother of the  7 Jan 1823
                    governor of Pennsylvania.
FINLEY, Asa - Saline Co., offers $10 reward for return of Negro Sy.  4 Sep 1824
    - again offers reward for "Sie," this time $20.  28 Dec 1826
    - JP, Arrow Rock Twp, stray taken up by Polly Harvy.  11 Jun 1831
FINNELL, Jonathan - Prairie Twp Howard Co., took up a strawberry roan  20 Feb 1829
    filly appraised at $25 by Loverance Evans & Wm.
    Finnell. A. Q. Thomson JP.
    William - appraised a stray taken up by Asa Kerly.  12 Jul 1827
FISHER, Abraham - appraised a stray taken up by Abner Weaver; signed"x."  14 Aug 1829
    Caleb - Clear Creek Twp Cooper Co., took up a dark bay horse  26 May 1826
    ae 4y appraised at $20 by Mansfield Hatfield & James
    Harper. Robert Steel JP.
    James D. - appraised a stray taken up by Lewis Day.  17 Mar 1832
    John - appraised a stray taken up by Harmon Smelser.  2 May 1828
    Thomas - JP, Callaway Co., stray taken up by Elijah Stephens.  11 Dec 1824
FLEMING, Peter - appraised a stray taken up by John M. Savage.  3 Nov 1832
FLETCHER, James - JP, Lexington Twp Lafayette Co., stray taken up  21 Apr 1826
                    by Elbert Linch.
    - " by Jefferson Cary.  29 Feb 1828
    Mordecai - appraised a stray taken up by Tyre March.  3 Dec 1831
FLINN, Luke - appraised a stray taken up by Edward Ford.  10 Mar 1832
FOLEY, Elijah - Missouri Twp Boone Co., took up a bay horse ae 4y  12 Aug 1825
    appraised at $18 by Wm. S. Burch & Wm. Harris.
                    John Henderson JP.
FORD, David - runaway apprentice of cabinet-maker Elijah Mock. Age  16 Nov 1826
    about 18, sallow, deformed leg. "May have gone to Hurricane."
    Edward - Montgomery Co., took up a bay mare ae 2y appraised at $20  10 Mar 1832
    by Luke Flinn & James Jones. John Custuer JP.
    Pleasant - appraised a stray taken up by Benjamin Bowles.  20 Jul 1826

FORD, Thomas - of St. Charles, testifies in favor of Jesse T. Wood.     26 Apr 1825
FORMAN, William - JP, Ralls Co., stray taken up by James Chitwood.     30 Apr 1831
FOWLER, John M. - Prairie Twp Chariton Co., took up a sorrel mare ae 4y
     appraised at $20 by Abraham Lock & John W. Gentry.     14 Dec 1827
                       Hiram Craig JP.
   Robert Y. - warns the public not to accept a note he gave David P.
     Boggs which he says was "fraudulently obtained."     2 Oct 1824
FOX, Ezra- appraised a stray taken up by Jordan Sizemore.     15 Aug 1828
     - " by Jacob Whittenburgh (15 Aug 1828) & James B. Reavis     11 Dec 1830
     - Union Twp, Ralls Co., took up two strays appraised at $40 by
     Elliott Willbourn & Jordan Sizemore. Jacob Whittenburgh JP.     29 Jan 1831
     - took up a sorrel mare ae 3y appraised at $30 by Jordan
     Sizemore & James Davis.  Whittenburgh JP.     9 Jul 1831
   James C. - appraised a stray taken up by David E. Sloan.     5 Feb 1830
FRAKER, George - appraised a stray taken up by Charles Litrell.     15 May 1824
     - " by David E. Sloan.     5 Feb 1830
FRENCH, Charles - dissolves partnerhip with George Tompkins.     15 May 1824
   Hugh - Boone Co., took up a roan filly appraised at $20 by George
     Tally & David Wilson.  James E. Fenton JP.     ·12 May 1826
FRISTOE, Markham - Sheriff of Lillard Co.     14 Aug 1824
FRUIT, Enoch - road reviewer, Callaway Co.     14 Jan 1823
     - JP, Nine-Mile-Prairie Twp Callaway Co., stray taken up
     by Edward Boone.     4 Dec 1830
FUGATE, James - Spencer Twp Ralls Co., took up a chestnut sorrel mare
     appraised at $24 by James Underwood & Solomon Onstott.     13 Aug 1831
                    Peter Grant JP.
FUGETT, B. C. - appraised a stray taken up by Francis Brown.     27 Feb 1829
GAGE, Thomas P. - his land on sale for debt.     18 Jan 1827
GAITHER, Mrs. Mary - her former house and lot in Fayette for sale or
     trade for property in Columbia.     29 May 1830
GALBRAITH, William H. - appraised a stray taken up by Chatham Ewing Sr.     9 Dec 1825
GALBREATH, John G. - appraised  a stray taken up by George W. Burt.
GARMAND, Leonard - paid a $1 fine in Callaway Co. Circuit Court.     14 Jan 1823
GARNER, Jesse W. - Captain of the Fayette Guards.     10 May 1827
GARNETT, John - dissolves partnership with William Provines, Garnett
     will continue the business.     17 Sep 1831
GARRET, William B. - Aux Vasse Twp Callaway Co., took up a bay horse
     ae 7-8y appraised at $22.50 by Thomas Kitchings &     8 Dec 1832
     James Shannon.  James Stewart JP.
GARTIN, Hugh - Moreau Twp Cole Co., JP, stray taken up by Wm. Newman.     29 Jul 1825
GARY, Gideon - asks his debtors to settle up as he intends to move to
     St. Louis on 25 August.     5 Aug 1823
   Robert - Spencer Twp Ralls Co., took up a gray mare ae 7y appraised
     at $47.50 by John G. Clarke & Aru Lanicle; Ralph D. Briscoe JP.18 Jun 1831
   Sarah - advertises her household and kitchen furniture for sale -
     chairs, tables, bedsteads, stove, bureau, a large press.     10 Apr 1824
GASLIN, William - appraised a stray taken up by John Grayum.     10 Aug 1826
GEE, Morris and William - appraised a stray taken up by Mark Noble.     18 Jan 1828
GENTRY, Bartlett and Nicholas - among a group entering the Santa Fe trade,
     leaving Blue Spring 1 June.     8 May 1829
   David M. - appraised a stray taken up by Josiah Short.     4 Dec 1824
   John W. - appraised a stray taken up by John M. Fowler.     14 Dec 1827
   Reuben E. - offers 160 acres for sale, two miles from Franklin.     21 Oct 1825
GIBBS, Robert F. - appraised a stray taken up by John Willingham.     6 Aug 1831
   Samuel - appraised a stray taken up by Herman Bedstrup.     2 Jun 1826
GIBSON, John - fined $1 in the Callaway Co. Court.     6 Jan 1824
   William - Saline Twp Cooper Co., took up a mule ae 11y appraised
     at $27.50 by William Houx & David Lilley; Levin Cropper JP.21 Dec 1827
GILBREATH, Hugh - licensed to operate a ferry, Howard Co.     5 Jun 1829
GILLET, John S. - town of Chariton, took up a yellow sorrel horse ae 3y
     appraised at $35 by John Tooly & James A. Kerr.     9 Aug 1827
                  Henry T. Williams JP.
GILMAN, Mary - lots for sale in Boonville by her attorney Gilman Peck.     9 Jan 1829
GINNINS, Thomas - appraised a stray taken up by Allen Coats.     16 Apr 1831
GITTINGS, Michael - notice that the Saline Co. Court has rendered a
     judgment against him for debt and costs paid by     4 Feb 1823
     Jacob Ish.
GIVENS, Thomas J. (P?) - attorney in Fayette.     30 Oct 1829

GLASGOW, Nathan - notifies that his apprentice Harrison S. Elliott has run away.    3 Dec 1831

GLASCOCK, Eli - Blew Twp Lafayette Co., took up a yellow bay mare ae 8-9y appraised at $16 & a gray mule ae 4y appraised at $20 by Henry C. Davis & Jabez Jones. Lewis Jones JP.    22 Mar 1827

GODMAN, John - appraised a stray taken up by R. Baker.    24 Mar 1832

GOODDING, Joseph - JP, Sugar Creek Twp Randolph Co., stray taken up by Peter Blanset.    5 Feb 1831

GORDEN, George W. - offers the land where he lives for sale, 3 miles north of Columbia, 160 acres.    3 Dec 1831

GORDON, David - Columbia Twp Boone Co., took up a bay mare ae 3y appraised at $22.50 by Sinclair Kirtley & Lewis Collins.    27 Mar 1829
   Warren Woodson JP.

~ J. B. - an attorney in Columbia, partner of A. A. King.    26 Feb 1831

John C. - JP, Jefferson Twp Cole Co., stray taken up by James Steward.    3 Jul 1824

   - appraised a stray taken up by Jonathan Ramsey.    15 Feb 1826

GORHAM, Thomas - offers $5 reward for runaway mulatto Nelson.    1 May 1824

GRAHAM, Daniel - appraised a stray taken up by Benjamin Ellis Jr.    16 Dec 1825

GRANT, Peter - JP, Salt River Twp Ralls Co., stray taken up by James Weldon.    16 Jul 1825

   - " by David Onstott.    13 Aug 1831

Thomas D. - offers the jack "Tontalego" for sale.    18 Dec 1831

GRAY, John - appraised a stray taken up by William Jones Sr.    16 Jun 1826

GRAYUM, John - Perce Twp Boone Co., took up a sorrel mare ae 4y appraised at $27.50 by Peirce Ward & Wm. Gaslin. John Anderson JP.    10 Aug 1826

GREATHOUSE, William - appraised a stray taken up by James Chitwood.    30 Apr 1831

GREEN, Martin - Hugh King sentenced to death for his murder, St. Louis.    3 May 1827

Stephen - appraised a stray taken up by Philip Prather.    11 Dec 1829

Wesley S. - Presley Halley's stud horse "Josephus" is located at Green's farm in Howard Co.    15 Feb 1825

Willis M. - will practice medicine in Chariton.    6 Sep 1827

GREENING, John - Boonville; took up two mares appraised at $48 by Robert Greening & Samuel Huddleson. Hardeman Stone JP.    1 Feb 1827

GRIFFIN, Berry G. - Columbia; warns public not to accept bonds he gave James E. Fenton; he says "fraudulently obtained."    23 Dec 1830

GRIGSBY, J. T. - with others, offers lots for sale in Florida, Monroe Co.    16 Apr 1831

GRINDSTAFF, Isaac - bankrupt.    1 May 1830

GRISHAM, William - appraised a stray taken up by John Wilborn.    10 Aug 1826

GROSS, Isaac, Jacob,   - all give testimony regarding the recent
Margaret, Stephen   - Indian disturbances in the area where they reside, in Randolph Co.    18 Sep 1829

GUINN, Joshua - Jefferson Twp Saline Co., took up a bay mare ae 10-11y appraised at $20 and a yellow bay filly appraised at $10, appraisers not named.    24 Aug 1826

GUM, Jonathan - Franklin Twp Howard Co., took up a blind bay mare ae 12y appraised at $4 by Joseph Alorton & Thomas Hays.    25 Jan 1826
   John Bird JP.

   - took up a dark bay mare ae 7y appraised at $20 by Thomas Dueson & John Lee. George Chapman JP.    15 Feb 1826

   - took up a dun mare mule ae 10-12y appraised at $30 by Dueson & Lee. Chapman JP.    24 Mar 1826

GUNN, Calvin - St. Charles Co., sues Robert McCloud to foreclose mortgage.    2 Sep 1823

GUTHRIE, Samuel T. - Round Prairie Twp Callaway Co., took up a bay mare ae 13y appraised at $15 by Robert Criswell and Joseph Nevins. JP illegible.    29 May 1824

GUY, John - appraised a stray taken up by Andrew Hamilton.    23 Jul 1831

GWINN, Bartlett - JP, Jefferson Twp Saline Co., stray taken up by William Gwinn.    14 Jun 1827

William - Jefferson Twp Saline Co., took up a sorrel horse appraised at $30 by John Wood & John McMahon.    14 Jun 1827

HADEN, Rev. J. H. - to preach in Fayette on Sept. 21st.    12 Sep 1828

HALDERMAN, John A., M.D. - Fayette; dissolves partnership with McLean.    20 Nov 1829

HALL, Reuben - bankrupt.    12 Apr 1825

Thomas - of Callaway Co.; Joseph Ormrod of Boonville warns the public against Hall who, he says, violated a contract and is "not worthy of confidence."    16 Jun 1832

HALLEY, Presley W. advertises his stud "Josephus" at Wesley T. Green's in Howard Co. First on 15 Feb 1825, later    9 Mar 1827

HAM, Jabez - paid a $5 fine in the Callaway County Circuit Court.                          14 Jan 1823
HAMES, Thornton - Cedar Twp Boone Co., took up a black mare ae 8y
    appraised at $37 by John McDow & James Sullens.                                  2 Jun 1826
                    James Callaway JP.
HAMILTON, Andrew - Nine-Mile-Prairie Twp Callaway Co., took up a sorrel
    horse ae 12-13y appraised at $40 by Nat Craig &                                  23 Jul 1831
    John Guy.  Archibald Allen JP.
HANNAH, Alexander - will manage the cabinet shop of Justinian Williams
    while Williams is in Virginia.                                                  22 Jul 1825
HANNON, Esem - JP, Rocky Fork Twp Boone Co., stray taken up by
                  Abraham Winscott.                                    5 Feb 1831
    - " by Major Barkwell.                                                             7 Jul 1832
HARDEMAN, John - offers apple trees and hemp seed for sale.                                 25 Mar 1823
    - licensed to operate a ferry, Howard Co.; 16 Dec 1823 and                        6 Sep 1827
HARDIN, Benjamin - JP, Randolph Co., stray taken up by Samuel Hardin.                       25 Dec 1829
    Charles - tanner and currier, Columbia, advertises that his
    apprentice Edley Cornet has run away.                                              9 Dec 1823
    - his apprentice David Colier has run away and he
    offers "one cent and two cows' horns" reward.                                     14 Aug 1824
    - wants one or two apprentices.                                                   22 Feb 1825
    - David  Colier has run away again.                                               19 Jun 1830
    Martin - his brother William G. in Knox Co. TN asks for information;              28 Jun 1827
    Martin is deaf and dumb, came to Missouri in 1824,
    may be in Howard Co.
    Samuel - Randolph Co., took up a brown horse ae 4y appraised at
    $25 by Josiah Davis & George Watts. Benjamin Hardin JP.                           25 Dec 1829
HARDWICH, Lewis - William White will not pay a note he gave Hardwich
    which he says was "fraudulently obtained."                                         9 Jul 1825
HARGUS, Isaac D. - appraised a stray taken up by John Bybee.                                12 Apr 1825
HARPER, Henry - appraised a stray taken up by Thomas Davis; signed "x."                     29 Sep 1832
    James - appraised a stray taken up by Caleb Fisher.                               26 May 1826
HARRIS, Hezekiah - Luke, a black man, was executed for Harris' murder
                 at Boonville.                                        7 Sep 1826
    James - appraised a stray taken up by Gilpin Tuttle.                               1 May 1829
    - Cedar Twp Boon Co., took up two strays appraised by James                       24 Sep 1831
    Dunn & Wm. Ambress. James Callaway JP.
    - JP, Cedar Twp, stray taken up by Isaiah Austin.                                  8 Dec 1832
    R. B. - JP, Clear Creek Twp Cooper Co., stray taken up by                         14 Aug 1829
                 Abner Weaver.
    Robert - appraised a stray taken up by Rumsey Saling.                              23 Jul 1831
    Tyre - JP, Perce Twp Boone Co., stray taken up by Josiah Short.                    4 Dec 1824
    - " by Short again (19 Feb 1831) and by George Sexton                             16 Jun 1832
    William - appraised a stray taken up by Elijah Foley.                             12 Aug 1825
HARRISON, George - next friend of Mary Strode in her divorce suit.                          7 Aug 1824
    - dissolved partnership with John Bostick.                                        23 Jul 1831
    - offers 1¢ reward for Stephen Johnson, apprentice saddler.                       27 Oct 1832
    James & Co. - "new and fashionable goods" in Fayette.                             14 Mar 1828
    John - with Alonzo Pearson, appointed to lease the school
    land in Chariton Twp.                                                             25 Feb 1823
    Thomas - JP, Nine-Mile-Prairie Twp Callaway Co., stray taken
               up by Samuel Dyer.                                    12 Aug 1825
    - " by Henry Moxley                                                                12 May 1826
    - took up a sorrel mare ae 14y appraised at $20 by                                19 Jun 1830
    David H. Dunkin & Joel Palmer. Archibald Allen JP.
    Thomas Sr. - took up a sorrel mare ae 4y appraised at $22.50                      20 Nov 1830
    by Thomas Jr. & Wm. McCormack. A. Allen JP.
    - appraised a stray taken up by Jesse D. Oldham.                                  10 Mar 1832
    - took up a bay mare appraised at $40 by Samuel                                   29 Sep 1832
    Hopson & G.L. Ballinger. J. Curd JP.
    Thomas H. - of Callaway Co.; his barn burned 12 July and arson                    29 Jul 1825
    is suspected. Harrison's brother-in-law Joseph
               Potts burned to death.
    William H. - a tailor in Franklin.                                                29 Jul 1825
HARRYMAN, Charles - one of a group entering the Santa Fe trade, leaving                      8 May 1829
    Blue Spring 1 June.
HARTGROVE, Benjamin & Frederick - licensed to operate a ferry, Howard Co.                   11 Dec 1829
HARTT, G. C. - bankrupt, Cooper Co.                                                          1 May 1829
HARVEY, John - with Patrick Woods, appointed to lease school lands. (cont.)                  11 Feb 1823

HARVEY, John ( cont.) - collector, Howard Co.                                    16 Dec 1823
          - JP, stray taken up by Joseph Montgomery.                             19 Apr 1825
          - " by James Denny.                                                    11 Jan 1828
HARVY, Polly - Arrow Rock Twp Saline Co., took up a bay horse ae 4y             11 Jun 1831
          appraised at $40 by James Ray & John Thornton. Asa Finley JP
HATFIELD, Alexander - appraised a stray taken up by Abner Weaver.                14 Aug 1829
          Charles - Salt Spring Twp Randolph Co., took up a sorrel mare
               ae 3y appraised at $10 by James Wells, James Cooley,              17 Apr 1829
               & Thomas Sears. Blandamin Smith JP.
          Henry - Coleneck Twp Cooper Co., took up a strawberry roan
               horse ae 6y appraised at $30 by James L. Collins &               19 Dec 1828
               Nimrod Rector. John Dade JP.
          Mansfield - appraised a stray taken up by John Rice.                   25 Sep 1824
               - " by Caleb Fisher.                                              26 May 1826
HATTON, Charles B. - appraised a stray taken up by William Scott.                 5 Feb 1824
          - " by James R. Wood.                                                  15 Jan 1831
          R. M. - appraised a stray taken up by Alexander Ellington.             30 Jun 1832
          Thomas - road overseer, Callaway Co.                                   14 Jan 1823
HAYES, Charles M. - Boone Co., took up a bay mare ae 3y appraised at $30
               (Columbia Twp/) by Elisha McClelland & James                      3 Nov 1832
               Richardson. Warren Woodson JP.
          Delina - nee Cobb, suit for divorce vs James Hayes in the
               State Legislature.                                                15 Jan 1831
HAYNES, Joel - Bourbon Twp Callaway Co., took up a black mare ae 7y
          appraised at $25 by David McClain & Thomas P. Stephens.                29 Sep 1832
               Isaac Black JP.
HAYS, E. J. - appraised a stray taken up by Joseph Montgomery.                   19 Apr 1825
          John B. - offers his house and lot in Columbia for sale.               5 Mar 1831
          Thomas - appraised a stray taken up by Jonathan Gum.                   25 Jan 1826
          William - of Saline Co., offers $100 reward for a bay horse and a
               bay mare he says were stolen by John Kirk & Wm. Mann.             22 Jul 1823
HEARD, Jane - applies for renewal of a lost land certificate, T50 R15.           18 Sep 1824
HEDRICK, Jonathan - appraised a stray taken up by Harmon Smelser.                 2 May 1828
HELM, Lina - appraised a stray taken up by Baker Martin.                         28 Jul 1832
HENDERSON, Daniel - appraised a stray taken up by Samuel Dyer.                   12 Aug 1825
          James - with others, offers lots for sale in the town
               of Washington, Callaway Co.                                      26 Mar 1831
          - appraised a stray taken up by Isaac P. Howe.                         10 Mar 1832
          John - JP, Missouri Twp Boone Co., stray taken up by
               William Scott.                                                     2 Aug 1825
          - " by Grove Cook (1 Feb 1827), James R. Wood (5 Jan 1831)
               and Alexander Ellington                                           30 Jun 1832
          William P. - appraised a stray taken up by Willis W. Snell.            14 Jul 1832
HENSLEY, Thomas - runaway apprentice of John R. Peters, a carpenter
               in Liberty. Age about 16, dark eyes and hair.                     24 Jul 1830
HERIFORD, John - appraised a stray taken up by Elijah Stephens.                  11 Dec 1824
HERRIFORD, Paul - road reviewer, Callaway Co.                                    14 Jan 1823
HICKAM, Ezekiel - appraised a stray taken up by James Nichols.                   23 Jul 1831
          J. W. - JP, Missouri Twp Boone Co., stray taken up by James Nichols.   23 Jul 1831
          - " by Simeon Coppage.                                                  7 Apr 1832
HICKLIN, James - Lafayette Co., advertises 3 Negro boys and a girl for sale.     14 Aug 1829
          Jonathan - appraised a stray taken up by Redden Crisp.                 21 Jan 1823
HICKMAN, Capt. David - Abraham Spears' stud horse "Potomac" is located
               at Hickman's farm in Boone Co.                                    21 Mar 1828
          David M. - wool carding, Columbia.                                      2 Jun 1832
          Edwin T. - JP, Silver Creek Twp Chariton Co., stray taken up
               by Asa Kerly.                                                     12 Jul 1827
          H. A. - with others, offers lots for sale in Florida, Monroe Co.       16 Apr 1831
          James - with James Mahan, commissioner for a bridge over
               Sulphur Creek between Franklin and Fort Hempstead.                17 Jun 1823
          William - appraised a stray taken up by Samuel Pace.                     3 Dec 1831
HICKS, Y. E. - JP, Boone Co., stray taken up by Elijah Winn.                     25 Jan 1828
HILL, John T. - of Columbia, offers a reward for his lost Santa Fe pony.          9 Jul 1831
          William - found guilty of the murder of William M. Perry, Potosi,
               7 Sept 1825; a reward of $1000 for his capture offered            7 Oct 1825
               by John & Samuel Perry. Hill is about 50, 6'2", gray hair.
          William - lost two notes between Franklin and Fayette.                 26 Jul 1827

MIN                              13

HINKSTON, Robert - Columbia Twp Boone Co., took up a sorrel mare ae 6y
    appraised at $60 by Thomas Maupin & John Cary.         4 Sep 1824
HINSON, Lydia - sues Griffin Hinson for divorce, by next friend
    Nicholas Owens. Clay Co. Court.         17 Apr 1824
HITCHCOCK, Isaac - bankrupt, Lafayette Co.         7 Apr 1826
HIXSON, James B. - runaway apprentice of George Wallis, a hatter in
    Liberty. Ae about 19, fair hair, blue eyes.         17 Apr 1829
HOLDEN, Edward M. - JP, Jackson Twp Monroe Co., stray taken up by R. Baker.   24 Mar 1832
HOLMAN, Henry - appraised a stray taken up by James Toney.         23 Jul 1831
    John - offers reward for his sorrel horse, strayed from Chariton.   19 Apr 1825
HOOD, Robert - wants to buy cornfed pork, pork barrels, venison hams.    29 Jul 1823
    - dissolves partnership with James Scott and John Stothart
                      in Lexington.         7 Sep 1826
HOOK, Henry - advertises for 6 to 8 journeymen carpenters.         9 Oct 1829
HOOZER, Christian - Grand River Twp, took up a bay filly appraised at $25
    and black colt, $15, by Reuben & Isaac Clark.         17 Apr 1824
HOPE, Adam - JP, stray taken up by William Bryant (Cote sans Dessein Twp,
                            Callaway Co. )         7 Jan 1823
HOPPER, James - appraised a stray taken up by John B. Dennis.         23 Jun 1832
HOPSON, Samuel - appraised a stray taken up by Thomas Harrison Sr.     29 Sep 1832
HOUX, George - will take lard, tallow, beeswax, venison for any kind of
    saddlery until 1 Nov.         10 Jun 1823
    William - appraised a stray taken up by William Gibson.         21 Dec 1827
HOWARD, Abraham - appraised a stray taken up by Wm. McLaughlin.       29 Feb 1828
    Cornelius - Loutre Twp Montgomery Co., took up an iron gray filly
    appraised at $6 by James Ellis Jr. and Joseph         6 Jan 1826
    Thurman. A. Kibbe JP.
    Joseph B. - dissolved partnership with Robert Barr & James Tilton.   8 Mar 1826
    - again dissolved partnership with J.Tilton.         29 Jan 1830
HOWE, Isaac P. - Cedar Twp Callaway Co., took up a sorrel horse ae 3y
    appraised at $25 by James Henderson & Robert McKamey.       10 Mar 1832
    Horace Sheley JP.
HOXSEY, Rev. B. F. - gives an address on "The Effects of Ardent Spirits"
    at a public meeting in Columbia.         5 May 1832
HUBBARD, A. E. - appraised a stray taken up by Henry Lichlyter.      15 Apr 1823
    Asaph E. - JP, Jefferson Twp Monroe Co., stray taken up by
    Robert Donaldson.         11 Jun 1831
    Durrett - with Miner Neale, offers to race the horse "Georgian"
    against the horse "Tecumseh."         29 Jan 1831
    - appraised a stray taken by John Parker; signed "x."       21 May 1831
    - offers $100 reward for Negro Betsy and her 4 children.     2 Jun 1832
HUDDLESON, Samuel - appraised a stray taken up by John Greening.      1 Feb 1827
HUGHES, Berry - dissolved partnership with Edward M. Samuel and
    Samuel Moore, in Richmond.         4 Aug 1832
    John - notifies that his wife Jane has left his bed and board.    13 Nov 1829
    Mason - appraised a stray taken up by Jesse D. Oldham.         7 Jan 1832
    Roland - one of three commissioners for a brick school house to
    be built in Twp 50, Rng 16, Sect. 16.         12 Apr 1827
    - appraised a stray taken up by Wm. Patrick.         3 May 1827
    - trustee of Mt. Moriah Meeting House, asks bids for
                  carpenter work.         6 Mar 1829
HUGHS, William Sr. - offers two "first rate" tracts of land south of
    Columbia and a "first rate" jack.         7 Jan 1832
HUME, Reuben - appraised a stray taken up by William McDow.         17 Mar 1832
HUMPHRIES, James - road overseer, Callaway Co.         14 Jan 1823
HUNT, Daniel - Salt Spring Twp, Randolph Co., took up a bright sorrel
    mare ae 7y appraised at $20 by John D. Reed & Elisha     10 Jul 1829
    McDaniel. Blandamin Smith JP.
HURTER, Daniel - Rocky Fork Twp Boone Co., took up a sorrel horse ae 5y
    appraised at $47.50 by George Tally & John Smith.       6 Aug 1831
    Moses Baker JP.
HUTCHISON, Andrew - dissolved partnership with John Kelly.         28 Apr 1826
    James S. - appraised a stray taken up by Andrew Wallace.      4 Mar 1823
    John W. - appraised a stray taken up by ".         "
HUTSON, Lodwick - licensed to sell merchandise, Boone Co.         12 Aug 1823
INGLISH, James & John - appraised a stray taken up by James McKenny.    18 Jan 1826
    John - Moniteau Twp Cole Co., took up a bay horse appraised at $55
    by Jonathan Martin, John Williams, Abraham Kenny.       19 May 1826
                             James Maupin JP

INGLISH, Joseph - JP, Moniteau Twp Cole Co., stray taken up by Jesse Eads.  7 Jan 1823
INGRAM, Arthur - forms a partnership with Henry Reily; formerly it was
    Paul, Ingram & Reily.  12 Jun 1824
ISAACS, Robert - offers a tanyard for sale in Fayette.  13 Sep 1827
ISH, Jacob - obtained a judgment against Michael Gittings for debts and
    costs, Saline Co. Court.  4 Feb 1823
    William - "Head of Bear Creek," Saline Co., wants to buy a Negro
        girl, will trade cattle and cash.  2 Oct 1824
        - offers four Negroes for sale in Lafayette Co.  14 Aug 1829
IVEY, James - appraised a stray taken up by Wm. Patrick.  26 Mar 1831
JACKSON, C. F. - a merchant, moves to New Franklin.  25 Sep 1829
    Elbridge - offers "12 likely Negroes" for sale, Fayette.  5 Feb 1830
    George - JP, Prairie Twp Howard Co., stray taken up by James Denny.  17 Apr 1824
    - " by Wm. Patrick.  3 May 1827
    John - one of three commissioners for a brick school house to be
        built in Twp 50, Rng 16, Sec. 16.  12 Apr 1827
    W. M. - JP, Moniteau Twp Howard Co., stray taken up by
        Samuel Street.  25 Dec 1829
    JACOBS, Leonard - offers a new method of tanning, Boonville; recommended
        by Joseph Ormrod & Peter Wright.  14 May 1825
JAMES, Moses - bankrupt.  16 Sep 1823
JAMESON, James A. - appraised a stray taken up by John Nesbitt.  8 Dec 1832
JAMISON, John - appraised a stray taken up by John Parker; signed "x."  21 May 1831
JEANNERET, Charles E. - moving to St. Louis.  16 Nov 1826
JENKINS, Washington - attorney at law, Columbia.  20 Aug 1831
JOB, William - accused horse thief, broke jail in Cooper Co. Stout,
    about 5'10" tall, sandy hair, red complexion.  24 Apr 1824
JOHNSON, A. M. - appraised a stray taken up by Joseph Bozarth.  28 Mar 1828
    Andrew - licensed to operate a tavern, Howard Co.  16 Dec 1823
    Benjamin - Tabbo Twp Lafayette Co., took up a sorrel mare
        ae 9-10y appraised at $15 by James Linvill & John  10 Aug 1826
        Evans. Samuel Weston JP.
    - took up a sorrel mare ae 3y appraised at $30 by Allen
        Wamock, John Allison, and Wm. Norris.  16 Nov 1826
        David McWilliams JP.
    John - sues Samuel P. Walkup for debt, Boone Co.  27 Sep 1827
    Joseph - Missouriton Twp Ray Co., took up a sorrel mare ae 6y
        appraised at $40 by John Standley & Wm. Turner.  6 May 1823
        James Standley JP.
    Moses - Tabbe Twp Lafayette Co., took up a yellow bay mare
        ae 4y appraised at $40 by Allen & Abraham Wamuck.  26 Jun 1829
        Wm. Carpenter JP.
    Reasen - appraised a stray taken up by Edward Snow.  3 Nov 1832
    Richard - Richmond Twp Howard Co., took up a chestnut sorrel mare
        ae 6-7y appraised at $20 by Daniel Long & Thomas  26 Apr 1827
        Shields. Wm. B. Means JP.
    Stephen J. - runaway apprentice of George Harrison, saddler, who
        offers 1¢ reward. He 18-19, fair hair, blue eyes,  27 Oct 1832
        about 5'8 or 5'10".
    William B. - Franklin, offers $10 reward for runaway Negro Hampton.  18 Apr 1828
JOHNSTON, Isaac - appraised a stray taken up by Benjamin Barnes.  8 Mar 1827
    Lewis - lost a land certificate for Twp 51 Rng 27; it was
        assigned to Martin Trapp.  15 Mar 1825
    Robert - advertises his stud horse "Potomac" on Foster's
        Prairie 10m north of Fayette.  14 Aug 1829
JONES, Jabez - appraised a stray taken up by Eli Glascock.  22 Mar 1827
    James - bankrupt, Boone Co.  4 Jan 1827
    - appraised a stray taken up by Edward Ford.  10 Mar 1832
    Josias - appraised a stray taken up by Wm. Ramsey Sr.  12 Aug 1823
    Lewis - Blew Twp Lafayette Co., JP, stray taken up by Eli Glascock.  22 Mar 1827
    Mosias - appraised a stray taken up by James Wiseman.  8 Jan 1831
    - " by Foster Martin.  17 Sep 1831
    Richard - appraised a stray taken up by Simeon Coppage.  7 Apr 1832
    Shelton - partner of Thomas L. Barrett, Jewelry and watch-making
        materials, Columbia.  28 May 1831
    - partnership dissolved.  8 Dec 1832
    Stephen - appraised a stray taken up by Peter Mason; signed "x."  7 Jan 1832
    T. J. - JP, stray taken up by Hardin Steele.  18 Aug 1832

MIN    15

JONES, William Sr. - Missouri Twp Boone Co., took up a chestnut sorrel          16 Jun 1826
          horse ae 8-9y appraised at $40 by John Gray and
          Wm. Jones. John Henderson JP.
     William - bankrupt, town of Chariton.                                       2 Oct 1824
KAVANAUGH, Rev. William W. - delivered the opening address at the
          meeting of McGee Presbytery, Cumberland                                4 Sep 1830
          Pres. Church. He was from Cooper Co.
KEEN, James S. & Co. - commission house, Nashville MO.                           6 Nov 1830
KEENAN, William - with others, lots for sale in Florida, Monroe Co.             16 Apr 1831
KELLY, Edward vs Mary, divorce, Boone Co.                                       26 Aug 1825
     John - dissolves partnership with Andrew Hutchison.                        28 Apr 1826
     Thomas -appraised a stray taken up by Wm. Atteberry.                       27 Feb 1829
KELSAY, Samuel - JP, Cooper Co., stray taken up by Stephen Rogers.               3 Jul 1829
KEMPER, Enoch - Collector, Howard Co.                                           31 May 1827
KENNADAY, David - appraised a stray taken up by Henry Moxly.                    12 May 1826
KERLY, Asa - Silver Creek Twp Chariton Co., took up a bay horse ae 5y
          appraised at $40 by Wm. Finnel & Allen Mayo.                          12 Jul 1827
                              Edwin T. Hickman JP.
KENNY, Abraham - appraised a stray taken up by John Inglish.                    19 May 1826
KERR, James A. - appraised a stray taken up by John S. Gillet.                   9 Aug 1827
KERTLEY, James - Boone Co., took up a yellow bay mare ae 4y appraised at
          $25 by Wm. Cave & Robert Adkins. Richard Cave JP.                      5 Apr 1825
KIBBE, Amos (Amor?) - JP, Loutre Twp Montgomery Co., stray taken up by
                              Benjamin Ellis Jr.                                 16 Dec 1825
KILLGORE, Isham & John - appraised a stray taken up by John Willingham.          6 Mar 1829
     Isham & John C. -  " by Christopher Winscot.                               30 Oct 1830
KING, A. A. - an attorney in Columbia, partner of J. B. Gordon.                 26 Feb 1831
     Daniel - appraised a stray taken up by Wm. McClain.                        11 Jan 1828
     Hugh - sentenced to death for the murder of Martin Green, St. Louis.        3 May 1827
     Jeremiah - appraised a stray taken up by Wm. Bryant; signed "x."            7 Jan 1823
KIRK, John - accused of stealing a horse and mare from Wm. Hayes, Saline Co.    22 Jul 1823
KIRKPATRICK, David M. - appraised a stray taken up by Hardin Steele.            18 Aug 1832
KIRTLEY, James - appraised a stray taken up by Robert Nelson.                    5 Jul 1827
          - JP, Columbia Twp Boone Co., strays taken up by Samuel
                    Wright (11 Jun 1831) and by Thomas Callahan.                 17 Mar 1832
     Sinclair - appraised a stray taken up by David Gordon.                     27 Mar 1829
          - selling his farm and horses, wants to devote more
                    time to his profession.                                     24 Sep 1831
KITCHINGS, Thomas - appraised a stray taken up by Wm. B. Garret.                 8 Dec 1832
KRUPER, Henry - his pocketbook containing numerous accounts was stolen
                    in Howard Co.                                                9 Nov 1826
KUYKENDALL, Jesse - appraised a stray taken up by Wm. Perkins.                   8 Oct 1831
KYLE, David - opens a "new store" with Alexander McCausland - dry goods,
          hardware, groceries, etc.                                             29 Mar 1827
          - closing business, auctioning his goods, will sell his
                    house and lot.                                              25 Dec 1829
     P. - moves his business to New Franklin.                                   25 Sep 1829
LAMME, William - Franklin, wants "good leaf tobacco."                            5 Oct 1826
LANGLEY, Collet - paid a $1 fine in Callaway Co. Circuit Court.                 14 Jan 1823
     Isaac - appraised a stray taken up by Napoleon B. Ferguson.                 7 Apr 1832
     John - road overseer, Callaway Co.                                         14 Jan 1823
LANE, Hardage - offers $100 reward for runaway Negro Joe.                       19 Aug 1823
LANHAM, Richard - appraised a stray taken up by William Ramsey Sr.             12 Aug 1823
LANICLE, Aru - appraised a stray taken up by Robert Gary.                       18 Jun 1831
LAUGHLIN, Charles - Missouri Twp Boone Co., took up a bay mare ae 3y
          appraised at $30 by John Mayo & James Nichols.                         9 Jul 1831
                              William Lientz JP.
LAURENCE, James - appraised a stray taken up by Henry Moxly.                    12 May 1826
LATHROP, John W. - licensed to sell wines and spirits, Howard Co.              31 May 1827
LAY, Daniel - Richmond Twp Howard Co., took up a light gray mare ae 3-4y
          appraised at $30 by Asa Bartee & Reuben Proctor.                      16 Jan 1829
                              William Taylor JP.
     James H. - a tanner, advertises for his runaway apprentice
                    Liberty G. Teeter.                                          15 Mar 1826
LEE, Green - paid a $5 fine in the Callaway Co. Circuit Court.                  14 Jan 1823
     Joel - appraised a stray taken up by Wm. Taylor.                            5 Feb 1830
     John - appraised a stray taken up by Jonathan Gum. 15 Feb and 24 Mar,
                                                                                     1826
          MIN

                              16

LEE, Tinselly - appraised a stray taken up by Nathaniel Riggs.                                    26 Mar 1831
LEMON, Robert - appraised a stray taken up by Wm. McClain.                                        11 Jan 1828
       - offers a reward for a strayed sorrel horse, nr Columbia.                                 23 Jul 1831
LEVERIDGE, R. S. - advertises watches and clocks, Franklin.                                       22 Mar 1827
LEWIS, John - took up two colts appraised at $33 in Columbia Tp, Boone Co.                        17 Mar 1832
       Appraisers, Samuel Spires, Martin Bucklar. James Kirtley JP.
LICHLYTER, Henry - Richmond Twp Howard Co., took up a dark brown mare ae 3y
       appraised at $20 by A.E. Hubbard & Pleasant Wilson.                                        15 Apr 1823
                                          Joseph Sears JP.
LIENTZ, William - JP, Missouri Twp Boone Co., stray taken up by Wm. South.                        14 May 1831
LILLEY, David - appraised a stray taken up by Wm. Gibson.                                         21 Dec 1827
LINCH, Elbert - Lexington Twp Lafayette Co., took up a claybank mare ae 3y
       appraised at $27.50 by James Whitnett & Armenius Cary.                                     21 Apr 1826
                                          James Fletcher JP.
LINN, James S. - will pay no bills but his own.                                                   16 Nov 1827
       - notice warns the public "to prevent him from imposing
       himself on honest people." (With James Crowe; described                                    23 May 1828
       as "bully and blackguard." A typesetter.)
LINVILLE, James - appraised a stray taken up by Benj. Johnson.                                     10 Aug 1826
       Richard - licensed to operate a ferry, Clay Co.                                            25 Jan 1826
LITRELL, Charles - Bonne Femme Twp Howard Co., took up a bay mare ae 3y
       appraised at $25 by George Fraker & Joseph Logsdon.                                        15 May 1824
                                          John Meyers JP.
LOCK, Abraham - appraised a stray taken up by John M. Fowler.                                     14 Dec 1827
LOGSDON, Joseph - appraised a stray taken up by Charles Litrell.                                  15 May 1824
LOMAX, A. - appraised a stray taken up by Matthew Agee.                                           16 Sep 1825
LONG, Daniel - appraised strays taken up by Thomas Patton & Richard Johnson.                      26 Apr 1827
LORTON, John - Nine-Mile-Prairie Twp Callaway Co., took up two horses
       appraised at $65 by Alfred Petty & Wm. Boyes.                                              10 Mar 1832
                                          John K. Barry JP.
LOUGHLEY, Collet - appraised a stray taken up by Elijah Stephens.                                 11 Dec 1824
LOWREY, James S. - appraised a stray taken up by Wm. South.                                       14 May 1831
LOWTHIAN, Isaac - appointed guardian of James Snoddy, "of unsound mind."                          15 Mar 1826
LYNCH, Cornelius - appraised a stray taken up by James Nichols.                                   23 Jul 1831
LYON, Francis - paid a $1 fine in Callaway Co. Court.                                             6 Jan 1824
McBRIDE, Jacob - JP, Rocky Fork Twp Boone Co., stray taken up by
                                          John Roberts.                                            7 Jan 1832
       P. H. - testified in favor of Jesse T. Wood.                                               26 Apr 1825
       - JP, Columbia Twp Boone Co., stray taken up by John Wilborn.                              10 Aug 1826
McCAMPBELL, James - appraised a stray taken up by Francis Whitlock;                               20 Feb 1829
       signed "x."
McCAUSLAND, Alexander - advertises a "new store" with David Kyle - dry                            29 Mar 1827
       goods, hardware, groceries, etc.
       A. Jr. - licensed as an auctioneer, Franklin.                                              29 Jan 1830
McCLAIN, David - appraised a stray taken up by Ninian Ridgway.                                     9 Oct 1830
       - " by Joel Haynes.                                                                        29 Sep 1832
       William - Columbia Twp Boone Co., took up a black mare appraised                           11 Jan 1828
       at $25 by Robert Lemon & Daniel King. Jesse T. Wood JP.
McCLELLAND, Elisha - appraised a stray taken up by Charles M. Hayes.                               3 Nov 1832
McCLOUD, Robert - defendant, mortgage foreclosure suit by Calvin Gunn,                            2 Sep 1823
       St. Charles.
McCORMACK, William - Nine-Mile-Prairie Twp Callaway Co., took up a gray                           6 Nov 1830
       horse ae 10y appraised at $20 by Isaac Tate &
       George Burt. Archibald Allen JP.
       - appraised a stray taken up by Thomas Harrison Sr.                                        20 Nov 1830
McCRAY, Daniel - appraised a stray taken up by Solomon Odell.                                     29 Sep 1832
McDANIEL, Absalom - appraised a stray taken up by Benjamin Barnes.                                 8 Mar 1827
       Elisha - appraised a stray taken up by Daniel Hunt.                                        10 Jul 1829
McDONALDSON, Isaac - Moniteau Twp Howard Co., took up two brown fillies                           4 Jan 1828
       appraised at $40 by James G. Montgomery &
       Wm. Parton.    Wm. B. Means JP.
McDOW, John - appraised a stray taken up by Thornton Hames.                                        2 Jun 1826
       William - Cedar Twp Boone Co., took up a sorrel colt appraised                             17 Mar 1832
       at $13 by Reuben Hume & Peyton Colier. James Harris JP.
McDOWELL, John - advertises wool carding in Franklin; partner of                                  16 Jun 1826
                                          Robert Percival.

                              MIN
                               17

McFARLAND, James - JP, stray taken up by Reuben Smith.    15 Jan 1824
McGARY, Hugh H. - appraised a stray taken up by Thomas Davis.    29 Sep 1832
McGAUGH, John - Richmond Twp Ray Co., took up a sorrel mare ae 6-7y
    appraised at $45 by Wm. Wilkinson & Elijah Curtis.    30 Jul 1831
                  Joseph H. Ball JP.
McGEE, John S. - JP, Jackson Twp Monroe Co., stray taken up by Elijah Bunton.  11 Jun 1831
McGIRK, John W. - appointed guardian of James Snoddy, "of unsound mind."    15 Mar 1826
McGLOTHLIN, John - Clay Twp Lafayette Co., took up a dark bay horse ae 3y
    appraised at $5 by Wm. Rupe & Henry Triglar.    10 Aug 1826
                  W.Y.C. Ewing JP.
McILVAIN, J. H. - advertises "cast and wrought" iron, Franklin.    1 Aug 1828
McKAYMEY, Robert - with others, offers lots for sale in Washington,
                Callaway Co.    26 Mar 1831
    - appraised a stray taken up by Isaac P. Howe.    10 Mar 1832
McKEE, Henry- St. Louis; wants to buy flax seed.    9 Oct 1830
McKENNY, James - Marion Twp Cole Co., took up a bay roan horse ae 7-8y
    appraised at $20 by Thomas Smith, James English &    18 Jan 1826
    John Inglish. William Wade JP.
McLAUGHLIN, D. - paid a $1 fine in the Callaway Co. Court.    14 Jan 1823
    William - courthouse and jail commissioner, Callaway Co.    14 Jan 1823
    - Auxvasse Twp Callaway Co., took up a chestnut
    sorrel horse ae 9y appraised at $25 by Willis    29 Feb 1828
    Alexander & Nathaniel Howard & Abraham Howard.
                  Thomas Baker JP.
McLEAN, W. B. - appraised a stray taken up by James Denny.    11 Jan 1828
McMAHON, John - appraised a stray taken up by Wm. Gwinn.    14 Jun 1827
McPHEETERS, Addison - Secretary of the Bonne Femme Academy announces    5 Jun 1830
    the successful results of the semi-annual exam.
McWILLIAMS, David - JP, Tabbo Twp Lafayette Co., stray taken up by
                Benjamin Johnson.    16 Nov 1826
MADDOX, Larkin and Sherwood - appraised a stray taken up by Willis Snell.    17 Mar 1832
MAGNOR, Jeremiah - of Liberty; with Lewis Scott advertises for a
    runaway apprentice, Albert Endecott.    16 Jan 1830
MAHAN, James - with James Hickman, commissioner for a bridge over
    Sulphur Creek between Franklib & Fort Hempstead.    17 Jun 1823
MANN, William - accused of stealing a horse and a mare from William
                Hays, Saline Co.    22 Jul 1823
MARCH, Tyre - Boone Co., took up a brown bay horse ae 10y appraised at
    $22.50 by Isham Fletcher & Solomon Mordecai. John Corlew JP.    3 Dec 1831
MARR, John - lost a land certificate, Franklin district.    22 Feb 1825
MARSHALL, J. (Joseph) - offers his Boone Co. farm for sale, 160 acres
    with 50 in cultivation.    28 Aug 1830
    - offers live stock and furniture for sale.    4 Dec 1830
    L. P. - "books and stationery," Franklin.    19 Jun 1829
    - moves to New Franklin.    25 Sep 1829
    - commission merchant, has bought Lamme & Bros. warehouse
    and wants to buy hemp.    22 Jan 1830
MARTIN, Baker - Clay Twp Lafayette Co., took up a bay mare "mired in the
    Missouri River," ae 3y, appraised at $15 by Lina Helm &    28 Jul 1832
    Thomas Morris. W. C. Y. Ewing JP.
    Foster - Cedar Twp Boone Co., took up a gray horse ae 6y
    appraised at $30 by Mosias Jones & Mark Sappington.    17 Sep 1831
                Tyre Martin JP.
    Henry - JP, Union Twp Ralls Co., stray taken up by Geo. Saling.    11 Jan 1828
    Isaac - JP, Missouriton Twp Ray Co., stray taken up by    18 Mar 1823
                Lovell Snowden.
    J. & J. (John & Joseph) - bootmakers in Columbia.    11 Dec 1830
    - discontinue partnership, John will continue business.    17 Mar 1832
    James - appraised a stray taken up by Aquilla Barns.    8 Mar 1826
    Jonathan P. - appraised a stray taken up by John Inglish.    19 May 1826
    Meredith - appraised a stray taken up by Wm. Ramsay.    7 Jul 1832
    Tyre - JP, Cedar Twp Boone Co., stray taken up by Wm. Ramsay Sr.    12 Aug 1823
    - " by James Wiseman (8 Jan 1831) & Wm. Ramsay Sr.    7 Jul 1832
    William - JP, Round Prairie Twp Callaway Co., stray taken up by
                John Nesbit.    8 Dec 1832
    William B. - Court justice, Ray Co.    25 Feb 1823

MASON, Peter - Callaway Co., took up a bright bay horse ae 4y appraised
    at $20 by Mordecai Bell & Stephen Jones. George Bartley JP.    7 Jan 1832
MATHEW, Willis G. - Columbia; advertises for a pocketbook, with notes,
    etc. stolen "during the last races in St. Louis."    3 Dec 1831
MATHIS, James B. - appraised a stray taken up by Elijah Bunton.    11 Jun 1831
MAUPIN, James - JP, Moniteau Twp Cole Co., stray taken up by John Inglish.    19 May 1826
    Thomas - appraised a stray taken up by Robert Hinkston.    4 Sep 1824
MAXEY, Boze - received payment for services, Howard Co.    16 Dec 1823
    Walter - Cedar Twp Boone Co., took up a bright sorrel mare ae 13y
    ($25) a bright bay mare 9y ($20) a brown filly ($20) and    26 Apr 1825
    a bay colt ($10), all appraised by James Bradley and
    Jacob Billet. James Callaway JP.
MAY, Henry - road reviewer, Callaway Co.    14 Jan 1823
MAYO, Allen - appraised a stray taken up by Asa Kerly.    12 Jul 1827
    John - appraised strays taken up by John Wilborn (10 Aug 1826)
    and Charles Laughlin.    9 Jul 1831
MEAD, David - appraised strays taken up by Benjamin Cornelius    16 July 1825
    and by Joseph Bozarth.    28 Mar 1828
    Stephen C. - licensed to sell wines and spirits, Clay Co.    20 May 1823
MEANS, James - Moniteau Twp Howard Co., took up an iron gray horse ae 5-6y
    appraised at $25 by Daniel Long & Neal Murphy. Means JP.    21 Jun 1827
    William B. - JP, Moniteau Two Howard Co., stray taken up by
    Benjamin Cornelius.    16 Jul 1825
    - sues Samuel Alexander for debt, Howard Co. Court.    7 Dec 1827
MILLER, John - appraised a stray taken up by Jesse Eads.    7 Jan 1823
    William - Ray Co. Sheriff.    25 Feb 1823
MILLION, William - appraised a stray taken up by Samuel Street.    25 Dec 1829
MILLS, F. P. - attorney, Columbia, partner of W. K. Van Arsdall.    25 Dec 1830
MITCHELL, Moses - will not pay two notes he executed in Santa Fe.    16 Nov 1827
MOBLEY, John H. - appraised a stray taken up by David Enyart.    12 Jul 1827
MOCK, Elijah - offers 6-1/2¢ reward for runaway apprentice David Ford -
    "about 18, sallow, with a deformed leg. . . may have gone    16 Nov 1826
    to Hurricane."
    - advertises a "cabinet warehouse" in Fayette, "turning and
    carving in the neatest manner."    21 Dec 1827
MONROE, Rev. Andrew - will preach in Fayette Thursday at 11.    25 Jul 1828
MONTGOMERY, James G. - appraised a stray taken up by Isaac McDonaldson.    4 Jan 1828
    Joseph - Prairie Twp Howard Co., took up a black horse ae 4y
    appraised at $20 by E. J. Hays & David Elliott.    19 Apr 1825
    John Harvey JP.
MOORE, James - Fulton Twp Callaway Co., took up a sorrel horse ae 10-12y
    appraised at $25 by Wm. Smart & Felix G. Nichols.    31 Jul 1830
    Wm. Armstrong JP.
    John H. - accused of perjury, broke jail in Cooper Co. Slender,
    about 30, 6' tall, red hair, red complexion.    24 Apr 1824
    Robert - paid a $1 fine in the Callaway Co. Court.    14 Jan 1823
    Samuel - professor at Boonville Academy.    18 Apr 1828
    - dissolved the partnership of Edward M. Samuel, Abraham
    Croysdale, and himself, in Liberty. Moore and Samuel will    5 Feb 1831
    continue the business.
    - dissolved partnership with Edward M. Samuel and Berry
    Hughes, in Richmond.    4 Aug 1832
    Samuel T. - near Ham's Prairie, Elizabeth Twp Callaway Co., took up
    a dark bay horse ae 9y appraised at $15 by Irvine    5 Aug 1825
    Hockaday & James Rose. Bethel Allen JP.
MORDECAI, Solomon - appraised a stray taken up by Tyre March.    3 Dec 1831
MORRIS, Robert - offers "five genets and a jack" for sale.    15 Jan 1824
    - "On Hinkson Creek near Old St. Charles Road" advertises
    a Santa Fe voyage (waggons); "will take merchandise."    15 Mar 1827
    Thomas - appraised a stray taken up by Baker Martin.    28 Jul 1832
    Wilson - appraised a stray taken up by Thomas Wisdom.    7 Jul 1832
MOSS, Mason - offers a reward for a runaway Negro, Jos, in Boone Co.    14 Sep 1832
MOURNING, Daniel - Columbia Twp Boone Co., took up a sorrel horse ae 8y
    appraised at $50 by Wm. Wright & Joseph Renfro.    25 Jun 1831
    James Barnes JP.
MOXLY, Henry - Nine-Mile-Prairie Twp Callaway Co., took up a roan horse
    ae 4y appraised at $40 by James Lawrence & David Kennaday.    21 May 1826
    Thomas Harrison JP.

MIN      19

MOXLEY, Thomas - Nine-Mile-Prairie Twp Callaway Co., took up a black
     filly ae 2y appraised at $25 by Henry Moxley & John     19 Jun 1830
     Todd. John K. Berry JP.
MULKY, Christopher - appraised a stray taken up by John Smelser;
     signed "x."     4 Sep 1829
MULLINS, David - appraised a stray taken up by John W. Rawlings.     7 Mar 1828
MUNRO, Daniel - Franklin Twp Howard Co., took up a sorrel mare ae 4y and
     a colt, appraised at $35 by John Broadhurst & Boswell     25 Mar 1823
     Pulliam. George Chapman JP.
MURPHY, Jeremiah - appraised a stray taken up by Wm. Taylor.     5 Feb 1830
     Neal - appraised a stray taken up by James Means.     21 Jun 1827
MURRAY, James - Clay Twp Lafayette Co., took up a bay horse ae 5y
     appraised at $35 by John Fielder & James Person.     23 Jun 1832
     W.Y.C. Ewing JP.
     Thomas - appraised a stray taken up by Jesse Eads.     7 Jan 1823
MYERS, Jacob - lost 3 banknotes on the road from New London to Fayette.     14 Dec 1826
     James and Mrs. Thursey - of Randolph Co., gave testimony as to
     recent Indian disturbances. Shown as     18 Sep 1829
     "near Salt River."
     John - with Thomas Winn, appointed to lease school lands in
     Bonne Femme Twp, Howard Co.     11 Feb 1823
     - JP, strays taken up by Charles Litrell (15 May 1824) and
     by John Bybee.     12 Apr 1825
MYRTLE, Reuben - Randolph Co., gave testimony about the recent "hostile
     and outrageous" Indian disturbances.     18 Sep 1829
NASH, Ira P. - probably leaving state, wants to settle accounts.     12 Aug 1823
NEALE, Miner - with Durrett Hubbard, offers to race the horse "Georgian"
     against "Tecumseh."     29 Jan 1831
     - with George W. Osborne & Richmond Curl, advertises
     "Georgian" at stud.     19 Mar 1831
NEILL, Henry - JP, Cote sans Dessein Twp Callaway Co., stray taken
     up by Napoleon B. Ferguson.     7 Apr 1832
NELSON, Robert - Columbia Twp Boone Co., took up an iron gray mare ae 3y
     appraised at $25 by James Kirtley & Andrew Spence.     5 Jul 1827
     John Williams JP.
     - appraised a stray taken up by Sampson Wright.     11 Jun 1831
NESBIT, John - Round Prairie Twp Callaway Co., took up a bay mare ae 8y
     appraised at $25 by Samuel Shaw & James A. Jameson.     8 Dec 1832
     William Martin JP.
NEVINS, James - Road commissioner, Callaway Co.     14 Jan 1823
     - JP, Round Prairie Twp, Callaway Co., stray taken up
     by Daniel Vinston.     11 Nov 1823
     Joseph - appraised a stray taken up by Samuel T. Guthrie.     29 May 1824
NEWELL, R. W. - fined $20 in the Callaway Co. Court.     6 Jan 1824
NEWMAN, William - Moreau Twp Cole Co., took up a sorrel mare ae 4y
     appraised at $20 by Edward Carter & Henry Sailing.     29 Jul 1825
     Hugh Gartin JP.
NEWTON, Samuel - commissioner, advertises lots in Independence, county
     seat of Jackson Co.     14 Jun 1827
NICHOLS, Felix - appraised a stray taken up by James Moore.     31 Jul 1830
     James - Missouri Twp Boone Co., took up an iron gray filly ae 3y
     appraised at $25 by Ezekiel Hickam & Cornelius Lynch.     23 Jul 1831
     J. W. Hickam JP.
NOBLE, Mark - Salt Spring Twp Chariton Co., took up a black mare ae 2y
     appraised at $27 by William & Morris Gee; Blandamin Smith JP.     18 Jan 1828
NOLLEY, Daniel - appraised a stray taken up by Lewis Day (17 Mar 1832)
     and by Willis W. Snell.     14 Jul 1832
NORRIS, William - appraised a stray taken up by Benjamin Johnson.     16 Nov 1826
NORWOOD, Charles - appraised a stray taken up by James Steward.     3 Jul 1824
O'BRIAN, John - a convicted horse thief, broke jail; age about 27,
     6' tall, 190 pounds, black hair and beard,"very talkative."     22 Jul 1825
ODELL, Solomon - Fishing River Twp Ray Co., took up two horses appraised
     at $70 by Daniel McCray & Matthew Roland. Isaac Odell JP.     29 Sep 1832
ODLE, Delilah, Jeremiah, and John - paid for services to Howard Co.     16 Dec 1823
OLDHAM, Jesse D. - Callaway Co.; offers $20 reward for runaway Negroes.     4 Sep 1830
     - Nine-Mile-Prairie Twp; took up a mule colt appraised at
     $12 by Mason Hughes, Thos. Harrison Sr. A. Allen JP.     10 Mar 1832

MIN

20

ONSTOTT, David - Salt River Twp Ralls Co., took up a roan mare appraised at $40 by Adam Utterback & Jonathan Abbay. Peter Grant JP. 13 Aug 1831

Solomon - Spencer Twp Ralls Co., took up an iron gray horse ae 5y appraised at $24 by James Fugate & James Underwood. Peter Grant JP. 13 Aug 1831

ORMROD, Joseph - recommends a new tanning method by Leonard Jacobs. 14 May 1825

- Boonville; warns the public against Thomas Hall of Callaway Co. who violated a contract and is "not worthy of confidence." 16 Jun 1832

ORR, Jacob - his wife Cynthia has left his bed and board. 5 Jul 1827

Patrick - Constable, Howard Co. 16 Dec 1823

OSBORNE, George W. - advertises the horse "Georgian" at stud. (With associates Miner Neale & Richmond Curl.) 19 Mar 1831

OWEN, I. P. - asks that his mail be sent to Franklin because of the inefficiency of the Fayette Post Office. 31 Oct 1828

OWENS, John - licensed to sell liquor and to operate a billiard room, Clay Co. 25 Jan 1826

Thomas - appraised a stray taken up by Major Barkwell. 7 Jul 1832

OWINGS, James - a coppersmith at Bass' Lick, 7 miles from Fayette. 24 Aug 1826

OWSLEY, Anthony - Missouri Twp Boone Co., took up an iron gray horse ae 5y appraised at $40 by John Austin & John Williamson. Dabney Pettis JP. 7 Jan 1832

PACE, Jonathan - appraised a stray taken up by Isaiah Austin. 8 Dec 1832

Samuel - Cedar Twp Boone Co., took up two fillies appraised at $60 by Wm. Hickman & Ambrose Estes. William Shields JP. 3 Dec 1831

PALMER, Joel - appraised a stray taken up by Thomas Harrison. 19 Jun 1830

PARKER, John - Columbia Twp Boone Co., took up an iron gray horse ae 6y appraised at $50 by John Jamison & Durrett Hubbard. Warren Woodson JP. 21 May 1831

Oliver - testified in favor of Jesse T. Wood. 26 Apr 1825

- sues Joseph & William Woods for $489.60. 27 Nov 1829

- advertises wool carding in Columbia. 22 May 1830

- dissolves partnership with T. G. Berry, Columbia. (Had previously dissolved, 4/10/1829, and asks debtors of the late firm to pay, 1/22/31.) 10 Apr 1829

PARKISON, George - lost land certificate, Twp 51 Rng 26, Franklin Dist. 22 Feb 1825

PARMER, Martin - lost a land certificate originally given to Alexander Galbraith - Tp49, Rng 20, Franklin Dist. 8 Mar 1825

PARTON, William - appraised a stray taken up by Isaac McDonaldson. 4 Jan 1828

PATRICK, William - Prairie Twp Howard Co., took up a bay mare ae 4y appraised at $14 by Roland Hughes & J.T. Cleveland. G. Jackson JP. 3 May 1827

- Salt River Twp Ralls Co., took up a bay colt appraised at $25 by James Ivy & Richard Bryant. Wm. Bybee JP. 26 Mar 1831

PATTON, Thomas - Moniteau Twp Howard Co., took up a bay horse ae 4y appraised at $20 by Daniel Long & James J. Averett. Wm. B. Means JP. 26 Apr 1827

PATTERSON, Thomas - appraised a stray taken up by James Denny. 17 Apr 1824

PATTON, Thomas - a coppersmith in Columbia, advertises miscellaneous work including brass bells. 27 Feb 1829

William - sues wife Martha for divorce, Boone Co. Circuit Court. 17 Jul 1824

PAVEY, Jesse H. - offers his slaves for sale as he no longer intends to be a slaveholder, Columbia. 19 Feb 1831

PAYNE, J. U. - "Santa Fe goods" for sale. 14 Apr 1831

PEARSON, Alonzo - appointed to lease school lands in Chariton Twp, with John Harrison. 25 Feb 1823

- announces the opening of Pleasant Grove Academy; boarding $10 per quarter. 31 Jul 1824

PECK, Gilman M. - attorney for Mary Gilman, Boonville. 9 Jan 1829

PEEBELS, Mrs. - opens a tavern in Franklin; also offers millinery, mantua-making, sewing for gentlemen. 24 Mar 1826

PEERCE, Mrs. H. T. (Harriet) will commence a summer school for young ladies in Fayette. 8 Feb 1826

- school for young ladies in Columbia. 1 May 1830

William & wife - school for boys and girls, Columbia. 22 Aug 1828

PENN, William N. - with others, lots for sale in Florida, Monroe Co. 16 Apr 1831

MIN

21

PENNINGTON, William - appraised a stray taken up by Grove Cook.                    1 Feb 1827
PERCIVAL, Robert - advertises wool carding, Franklin; partner of
                 John McDowell.                                                   16 Jun 1826
PERKINS, William - Union Twp Monroe Co., took up a brown filly appraised
                 at $19 by John & Samuel Riggs, and a yellow bay mare             8 Oct 1831
                 ae 4y appraised at $37.50 by Jesse Kuykendall &
                 Jonathan Riggs. George Saling JP.
PERRY, Thomas - appraised a stray taken up by Richard Earickson.                   9 Jan 1829
PERSON, James - appraised a stray taken up by James Murray.                       23 Jun 1832
PERVANT, Peter - "on Snyebar," Clay Twp Lafayette Co., took up a chestnut
                 sorrel mare ae 18-20 with a colt, appraised at $5 by             15 Dec 1832
                 Wiley Thompson & Wm. Stacy. W.Y.C. Ewing JP.
PETERS, John R. - a carpenter in Liberty, advertises for his runaway
                 apprentice Thomas Hensley.                                       24 Jul 1830
PETTIS, Dabney - JP, Missouri Twp Boone Co., stray taken up by
                 Anthony Owsley (7 Jan 1832) and by John B. Dennis.               23 Jun 1832
PETTY, Alfred - appraised a stray taken up by John Lorton.                        10 Mar 1832
PHARIS, Alzada - sues Lewis Pharis for divorce, Howard Co. Circuit Court,
                 by next friend Jesse Cornelius.                                   5 Apr 1827
PHILLIPS, Warner - appraised a stray taken up by George Titus.                     1 Oct 1831
POMEROY, Rev. Augustus - will preach Saturday and Sunday at the
                 courthouse in Fayette.                                            2 Nov 1826
PORTER, Rev. A. - a professor at Boonville Academy.                               18 Apr 1828
        William C. - the jailer, Cooper Co.                                       24 Apr 1824
POTTER. Joshua - appraised a stray taken up by Wm. S. Banks.                      14 Dec 1826
POTTS, Joseph - brother-in-law of Thomas H. Harrison of Callaway Co.,
                 burned to death when Harrison's barn burned; ae 13? or           29 Jul 1825
                 18?. Arson suspected.
POWELL, T. - advertises his "new store" in Franklin.                             16 Sep 1825
PROVINES, William, M.D. - now in Columbia.                                         5 Mar 1831
                 - dissolves partnership with A.M. Robinson.                      10 Sep 1831
                 -      " with John Garnett.                                      17 Sep 1831
PRATHER, Philip - Prairie Twp Howard Co., took up two sorrel horses
                 appraised at $70 by Stephen Green & John Baker.                  11 Dec 1829
                 A. Q. Thompson JP.
PREWITT, David - Collector, Howard Co.                                             5 Aug 1825
         Joel - one of three commissioners for a brick school house to
                 be built in sec. 16, twp 50, rng 16.                             12 Apr 1827
PROCTOR, Reuben - appraised a stray taken up by Daniel Lay.                       16 Jan 1829
PULLIAM, Ann R. - her marriage to William Chick was declared null and
                 void by the General Assembly.                                    18 Jan 1825
         Boswell - appraised a stray taken up by Daniel Munro.                    25 Mar 1823
PURCELL, Macam - Rocky Fork Twp Boone Co., took up a bay mare and a
                 sorrel mare appraised at $70 by Henry Cave Jr &                   4 Aug 1832
                 Zadock Riggs Jr. Silas Riggs JP.
PURDIN, C. B. - a chairmaker in Columbia, will also do house- and
                 sign-painting.                                                   24 Sep 1831
RAINES, Henry - Boons Lick Twp Howard Co., took up a sorrel mare ae 3y
                 appraised at $17.50 by Charles Callaway & J. W. Elliott.         24 May 1827
                 John Bird JP.
RAMSAY, James - found two black mules, asks owner to claim.                        8 Feb 1828
        William - Cedar Twp Boone Co., took up a gray horse ae 5y
                 appraised at $25 by Mark Sappington & Meredith Martin.            7 Jul 1832
                 Tyre Martin JP.
RAMSEY, Jonathan - took up a dark bay horse ae 6y appraised at $28 by
                 Christopher & Hardin Casey & John C. Gordon.                     15 Feb 1826
                 Jesse F. Royston JP.
        William Sr. - Cedar Twp Boone Co., took up a bay horse ae 10-12y
                 appraised at $27.50 by Josias Jones & Richard                    12 Aug 1823
                 Lanham. Tyre Martin JP.
RAWLINGS, John W. - Moniteau Twp Howard Co., took up a brown horse
                 ae 15y appraised at $15 by David Mullins & Joseph                 7 Mar 1828
                 Sidebottom. Thomas Rawlings JP.
         Thomas - see above.
RAY, Benjamin B. - county court justice, Howard Co.                               16 Dec 1823
     James - appraised a stray taken up by Polly Harvy.                           11 Jun 1831
READ, Robert - fined $2.50 in the Callaway Co. Court.                             18 Dec 1824

          MIN
                                    22

REAVIS, James B. - Salt River Twp Ralls Co., took up a bay horse ae 8y      11 Dec 1830
    appraised at $50 by Ezra Fox & Ben Davis. Wm Bybee JP.
    Mark - Missouri Twp Boone Co., took up a black horse ae 12y           5 Feb 1831
    appraised at $25 by Wm. Barnes & Milton Berry.
                    John Henderson JP.
RECTER, Daniel - appraised a stray taken up by Zachariah Benson.            16 Dec 1825
RECTOR, Mrs. Eliza - will open her school in Fayette on 9 March.             6 Mar 1829
    Enoch - bankrupt.                                                  16 Sep 1823
    Nimrod - appraised a stray taken up by Henry Hatfield.             19 Dec 1828
REDMAN, Dr. J. W. - opens an office in Franklin.                            21 Apr 1826
    Rev. William H. - will preach in Franklin "Sunday next."            6 Jan 1826
        - will preach at the annual meeting of the                30 Aug 1827
                Fayette Bible Society.
REED, John - appraised a stray taken up by Daniel Hunt.                     10 Jul 1829
    John D. - appraised a stray taken up by George Titus.               1 Oct 1831
    William - accused horse thief, broke jail at Boonville. Slender,   29 Feb 1828
        5'10" tall, dark hair, blue eyes, fair skin.
        - accused horse thief, broke jail at Lexington. Age 21-2,          11 Apr 1828
        dark hair, blue eyes, middling stature, "somewhat fat."
        Fled with Humphrey Smith.
REILY, Henry - formed a partnership with Arthur Ingram.                     12 Jun 1824
RENFRO, Isaac - convicted of the murder of Absalom T. Woods in the           2 Jul 1825
    Cooper Co. Circuit Court, re-tried in Howard Co. but "one
    juror being alien" will be re-tried again.
    - broke jail; age about 50, 5'6" tall, blue eyes, gray hair.       22 Jul 1825
    Joseph C. - appraised a stray taken up by Robert Gary.             25 Jun 1831
    Mark S. - appraised a stray taken up by Roger Wigginton.           17 Sep 1831
RENICK, Burton L. - appraised a stray taken up by Chatham Ewing Sr.          9 Dec 1825
    Henry - JP, Lillard Co., stray taken up by Redden Crisp.           21 Jan 1823
    - ", Lafayette Co., stray taken up by Chatham Ewing Sr.             9 Dec 1825
    William - appraised a stray taken up by Redden Crisp.              21 Jan 1823
RENNY, Peter - merchant's license, Boone Co.                                12 Aug 1823
RENSHAW, Absalom - appraised a stray taken up by James Turner.              29 Apr 1823
REYNOLD, Th. - attorney in Fayette.                                         22 May 1829
REYNOLDS, William - treasurer of the Boons Lick Library Association.        29 May 1829
RICE, Edward - defendant, mortgage foreclosure by the State of Missouri.     7 May 1825
    Jeremiah - of Franklin, recommends a new tanning method            14 May 1825
            by Leonard Jacobs.
    John - Clear Creek Twp Cooper Co., took up a bay mare appraised    25 Sep 1824
        at $20 by Mansfield Hatfield & Hugh Allison. John Briscoe JP.
    Dr. Oliver - has moved to Fayette, lives at Henry Burnham's        29 Apr 1823
                   "near town."
RICHARDS, Lewis - of Clay Co.; his wife Jane has left his bed & board.      28 Feb 1824
RICHARDSON, James - appraised a stray taken up by Charles M. Hayes.          3 Nov 1832
RICKISON, Nathaniel - of Randolph Co., testifies in regard to the          18 Sep 1829
            recent Indian disturbances.
RIDGWAY, Ninian - Bourbon Twp Callaway Co., took up a black horse ae 4y      9 Oct 1830
    appraised at $45 by David McClain & Thomas Ferree.
                Isaac Black JP.
RIDWAY, John D. - appraised a stray taken up by Roger Wigginton.            17 Sep 1831
RIGGS, John, Jonathan, and Samuel - appraise strays taken up by             8 Oct 1831
                Wm. Perkins.
    Nathaniel - appraised a stray taken up by James Weldon, signed "x." 16 Jul 1825
    - Salt River Twp Ralls Co., took up an iron grey filly             26 Mar 1831
    appraised at $25 by Jonathan Abbay & Tinselley Lee.
                Wm. Bybee JP.
    Peter - appraised a stray taken up by Rumsey Saling.               23 Jul 1831
    Reuben - Rocky Fork Twp Boone Co., took up a bay filly appraised   21 Jan 1823
    at $25 & a sorrel colt at $10 by James & Enoch Turner &
    Wm. Toalson. James R. Abernathy JP.
    Silas - JP, Rocky Fork Twp Boone Co., stray taken up by Macam Purcel.  4 Aug 1832
    Timothy - received payment for use of his house as Ray Co. Court.  25 Feb 1823
    Zadock - appraised a stray taken up by Wm. A. Bates.                3 Aug 1826
    Zadock Jr. - appraised a stray taken up by Macam Purcel.            4 Aug 1832
RINGO, John - warns the public not to accept a note given him by             4 Sep 1829
                S. Brownejohn.

RINGO, Samuel Jr. - joins the firm of Hickman & Lamme; the partnership      2 & 12 Dec
    is in Liberty.                                                        1825
ROBERTS, John - took up a horse, mare, and filly in Rocky Fork Twp, Boone      7 Jan 1832
    Co., appraised at $80 by James & Nathan Roberts.
                          Jacob McBride JP.
    William - appraised a stray taken up by David Enyart.          12 Jul 1827
ROBINSON, Dr. A. - now located at G. Robinson's near Salt Creek Bridge.    12 Apr 1825
    Dr. Alexander M. - in Columbia, partner in a drug store with    17 Jul 1829
        James H. Benson & James C. Boggs.
        - dissolves partnership with Wm. Provines.          10 Sep 1831
    John M. - offers "likely Negroes" for sale near Salt Creek bridge.  23 Sep 1825
    S. S. - offers five slaves for sale.                  26 Feb 1831
ROCHESTER, J. C. - Assessor, Cooper Co.                    22 Apr 1823
ROBNETT, Joseph - Cedar Twp Boone Co., took up a bay mare ae 4y appraised    5 Jun 1830
    at $35 by Pleasant Robnett & Theodore Beavin.
                    Wm. Shields JP.
ROGERS, Stephen - Cooper Co., took up a black mare ae 3y appraised at $25    3 Jul 1829
    by Robert Rogers & Elijah Anderson. Samuel Kelsay JP.
ROLAND, Matthew - appraised a stray taken up by Solomon Odell.        29 Sep 1832
ROSE, James - appraised a stray taken up by Samuel T. Moore.         5 Aug 1825
ROUTHWELL, James - has leased Sibley's Ferry.                29 Jul 1823
ROYSTON, James F. JP, stray taken up by Jonathan Ramsey.          15 Feb 1826
RUBEY, Dr. Robert C. - in Chariton, located over Dr. Bull's store.     3 Jul 1824
RUCKER, Wilton - appraised a stray taken up by Isaiah Austin.        8 Dec 1832
RUKEY, John - licensed to sell wines and spirits, Clay Co.          20 May 1823
RUNNION, Isaac - appraised a stray taken up by Wm. Wright.         14 Dec 1827
    John Jr. - licensed to sell wines and spirits, Howard Co.      31 May 1827
RUPE, William - appraised a stray taken up by John McGlothlin.       10 Aug 1826
SAILING, Henry - appraised a stray taken up by Wm. Newman.         29 Jul 1825
SALING, George - Union Twp Ralls Co., took up a red roan filly, no        11 Jan 1828
    appraisers shown, $25. Henry Martin JP.
    - appraised a stray taken up by Wm. Perkins.             8 Oct 1831
    Rumsey - Union Twp Monroe Co., took up a strawberry roan horse    23 Jul 1831
        appraised at $22 (it was 13y old) by Peter Riggs &
        Robert Harris. Reese Davis JP.
SAMUEL, Edward M. - dissolves partnership with Abraham Croysdale &    5 Feb 1831
        Samuel Moore in Liberty, but will continue in a new
        partnership with Moore.
        - dissolves partnership with Moore & Berry Hughes        4 Aug 1832
        in Richmond.
SAMUEL, F. S. & G. M. - move to New Franklin.                25 Sep 1829
    Presley - sergeant in the Franklin Guards.             22 Jul 1823
    Sam - (alias Earls) - convicted of the murder of Charles Rouse    18 Jun 1831
        in New London a year ago.
SANDFORD, John D. - appraised a stray taken up by Edward Atteberry.    15 Feb 1826
SANDERS, Bryant - opens a House of Entertainment in Lexington,        29 Feb 1828
                        Lafayette Co.
SAPPINGTON, John - appraised a stray taken up by James Wiseman.      8 Jan 1831
    Mark - appraised strays taken up by Foster Martin (17 Sep 1831)    7 Jul 1832
        and by Wm. Ramsay.
SAVAGE, John M. - Boonville Twp Cooper Co., took up a brown filly appraised    3 Nov 1832
    at $25 by Peter Fleming & Joseph Chambers.
                 George Crawford JP.
SCHOOLING, Robert - JP, "Persia" Twp Boone Co., stray taken up by      3 Nov 1832
                       Edward Snow.
SCONCE, Robert - Salt Spring Twp Cooper Co., took up a chestnut sorrel    18 Jan 1827
    mare ae 3y appraised at $37.50 by John Wheldon &
    Abraham Dule. James Wells JP.
SCOTT, James - asks debtors to pay; represented by Greenup Bird.      29 Jun 1826
    - dissolves partnership with Robert Hood & John Stothart,    7 Sep 1826
                            Lexington.
    Lewis - appraised a stray taken up by Zachariah Benson.        16 Dec 1825
    - of Liberty; with Jeremiah Magnor, advertises for runaway    16 Jan 1830
        apprentice Albert Endecott.
    William - Missouri Twp Boone Co., took up a sorrel horse ae 10y    5 Feb 1824
        appraised at $24 by Benjamin Watson & Charles B. Hatton.
                  John Henderson JP.

SEARCY, Alexander - advertises wool carding in Fayette, with James Spencer.  1 Aug 1828
SEARS, Joseph - JP, Richmond Twp Howard Co., stray taken up by
                                                      Henry Lichlyter.  15 Apr 1823
     Thomas - appraised a stray taken up by Charles Hatfield.  17 Apr 1829
SEMPLE, James - moving to Louisville, asks his debtors to pay.  18 Dec 1824
     - his land sold for debt.  18 Jan 1827
SERICHFIELD, Henry - appraised a stray taken up by James Denny.  17 Apr 1824
SETTLE, Martin - formerly of Kentucky, information wanted by Levi G. Ewers
     of Leasburg, Va. A note adds that Settle moved to Mo.   5 Jun 1824
     in Sept. 1822 and lives about 6 miles from Franklin.
SEXTON, George - Persia Twp Boone Co., took up a bay mare ae 10y appraised
     at $40 by Reuben Elliott & Fielding White. Tyre Harris JP.  16 Jun 1832
SHANKLIN, Elijah - appraised a stray taken up by Wm. Brooks.  12 Aug 1825
SHANNON, James - appraised a stray taken up by Wm. B. Garret.  8 Dec 1832
SHARP, Jacob L. - appraised a stray taken up by Benjamin Ellis Jr.  16 Dec 1825
     John V. - shown as a pauper on Cooper Co. list.  15 Jan 1824
SHAW, John - licensed to operate a tavern, Howard Co.  16 Dec 1823
     Samuel - appraised a stray taken up by John Nesbit.  8 Dec 1832
SHELEY, Horace and Van - lots for sale in Washington, Callaway Co.,
                                                with others.  26 Mar 1831
     Horace - JP, Cedar Twp Callaway Co., stray taken up by Isaac P. Howe.  10 Mar 1832
SHEPHERD, G. W. - wants a "first-rate journeyman tailor."  27 Sep 1827
     George W. - bankrupt, Cooper Co.  1 Mar 1826
     James - appointed to lease the school lands in Richmond Twp,
     Howard Co., with Wm. Ward.  4 Feb 1823
     Jonah H. - Captain of the Fayette Light Horse.  28 Mar 1828
SHIELDS, John - received payment for use of his house as court, Ray Co.  25 Feb 1823
     Thomas - appraised a stray taken up by Richard Johnson.  26 Feb 1827
     William - JP, Cedar Twp Boone Co., strays taken up by Benjamin
     Barnes (8 Mar 1827), Jos. Robnett (5 Jun 1830) and
                                                  Samuel Pace.  3 Dec 1831
SHIRLEY, James A. & Co. - "new goods" in Fayette: dry goods, groceries,
                          queensware, medicine, drugs, etc.  16 Jan 1829
SHORT, Cornelius - appraised a stray taken up by Thomas Wisdom.  7 Jul 1832
     Josiah - Perce Twp Boone Co., took up a sorrel horse ae 4y appraised
     at $25 by David Gentry & John Short. Tyre Harris JP.  4 Dec 1824
     - took up a dark brown horse ae 7y appraised at $30 by Tyre
     Berry & Eppy Elliott. Tyre Harris JP.  19 Feb 1831
SIBERT, William - Franklin Twp Howard Co., took up a bay mare ae 4y
     appraised at $18 by Samuel Teeter & J. R. Burckhartt.  5 Dec 1828
                                        N. S. Burckhartt JP.
SIDEBOTTOM, Joseph - appraised a stray taken up by John W. Rawlings.  7 Mar 1828
SILLON, Jeffrey - road reviewer, Callaway Co.  14 Jan 1823
SIMPSON, Joseph - wants cornfed pork, tallow, lard, honey, beeswax,
                                   and venison hams.  12 Aug 1823
     - has a "new store" on the ne corner of the Public
     Square, Franklin.  15 May 1824
     - offers mules, jennies, Spanish horses for sale, Franklin.  19 Oct 1827
     Mary - thanks the customers of her late husband Joseph, will
     continue the business in Franklin & Fayette.  7 Mar 1828
SIZEMORE, Jordan - Union Twp Ralls Co., took up a gray horse ae 9y appraised
     at $40 by Ezra Fox & Robert Swinney. John Burton JP.  23 Aug 1827
     - appraised a stray taken up by Jacob Whittenburgh.  15 Aug 1828
     -        " by Ezra Fox.  29 Jan 1831
SLACK, John - JP, Persia Twp Boone Co., stray taken up by Aquilla Barns.  8 Mar 1826
SLOAN, David E. - Union Twp Ralls Co., took up a bay mare ae 2y appraised
     at $40 by George Fraker & James Fox. John Burton JP.  5 Feb 1830
SLONE, John - road reviewer, Ray Co.  25 Feb 1823
SLY, Solomon - "cheap boarding" at the Wooden Nutmeg.  1 May 1824
SMART, William - appraised a stray taken up by James Moore.  31 Jul 1830
SMELSER, Harmon - Lamine Twp Cooper Co., took up a sorrel horse ae 6y
     appraised at $50 by Stephen Turley & John Fisher.  2 May 1828
                                        Samuel Turley JP.
     John - Tabbo Twp Lafayette Co., took up a bay mare ae 6y
     appraised at $44 by Christopher Mulky & Obadiah Bounds.  4 Sep 1829
                                        Wm. Carpenter JP.
SMITH, Blandamin - JP, Salt Spring Twp Chariton Co., strays taken up by
     Mark Noble (18 Jan 1828) & Charles Hatfield.  17 Apr 1829

          MIN
                                25

SMITH, Elkanah - appraised a stray taken up by Hardin Steele.                18 Aug 1832
Humphrey - of Clay Co., broke jail at Lexington. Accused of hog             11 Apr 1828
    theft and non-payment of costs in Ray Co. Age about 55,
    6' tall, "strong." Fled with William Reed.
John - appraised a stray taken up by Daniel Hurter.                          6 Aug 1831
John M. - appraised a stray taken up by Daniel Vinston.                     11 Nov 1823
Joseph & Samuel - appraised a stray taken up by Reuben Smith;               15 Jan 1824
    both signed "x."
Reuben - took up a dark bay mare ae 15-16 appraised at $10 and a            15 Jan 1824
    sorrel colt appraised at $25 by John Chilcoat, Joseph &
    Samuel Smith. James McFarland JP.
Thomas - appraised a stray taken up by James McKenny.                       18 Jan 1826
William - appraised a stray taken up by Gilpin Tuttle.                      23 Jul 1831
SNELL, Landon - appraised a stray taken up by Simeon Coppage.                7 Apr 1832
Willis W. - took up a sorrel mare ae 3y in Nine-Mile-Prairie Twp,          17 Mar 1832
    Callaway Co. Appraised at $25 by Larkin & Sherwood
    Maddox. Archibald Allen JP.
    - took up a dark bay horse ae 12y appraised at $17.50               14 Jul 1832
    by Daniel Nolley & Wm. P. Henderson. J. Curd JP.
SNODDY, James - found of unsound mind; John W. McGirk and Isaac Lowthian    15 Mar 1826
    appointed guardians. Howard Co.
    - James Allcorn, guardian, petitions to sell a slave.                6 Sep 1827
SNOW, Edward - Persia Twp Boone Co., took up a sorrel filly appraised        3 Nov 1832
    at $30 by Reasen Johnson, Brinsley Barnes. Rob't Schooling JP.
SNOWDEN, James - Justice of the Ray Co. Court.                              25 Feb 1823
SNOWDEN, Lovell - Missouriton Twp, Ray Co., took up a black filly           4 Mar 1823
    appraised at $15 by John Dodson & John Brunt.
                                        Isaac Martin JP.
    - on trial for the murder of John Wood in Lillard Co.                7 Aug 1824
    Verdict, manslaughter.
    - broke jail; described as ae 30, nearly 6' tall, with              14 Aug 1824
    dark hair and a pale complexion.
SOUTH, William - Missouri Twp Boone Co., took up a black mare ae 4y         14 May 1831
    appraised at $20 by Samuel L. South & James S. Lowrey.
                                        William Lientz JP.
SPEARS, Abraham - advertises his stud horse "Potomac" at the farm of        21 Mar 1828
    Capt. David Hickman in Boone Co.
SPENCE, Andrew - appraised a stray taken up by Robert Nelson.                5 Jul 1827
SPENCER, James - advertises wool carding at Fayette, with Alex'r Searcy.     1 Aug 1828
SPIRES, Samuel - appraised a stray taken up by John Lewis.                  17 Mar 1832
STACY, William - appraised a stray taken up by Peter Pervant.               15 Dec 1832
STANDLEY, James - JP, Missouriton Twp Ray Co., stray taken up by             6 May 1823
                                        Joseph Johnson.
John - appraised a stray taken up by Joseph Johnson.                         6 May 1823
William - Missouriton Twp, Ray Co., took up a jenny mule ae 12y            30 Sep 1823
    appraised at $22.50 by Joseph Johnson & Wm. Turner.
STEEL, Robert - JP, Clear Creek Twp Cooper Co., stray taken up by           26 May 1826
                                        Caleb Fisher.
STEELE, Hardin - took up a yellow bay mare ae 13-14 appraised at $22 by     18 Aug 1832
    David M. Kirkpatrick & Elkanah Smith. T. G. Jones JP.
STEPHENS, Elijah - Callaway Co., took up a gray horse ae 4y appraised       11 Dec 1824
    at $27.50 by Collet Loughley & John Heriford.
                                        Thomas Fisher JP.
Thomas P. - appraised a stray taken up by Joel Haynes.                      29 Sep 1832
STERKEY or STIRKEY, Jean - Andrew Turpin accused of his murder.             25 Sep 1824
STEWARD, James - Jefferson Twp Cole Co., took up a sorrel mare ae 8y         3 Jul 1824
    appraised at $25 by Charles Norwood & Daniel Colgan.
                                        John C. Gordon JP.
STICE, Peter - Rocky Fork Twp Boone Co., took up a dark bay mare ae 20-30   13 Jul 1826
    appraised at $5 by John Wilborn & Esrom Tipton.
                                        James E. Fenton JP
STOKES, John - appraised a stray taken up by Wm. Bryant; signed "x."         7 Jan 1823
STONE, Hardeman - JP, Boonville, stray taken up by John Greening.            1 Feb 1827
Samuel - advertises a new store in Columbia -dry goods, hardware,           9 Oct 1830
    queensware, etc.
STORRS, Asahel - licensed to sell wines and spirits, Howard Co.            31 May 1823
STOTHART, John - dissolves partnership with Robert Hood & James Scott.       7 Sep 1826
John D. - dissolves partnership with Thomas Campbell.                       25 Dec 1829

STRATTON, John - licensed as a merchant, Howard Co.   15 May 1824
STREET, Samuel - Moniteau Twp Howard Co., took up a bay filly ae 3y   25 Dec 1829
   appraised at $30 by John Wiley & Wm. Million.
                  W. M. Jackson JP.
STRODE, Mary - sues Stephen for divorce, Boone Co. Circuit Court,   7 Aug 1824
   by next friend George Harrison.
STROTHER, Thornton - sues Levi Woods for debt of $151.66, Clay Co.   14 May 1825
   - offers a reward for a stolen horse, Franklin.   25 Apr 1828
STUART, Jacob - executed for the murder of John Davidson.   19 Apr 1830
STURGEON, Humes - opens a grocery store in Fayette.   15 May 1824
   - defendant, mortgage foreclosure suit by Stephen   5 Aug 1825
   Trigg, Howard Co.
SULLENS, James - appraised a stray taken up by Thornton Hames.   2 Jun 1826
SUTTON, James - appraised a stray taken up by Thomas Crowson.   24 Mar 1832
   Roland - warns the public not to trade with his wife Elizabeth as   20 May 1823
   he will not pay her debts.
SWAIN, Daniel M. - appraised a stray taken up by Robert Donaldson.   11 Jun 1831
SWEARINGEN, Obed - appraised a stray taken up by Wm. Croley.   29 Feb 1828
SWEENEY, Joshua - appraised a stray taken up by Thomas Callahan.   17 Mar 1832
SWINNEY, Robert - appraised a stray taken up by Jordan Sizemore.   23 Aug 1827
SWITZLER, Lewis - licensed to operate a billiard hall, Howard Co.   15 May 1824
   Michael - licensed to operate a tavern, Howard Co.   16 Dec 1823
   - advertising a boarding house and stable, Franklin.   10 Jul 1829
TALLY, George - appraised a stray taken up by Hugh French.   12 May 1826
   - " by Daniel Hurter.   6 Aug 1831
   William - appraised a stray taken up by Robert Donaldson.   11 Jun 1831
TANNER, James - defendant in a mortgage foreclosure suit by Jere   1 May 1829
   Kingsbury, Howard Co.
TATE, Isaac - appraised a stray taken up by Wm. McCormack.   6 Nov 1830
TAYLOR, J. - opens a House of Entertainment in Randolph Co., "near   23 Oct 1829
   the courthouse."
   William - JP, Richmond Twp Howard Co., stray taken up by   15 Feb 1826
   Edward Atteberry.
   " by David Enyart (12 Jul 1827) & Daniel Lay   16 Jan 1829
   - Franklin Twp Howard Co., took up a sorrel mare ae 4y   5 Feb 1830
   appraised at $20 by Joel Lee & Jeremiah Murphy.
   - selling a brick house in Fayette, and woodland.   19 Feb 1830
TEETER, Liberty G. - runaway apprentice of tanner James H. Lay, ae ca 17.   15 Mar 1826
   Reward of 12½¢ offered.
   Samuel - selling school lands in Franklin Twp, with John Dade.   25 Feb 1823
   - appraised a stray taken up by Henry Hatfield.
TENNELL, Francis - see Hugh Tennill.   25 Feb 1825
TENNILL, Hugh - warns the public not to accept a note he gave Francis   25 Jan 1825
   Tennell; he has paid it but it was "fraudulently taken
   from me."
TENNELLE, George - defendant, mortgage foreclosure suit by   4 Sep 1824
   Susannah Cottee.
THOMPSON, A. Q. - JP, Prairie Twp Howard Co., stray taken up by   20 Feb 1829
   Jonathan Finnell.
   - " by Philip Prather.   11 Dec 1829
   John F. - Boonville, recommends new tanning method by   21 May 1825
   Leonard Jacobs.
THOMSON, Wiley - appraised a stray taken up by Peter Pervant.   15 Dec 1832
THORNTON, John - appraised a stray taken up by Polly Harvy.   11 Jun 1831
THURMAN, Joseph - appraised a stray taken up by Cornelius Howard;   6 Jan 1826
   signed "x."
TILTON, James - dissolved partnership with Robert Barr & Joseph Howard.   29 Jan 1830
   - dissolved partnership with James I. Howard.   29 Jan 1830
TIPTON, Esrom - appraised a stray taken up by Peter Stice.   13 Jul 1826
TITUS, George - Rocky Fork Twp Boone Co., took up a light sorrel filly   1 Oct 1831
   ae 3y appraised at $25 by Warner Phillips & John Reed.
                 James Barnes JP.
TOALSON, William - appraised a stray taken up by Reuben Riggs.   21 Jan 1823
TODD, John - appraised a stray taken up by Thomas Moxley.   19 Jun 1830
TOMPKINS, George - dissolved partnership with Charles French.   15 May 1824
TONEY, James - Callaway Co., took up a sorrel mare ae 9-10 y appraised   23 Jul 1831
   at $30 by Henry Holman & John Bartley. George Bartley JP.

TOOLE, George - bankrupt, some of his property sold.                           22 Jan 1831
TOOLY, John - appraised a stray taken up by John S. Gillet.                     9 Aug 1827
TRAMMELL, John - found a dark brown mule mixed in with his mules, in
    Lafayette Co.; asks the owner to claim.                                     2 Nov 1826
TRIGG, Dr. B. - advertises medicine and surgery, Boonville.                    20 Jun 1828
    Stephen - plaintiff, mortgage foreclosure suit vs Humes Sturgeon,
    Howard Co.                                                                   5 Aug 1825
TRIGLAR, Henry - appraised a stray taken up by John McGlothlin.                10 Aug 1826
TURNER, Enoch - appraised a stray taken up by Reuben Riggs.                    21 Jan 1832
TUMBLINSON, William - paid a $1 fine, Callaway Co. Circuit Court.              14 Jan 1823
TURLEY, Samuel - JP, Lamine Twp Cooper Co., stray taken up by Harmon Smelser.   2 May 1828
    Stephen - Collector, Cooper Co.                                            23 Dec 1823
    - appraised a stray taken up by Harmon Smelser.                             2 May 1828
TURNAGE, Michael - appraised a stray taken up by Jefferson Cary.               29 Feb 1828
TURNER, A. W. - appraised a stray taken up by Thomas Crowson.                  24 Mar 1832
    James - Franklin Twp Howard Co., took up a bay filly ae 2y
    appraised at $25 by Ephraim Turner & Absalom Renshaw.                      29 Apr 1823
    Jesse - JP, Rocky Fork Twp Boone Co., stray taken up by Wm. Baugh.         23 Sep 1825
    Talton - Chariton Twp Howard Co., took up two colts & a filly
    appraised at $15 each by Wm. Wright & Rhodias Fewell.                      27 Feb 1829
    - licensed to operate a ferry, Howard Co.                                  11 Dec 1829
    William - appraised a stray taken up by Joseph Johnson.                     6 May 1823
TURPIN, Andrew - accused of murdering Jean Sterky; notice by Benjamin
    Chambers, clerk of the Saline Co. Court, to the Sheriff                    25 Sep 1824
    of Saline Co., to pick Turpin up.
TUSSEY, Jona. - trustee of the Mt. Moriah Meeting House, asks bids
    for carpentry.                                                              6 Mar 1829
TUTTLE, Gilpin - Cedar Twp Boone Co., took up a black horse ae 8y appraised
    at $20 by James Harris & James Dunn. James Callaway JP.                     1 May 1829
    - took up a sorrel mare ae 4y appraised at $45 by Joseph
    Austin & Wm. Smith. James Callaway JP.                                     23 Jul 1831
UNDERWOOD, James - appraised  strays taken up by David Onstott &
    James Fugate.                                                              13 Aug 1831
UTTERBACK, Adam - appraised a stray taken up by David Onstott.                 13 Aug 1831
VAN ARSDALL, W. K. - attorney, partner of F.P. Mills, Columbia.                25 Dec 1830
VARNER, George - appraised a stray taken up by Major Barkwell.                  7 Jul 1832
VINSTON, Daniel - Round Prairie Twp Callaway Co., took up a strawberry
    roan mare ae 5y appraised at $40 by John M. Smith &                        11 Nov 1823
    Mark Cunningham. James Nevins JP.
VIVION, Hervey - trustee of Mt. Moriah Meeting House.                           6 Mar 1829
    Josiah - among a group entering the Santa Fe trade, leaving
    Blue Spring on 1 June.                                                      8 May 1829
WADE, William - JP, Marion Twp Cole Co., stray taken up by James McKenny.      18 Jan 1826
WALDEN, Austin F. - advertises a tanyard in Chariton.                          23 Sep 1823
WALKER, Dr. George K. - "lately fromeastward," now in Franklin.                28 Mar 1828
    - surgery, midwifery, medicine, in New Franklin.                           19 Jun 1829
    James R. - bankrupt.                                                       29 May 1824
WALKUP, Samuel P. - defendant, suit for debt by John Johnson, Boone Co.        27 Sep 1827
WALLACE, Andrew - Clear Creek Twp Cooper Co., took up a sorrel stud ae 8-9
    appraised at $10 by James S. & John H. Hutchinson &                        4 Mar 1823
    Henry Woolery.  John Briscoe JP.
WALLIS, George - a hatter in Liberty, offers 1¢ reward for runaway
    apprentice James B. Hixson, ca 19, fair hair, blue eyes.                   17 Apr 1829
WAMOCK, Allen - appraised a stray taken up by Benjamin Johnson.                26 Nov 1826
WAMUCK  Abraham & Allen - " stray by Moses Johnson.                            26 Jun 1829
WARD, Peirce - appraised a stray taken up by John Grayum.                      10 Aug 1826
    William - appointed to lease school lands in Richmond Twp.,
    Howard Co. (with James Shepherd).                                          4 Feb 1823
    - advertises wool carding at his home near Richmond, 10m
    from Franklin, 10¢ per lb.                                                 24 Jun 1823
    - advertises wool carding with Elijah Whitten.                            30 May 1828
WARE, Elias - appraised strays by Francis Whitlock (20 Feb 1829) and by
    (signed "x.")                         Francis Brown.                       27 Feb 1829
WARNER, Wynkoop - Sheriff of Callaway Co.                                      14 Jan 1823
WARREN, E. V. - JP, Chariton Twp Howard Co., stray taken up by Benj. Bowles.   20 Jul 1826
    William B. - JP, Chariton Twp Howard Co., stray taken up by               9 Jan 1829
    Richard Earickson.

MIN

28

WARSON, Reuben - has left his wife Rebecca "for just cause & provocation."    5 Jun 1824
WASHINGTON, Mrs. Ann E. - will give lessons in "all the ornamental    25 Jun 1825
    branches of female education" in Franklin.
  J. B. C. - opens a select school for young ladies and    25 Sep 1824
    gentlemen in Franklin.
WATKINS, Elisha - JP, Fort Osage Twp Jackson Co., stray taken up by    6 Feb 1829
    Zebediah Baker.
WATSON, Benjamin - appraised a stray taken up by Wm. Scott.    5 Feb 1824
WATTS, George - offers $10 reward for runaway Negro Jack, Howard Co.    23 Nov 1826
  - appraised a stray taken up by Samuel Hardin.    25 Dec 1829
WAYSERMAN, Jacob - advertises his blacksmith work.    16 Dec 1823
WEAVER, Abner - Clear Creek Twp Cooper Co., took up a black mare ae 5y    14 Aug 1829
    appraised at $45 by Abraham Fisher & Alexander Hatfield.
    R. B. Harris JP.
WEBSTER, Elizure D. - appraised a stray taken up by James Chitwood.    30 Apr 1831
WEEDEN, Rev. Caleb - will preach at Fayette 24 May.    17 May 1827
WELDON, James - Salt River Twp Ralls Co., took up a bright bay mare    16 Jul 1825
    appraised at $20 by Daniel Crump & Nathaniel Riggs.
    Peter Grant JP.
WELLS, James - JP, Salt Spring Twp Chariton Co., stray taken up by    18 Jan 1827
    Robert Sconce.
  - appraised a stray taken up by Charles Hatfield.    17 Apr 1829
  R. W. - attorney-at-law, now in Jefferson City.    21 Jun 1827
WEST, Joseph - offers a farm for sale 2m north of Bonne Femme Meeting    19 Mar 1831
    House; 160a, 30 fenced, a creek nearby.
WESTON, Samuel - JP, Tabbo Twp Lafayette Co., stray taken up by Benj. Johnson.10 Aug 1826
WHELDON, John - Salt Spring Twp Chariton Co., took up a bay horse ae 8y    11 Jan 1825
    appraised at $22.50 by James Cochran & Thomas Wright.
    James Willis JP.
  - appraised a stray taken up by Robert Sconce.    18 Jan 1827
WHITE, Crenshaw - appraised a stray taken up by Edward Atteberry.    15 Feb 1826
  Fielding - appraised a stray taken up by George Sexton.    16 Jun 1832
  Lewis - appraised a stray taken up by Wm. S. Banks.    14 Dec 1826
  William - warns the public not to accept a note he gave Lewis    9 Jul 1825
    Hardwich; it was "fraudulently obtained."
  William H. - opens a store in Columbia with Wm. Cornelius.    6 Nov 1830
WHITLOCK, Francis - Franklin Twp Howard Co., took up a brown mare ae 3y    20 Feb 1829
    appraised at $15 by Elias Ware & James McCampbell.
    James Allcorn JP.
WHITNITT, James - appraised a stray taken up by Elbert Linch.    21 Apr 1826
WHITTENBURGH, Jacob - Union Twp Ralls Co., took up a mare ae 3y    15 Aug 1828
    appraised at $30 by Ezra Fox & Jordan Sizemore.
    John Burton JP.
  - appraised a stray taken up by Ezra Fox.    29 Jan 1831
WHITTEN, Elijah - advertises wool carding with partner Wm. Ward.    30 May 1828
WIGGINTON, Roger - Bourbon Twp Callaway Co., took up a bright bay mare    17 Sep 1831
    ae 4y appraised at $40 by Mark S. Renfro & John D.
    Ridway. Isaac Black JP.
WILBOURN, Elliott - appraised a stray taken up by Ezra Fox.    29 Jan 1831
WILBORN, John - appraised a stray taken up by Peter Stice.    13 Jul 1826
  - Columbia Twp Boone Co., took up a bright bay horse ae 8y    10 Aug 1826
    appraised at $35 by John Mayo & Wm. Grisham. P.H. McBride JP.
WILCOX, Daniel P. - testified in support of Jesse T. Wood.    26 Apr 1825
WILEY, Isaac - appraised a stray taken up by Jefferson Cary.    29 Feb 1828
  John - appraised a stray taken up by Samuel Street.    25 Dec 1829
WILKERSON, Anthony T. - offers $10 reward for his runaway mulatto Washington. 14 Aug 1824
WILKINSON, William - appraised a stray taken up by John McGaugh.    30 Jul 1831
WILLIAMS, A. J. - Columbia; has sold out his stock of goods and wants    4 Dec 1830
    his accounts settled.
  Henry T. - JP, Chariton Twp Chariton Co., stray taken up by    14 Dec 1826
    Wm. S. Banks.
  - " by John S. Gillet.    9 Aug 1827
  John - JP, Columbia Twp Boone Co., stray taken up by Robert Nelson.    5 Jul 1827
  John D. - appraised a stray taken up by John Inglish.    19 May 1826
  Justinian - his cabinet shop managed by Alexander Hannah while    22 Jul 1825
    Williams is in Virginia.
  - opens a House of Entertainment in Boonville.    21 Apr 1826

MIN            29

WILLIAMS, William - of Clay Co.; his wife Catherine has left his bed
                    and board.            1 May 1824
WILLIAMSON, John - appraised a stray taken up by Anthony Owsley.     7 Jan 1832
            - " by John B. Dennis.                     23 Jun 1832
WILLINGHAM, John - Bourbon Twp Callaway Co., took up a bay filly ae 3y
           appraised (no amount shown) by John & Isham Kilgore.    6 Mar 1829
                                         Isaac Black JP.
         - took up a bay mare ae 11-12y appraised at $25 by George
           Cox & Robert F. Gibbs. Isaac Black JP.           6 Aug 1831
WILLIS, Anderson - appraised a stray taken up by R. Baker; signed "x."   24 Mar 1832
      James - JP, Salt Spring Twp Chariton Co., stray taken up by
                         John Wheldon.           11 Jan 1825
WILSON, Benjamin - appraised a stray taken up by James R. Wood.      15 Jan 1831
      David - appraised a stray taken up by Hugh French.           12 May 1826
         - " by Abraham Winscott.                         5 Feb 1831
      John - counsellor and attorney-at-law, Fayette.           22 Jan 1824
      Pleasant - appraised a stray taken up by Henry Lichlyter.     15 Apr 1823
WINN, Elijah - took up a bright bay mare ae 7-8y (in Boone Co.) appraised
           at $15 by William & Willis Angell. Y.E. Hicks JP.     25 Jan 1828
      Thomas - appointed to lease the school lands in Bonne Femme Twp,
           Howard Co. (with John Myers)                  11 Feb 1823
WINSCOTT, Abraham - Rocky Fork Twp Boone Co., took up a light chestnut
           sorrel horse ae 6-7y appraised at $20 by David Wilson    5 Feb 1831
           and John Ewens. Esem Hannon JP.
      Alfred - his wife Asenath has left his bed and board.       9 Oct 1830
      Christopher - Bourbon Twp Callaway Co., took up a bay horse
           ae 7y appraised at $45 by John C. & Isham         30 Oct 1830
           Kilgore. Archibald Allen JP.
      Dudley - his wife Nancy has left his bed and board.        1 Feb 1827
WISDOM, Thomas - Persia Twp Boone Co., took up a sorrel mare ae 3y
           appraised by Wilson Morris & Cornelius Short. (Appraisal   7 Jul 1832
           not shown.) Tyre Harris JP.
WISEMAN, James - Cedar Twp Boone Co., took up a black mare ae 9-10y
           appraised at $25 by Mosias Jones & John Sappington.    8 Jan 1831
                                   Tyre Martin JP.
WITHERS, Allen - offers a $5 reward for a green morocco pocket book
           lost on the road from Fayette to Franklin.       14 Dec 1826
WITT, E. B. - the public house he lately occupied was taken over by
                               Wm. Wright.       5 Apr 1827
         - takes over the "Tavern on the Hill" in Fayette.       4 Jul 1828
      Elisha - receives a merchant's license in Howard Co.      15 May 1824
      John - with others, offers lots for sale in Florida, Monroe Co.   16 Apr 1831
WOOD, James R. - Missouri Twp Boone Co., took up a bay mare ae 2y
           appraised at $30 by Benjamin J. Wilson & Charles B.    15 Jan 1831
           Hatton. John Henderson JP.
      J. T. - attorney-at-law, Columbia.                17 Jul 1824
         - moved his office to Mr. Harrison's building.        29 May 1830
      Jesse T. - Columbia; will present facts relative to "unsavory
           rumors" about him."                     12 Apr 1825
         - a long article in which he states that he was falsely    26 Apr 1825
         accused of stealing a Negro boy from Elijah Allen and
         Allen's mother Jane, of Boone Co. Several men testified
         as to Wood's truthfulness and good character: Thomas
         Ford and William Eckery of St. Charles, Daniel P. Wilcox,
         Oliver Parker, P. H. McBride, and Thomas G. Berby.
         - will practice law in Columbia.                7 May 1825
         - JP, Columbia, stray taken up by William McClain.     11 Jan 1828
         - partner of Calvin L. Ferry (attorneys).           8 Jan 1831
      John - of Lillard Co.; Lovell Snowden, on trial for his murder,
           was convicted of manslaughter.            7 Aug 1824
         - appraised a stray taken up by William Gwinn.      14 Jun 1827
      Levi - of Cooper Co., notifies the public that his wife Rachel
           has left him.               14 Dec 1826
WOODRUFF, William B. - bankrupt, Boone Co.             25 Jan 1826
           - appraised a stray taken up by Wm. A. Bates.      3 Aug 1826
WOODS, A. C. - JP, Chariton Twp Howard Co., stray taken up by Wm. Croley.   29 Feb 1828

MIN                   30

WOODS, Absalom T. - of Cooper Co.; Isaac Renfro was being re-tried
                                             for his murder.                           2 Jul 1825
       Adam - constable, Howard Co.                                                   16 Dec 1823
       Adam C. - JP, Chariton Twp, stray taken up by Wm. Wright.                      14 Dec 1827
       Joseph and William - defendants, suit for $489.60 by Oliver Parker.           27 Nov 1829
       Levi - defendant, suit by Thornton Strother, Clay Co.                         14 May 1825
       Patrick - appointed to lease the school lands in Prairie Twp,
            Howard Co. (with John Harvey).                                           11 Feb 1823
       Sarshel - appraised a stray taken up by Wm. Croley.                           29 Feb 1828
WOODSON, Warren - JP, Columbia Twp Boone Co., stray taken up by
                                             David Gordon.                           27 Mar 1829
       -   " by John Parker (21 May 1831), Thomas Crowson
                                  and Charles M. Hayes.                              24 Mar 1832
WOOLERY, Henry - appraised a stray taken up by Andrew Wallace.                        3 Nov 1832
WORKMAN, David - offers 1¢ reward for Christopher Carson, a runaway                   4 Mar 1823
                                  apprentice (saddler).                              12 Oct 1826
WRIGHT, Peter - recommends a new tanning method by Leonard Jacobs.                   14 May 1825
       Sampson - collector, Boone Co.                                                 6 Nov 1824
       Samuel - Columbia Twp Boone Co., took up a sorrel horse ae 7-8y
            appraised at $30 by Sampson Wright & Robert Nelson.                      11 Jun 1831
                                  James Kirtley JP.
       Thomas - appraised a stray taken up by John Wheldon.                          11 Jan 1825
       William - takes over the public house in Fayette lately occupied
                                  by E. B. Witt.                                      5 Apr 1827
            - Chariton Twp Howard Co., took up a chestnut sorrel
            horse appraised at $30 by Isaac Runnion & Joseph Brown.                  14 Dec 1827
                                  Adam C. Woods JP.
            - appraised a stray taken up by Richard Earickson.                        9 Jan 1829
            -   " by Daniel Mourning.                                                25 Jun 1831
WYAN, John - advertises wool carding in Boonville.                                    2 Jul 1825
YOUNG, Benjamin - neighbor of Augustine Creed, Ralls Co. near the south
                        fork of the Salt River. Creed was explaining the            14 Aug 1830
                        area where his stolen horse had disappeared.
       James C. - bankrupt, Saline Co.                                                3 Jul 1829
YOUNT, Eliza - sued George for divorce, Howard Co., by next friend                   11 Dec 1829
                                  Robert Brown.

                         - 0 -

                  *DOCTOR LOWRY,*

            **T**HANKFUL for the en-
                 couragement received in
            his profession, tenders his servi-
            ces to the citizens of Howard &
            Cooper Counties, in the practice
            of
            *Medicine, Surgery, and Mid-
                 wifery,*
            and hopes to merit patronage.
               He has on hand, and will re-
            tail, a quantity of

            *DRUGS & MEDICINES,*

               Also, some *Patent Medicines,*
            viz: Bauman's Drops, British
            Oil, Lee's Pills, &c.
               He can be consulted at his shop
            in Franklin.
               Franklin, April '23        4 tf.


    MIN                    31

ABERNATHY, J. R. - appraised a stray taken up by Jacob Whittenburg.  4 Jul 1829
ADAMS, John - Moniteau Twp, Howard Co.; took up two bay mares and a bay
   filly appraised at $50 by John W. Rawlings & Wm. L. Head.  8 Sep 1830
                                          John B. Clark JP.
**   Lowri - appraised a stray taken up by Richard Johnson.  14 Jul 1830
ALEXANDER, Samuel - his land sold to satisfy a claim of Joel Haden.  21 Feb 1829
ALLISON, William - Monitor Twp, Cooper Co.; took up a sorrel horse ae 12y
   appraised at $22 by Wm. Stephens & Wm. Swearingen.  14 Jul 1830
                                          David Jones JP.
ANGELL, Robert - appraised a stray taken up by John Roberts.  9 Jan 1830
ARTEBERRY, Simeon - took up a chestnut sorrel mare ae 12y appraised at
   $20 by Willis Skelton & John Willoby.  11 Jul 1829
                                          Frederick A. Bradford JP.
ASHCRAFT, Otho - appraised a stray taken up by John Hartgrave.  17 Nov 1830
AYRES, Benjamin - advertises the Green Tree Tavern, St. Charles.  28 Mar 1829
BAILY, Jacob - Chariton Twp, Howard Co.; took up a bright bay filly
   ae 2-3y appraised at $22.50 by Thomas Fristoe & John  8 Sep 1830
   Tooly.  James Turner JP.
BARNES, Abraham - will race his horse "Tecumseh" against W. H. Johnston's  7 Apr 1830
   "Georgian."
BARNETT, Zaccheus - Moniteau Twp, Howard Co.; took up a bay horse ae 6y
   appraised at $45 by Porter Jackman & John Rawlings.  7 Jul 1830
                                          Th. G. Rawlings JP.
BECKNELL, William - Arrow Rock Twp, Saline Co.; JP, stray taken up by  19 May 1830
                                          Jacob Nave.
BELLMAR, William - appraised a stray taken up by Wm. F. George.  16 Jan 1830
BERRY, Thomas G. - see Mr. Camplin.
BLACK, Abram - appraised a stray taken up by Garrison Patrick.  17 Nov 1830
   Abraham - Richmond Twp, Howard Co.; took up a gray mare ae 4y
   appraised at $40 by Watts D. Ewing & Samuel Hardin.  15 Dec 1830
                                          John B. Clark JP.
BOURN, John D. - appraised a stray taken up by Henry Burnam.  12 Dec 1829
BOWYER, Henry & Jesse - appraised a stray taken up by Charles Colter.  9 Jan 1830
BRADFORD, Frederick A. - JP, stray taken up by Simeon Arteberry.  11 Jul 1829
   - Prairie Twp, Chariton Co.; JP, strays taken up by
   James Morgan (7 July 1830) & Stephen McCollum.  18 Aug 1830
BRIDGES, Pemberton H. - his property in New Franklin sold to satisfy a  13 Oct 1830
   claim of William & David Lamme & C. F. Jackson.
BURCH, John - Chariton Twp, Howard Co.; took up a young jack appraised  26 May 1830
   at $50 by Thomas Perry & Thomas Morris.  Wm. B. Warren JP.
BURCKHARTT, N. - Franklin Twp, Howard Co.; JP, stray taken up by  14 Nov 1829
                                          Thomas McCullock.
BURNAM, Henry - Richmond Twp, Howard Co.; took up a bay horse colt ae 2y
   appraised at $20 by Gray Bynum & John D. Bourn.  12 Dec 1829
                                          John B. Clark JP.
   - took up a bay mare ae 7y appraised at $50 by James Owings  21 Apr 1830
   & Richard Burton.  Clark JP.
   Hickerson - defendant in a suit for $300 debt by Zachariah  20 Oct 1830
   Waller, Jackson Co.
BURNETT, James - Howard Co.; warns the public not to accept notes he gave  23 Jun 1830
   Nimrod Duncan & Andrew B. Walker.
BURTON, Richard - appraised a stray taken up by Henry Burnam.  21 Apr 1830
BUSTER, William - with John T. Marshall, warns the public not to accept a  5 Sep 1829
   note they gave Elias Rector, "conditions not complied with".
BYBEE, John - his wife Nancy has lefr his bed and board.  21 Feb 1829
BYNUM, Gray - appraised a stray taken up by Henry Burnam.  5 Dec 1829
CALAWAY, James - appraised a barrel of rum found by John B. Teeter.  31 Mar 1830
CALLAGHAN, Thomas - appraised a stray taken up by James Crawford.  9 Jan 1830
CAMPBELL, Isaac - a Christmas Eve ball to be held at his house in Chariton.
   Superintendents: James Daly, Charles Sterne, Berry Hurt,  5 Dec 1829
   Thomas Cockerill, Joseph Shepherd, John H. Turner,
   Willis M. Green, and George W. Samuel.
   R. S. - appraised a stray taken up by Thomas Knox.  24 Nov 1830
   Samuel - appraised a stray taken up by James Crawford.  9 Jan 1830
** ADAMS, William - next friend of Cealy Curtis, divorce, Chariton Co.  29 Aug 1829

CAMPLIN, Mr. - his inn at Columbia was the site of a Christmas Eve ball in Columbia.  Superintendents: Thomas G. Berry, Joseph B. Howard, Jesse T. Wood, A. M. Robinson, William S. Truett, L. N. Sanders, & J. Kirkbride.  — 5 Dec 1829

CARLILE, Thomas - Howard Co.; William Hughes testifies as to his good character.  — 15 Sep 1830

CATHEY, George - appraised a stray taken up by Alexander S. Miller.  — 12 Sep 1829

CHAPMAN, George - Franklin Twp, Howard Co.; JP, strays taken up by Eleazer McKee (23 Jun 1830) and by Thomas Knox.  — 24 Nov 1830

CHERRY, John - appraised a stray taken up by Thomas Kirkpatrick.  — 19 Dec 1829

CHRISMAN, Mrs. Catherine - "millinery, fancy silk and leghorn bonnets," etc., in Fayette.  — 23 Jan 1830

CHRISMAN & Co. - new store in the building formerly occupied by J. A. Shirley, Fayette.  — 30 Jan 1830

CLARK, John B. - JP, Richmond Twp, Howard Co., strays taken up by Henry Burnam (12 Dec 1829), Pleasant Wilson (23 Jun 1830) and Garrison Patrick.  — 17 Nov 1830

Also one stray in Moniteau Twp by John Adams.  — 8 Sep 1830

Robert P. - his house and lot in Boonville for sale or rent.  — 21 Apr 1830

COCKERILL, Thomas - see Isaac Campbell.

COLE, Halbert - appraised a stray taken up by James Doleson.  — 15 Dec 1830

COLMAN, Henry - wholesale and retail tin manufactory, Franklin.  — 4 Aug 1830

CONWAY, Thomas - five of his slaves sold to satisfy a claim of Wesley Green.  — 15 Dec 1830

COOK, John - Blue Twp, Jackson Co.; JP, stray taken up by Robert Rennick.  — 4 Aug 1830

COOLEY, John - bankrupt, Randolph Co.  — 6 Feb 1830

COLTER, Charles K. - Richmond Twp, Howard Co.; took up a black cow with a red heifer calf appraised at $7 by Henry & Jesse Bowyer.  Birch JP.  — 9 Jan 1830

CORNELIUS, John - appraised a stray taken up by Elmore Thompson.  — 15 Dec 1830

CRAWFORD, James - Columbia Twp, Boone Co.; took up a brown horse ae 2y appraised at $20 & a light sorrel horse ae 1y, $15, by Samuel Campbell & Thomas Callaghan.  J. T. Wood JP.  — 9 Jan 1830

John - Bonne Femme Twp, Howard Co.; JP, stray taken up by Richard Johnson.  — 14 Jul 1830

CUNNINGHAM, Joseph - appraised a stray taken up by Samuel Turley.  — 14 Apr 1830

CURRIN, Waddy T. - sues Joseph McReynolds, mortgage foreclosure, Howard Co.  — 24 Mar 1830

CURTIS, Cealy - sues Enoch Curtis for divorce, Chariton Co., by her next friend William Adams.  — 29 Aug 1829

DADE, John - Boonville Twp, Cooper Co.; JP, stray taken up by Sam'l Turley.  — 14 Apr 1830

DALY, James - see Isaac Campbell

DAVIES, George - Miami Twp, Saline Co.; took up a bay mare ae 6y appraised at $45 by Richard Malone & Joseph McReynolds. Samuel McReynolds JP.  — 17 Mar 1830

DAVIS, Baily - Rocky Fork Twp, Boone Co.; took up a sorrel mare ae 12y & a black mare colt, appraised at $25 by Peter Smith & David Wisdom.  Esem Hannah JP.  — 16 Jan 1830

DOLESON, James - Clear Creek Twp, Cooper Co.; took up a sorrel colt ae 1y appraised at $20 by Abraham Woolery & Halbert Cole. William Steele JP.  — 15 Dec 1830

DUESMORE, Samuel - appraised a stray taken up by James Morgan.  — 7 Jul 1830

DUNCAN, Nimrod - James Burnett warns the public not to accept a note he gave Duncan.  — 23 Jun 1830

DUNN, James - offers "a likely young Negro woman" for sale, Fayette.  — 5 Dec 1829

DYSART, John - Silver Creek Twp, Randolph Co.; JP, stray taken up by James Lesley.  — 16 Mar 1830

EATON, George - appraised a stray taken up by John Jackson.  — 16 Jan 1830

ENYART, Silus - appraised a stray taken up by Wm. F. George.  — 16 Jan 1830

ELLIOTT, John - Moses Hieott's property sold to satisfy a claim by Elliott.  — 2 Jun 1830

EPLY, Andrew - his property in Old Franklin sold to satisfy a claim of Lawrence Hall.  — 16 Jan 1830

ESTES, Peyton W. - Lafayette Co.; took up a dun horse ae 7y appraised at $20 & a dapple gray mare $35 by James Craig & Littlebury Estes.  David McWilliams JP.  — 7 Mar 1829

EWING, Watts D. - appraised a stray taken up by Garrison Patrick.  — 17 Nov 1830

    - "   by Abraham Black.  — 15 Dec 1830

FELAND, John - appraised a stray taken up by Thomas Kirkpatrick.  — 19 Dec 1829

```
FOSTER, Mark - appraised a stray taken up by Robert Rennick.                    4 Aug 1830
FOX, H. - appraised a stray taken up by Jacob Whittenburg.                      4 Jul 1829
FRISTOE, Thomas - appraised a stray taken up by Jacob Baily.                    8 Aug 1830
FROST, Joshua - runaway apprentice of Owen Tharp, Clay Co. He was "upwards
          of 14," fair, with light blue eyes and light hair. Reward            18 Aug 1830
          of 25¢ offered.
GARSHWILER, John W. - appraised a stray taken up by James Lesley.              16 Mar 1830
GEORGE, William F. - Prairie Twp, Howard Co.; took up a bay mare ae 15y
          appraised at $18 by Silus Enyart & Wm. Bellmar.
                                                 John Harvey JP.
GILL, J. - offers "a fine assortment of watch jewelry" from Philadelphia.       5 Dec 1829
GLASSCOCK, Charles - appraised a stray taken up by Charles Rice.               14 Jul 1830
          Stephen - Spencer Twp, Ralls Co.; JP, stray taken by Chas. Rice.       "
GOODING, Abraham - appraised a stray taken up by William Patrick.               4 July 1829
GRANT, Peter - Salt River Twp, Ralls Co.; JP, stray taken by James McGee.      28 Apr 1830
GREEN, Rev. Jesse - will preach in Fayette the 3rd Sunday in April.             7 Apr 1830
          Wesley S. - slaves of Thomas Conway sold to satisfy his claim.       15 Dec 1830
          Willis M. - see Isaac Campbell.
GREGG, Jacob - appraised a stray taken up by Robert Rennick.                    4 Aug 1830
          Jacob & John - offer land for sale in Chariton Co. - 221 acres -
               and two lots in Fayette.                                        14 Nov 1829
GUINN, Bartlett - Jefferson Twp, Saline Co., JP, stray taken up by
               Robert Rogers.                                                  15 Dec 1830
          Elijah & Mat C. - appraised the stray shown above.                     "
HADEN, Joel - Samuel Alexander's land sold to satisfy Haden's claim.           21 Feb 1829
HALL, Lawrence - Andrew Eply's property in Old Franklin sold to satisfy
               Hall's claim.                                                   16 Jan 1830
HANNAH, Esem - Rocky Fork Twp, Boone Co.; JP, stray taken by Baily Davis.      16 Jan 1830
HARDIN, Samuel - appraised a stray taken up by Abraham Black.                  15 Dec 1830
HARGROVE, Benjamin - Howard Co.; his land sold to satisfy a claim of
               Stephen Woods.                                                  30 Jan 1830
HARRIS, Peter B. - appraised a stray taken up by Eleazer McKee.                23 Jun 1830
HARRISON, James & Co. - property of Moses Hieott sold to satisfy their
                                                           claim.               2 Jun 1830
               - slave of Henry Kruper sold to satisfy their claim.            15 Dec 1830
HARTGRAVE, John - "near Arrow Rock Ferry, Cooper's Bottom;" took up a
               bay horse appraised at $40 by Otho Ashcraft & Edward            17 Nov 1830
               Mulhollan.  Thornton Strother JP.
HARVEY, John - Prairie Twp, Howard Co.; JP, stray taken up by Wm. George.      16 Jan 1830
HASE, Frederick C. - of Perry Co.; stated that John W. Steward, charged
               with the murder of George Maize on 11 Apr 1824,                  4 Jul 1829
               has escaped. Governor Miller offers $200 reward.
HAUGHN, Peter - appraised a stray taken up by Stephen McCollum.                18 Aug 1830
HEAD, William L. - appraised a stray taken up by John Adams.                    8 Sep 1830
HELM, Charles - appraised a stray taken up by John Reed Sr.                    29 Aug 1829
HICKS, Y. E. - Boone Co.; JP, stray taken up by John Roberts.                   9 Jan 1830
HICKSON, Allen - runaway apprentice of Thomas Hickson of Clay Co., three
               miles north of Liberty. Age 17 or 18. 1¢ reward.               15 Sep 1830
HIEOTT, Moses - his property sold to satisfy claims of John Elliott
               and James Harrison & Co.                                         2 Jun 1830
HOLLEY, Presley - advertises the stallion "Joseph" at stud six miles
               north of Fayette, one mile south of Foster's.                   31 Mar 1830
HOOD, Robert - advertises an agency and commission business, Boonville.        28 Apr 1830
HOWARD, Joseph B. - see Mr. Camplin.
HOWE, John H. - Cooper Co.; took up a bay horse ae 4y appraised at $45,
               appraisers not known.  John Miller JP.                          12 May 1830
HUGHES, Andrew - near Liberty; wants to hire a Negro blacksmith.                4 Jul 1829
          William - owner of a tanyard three miles west of Fayette, offers
               1¢ reward for apprentice Reuben Stewart, a runaway.             11 Jul 1829
               - testifies as to the good character of Thomas Carlile
               of Howard Co.                                                   15 Sep 1830
HUM, Jack - appraised a stray taken up by William Pearson.                      4 Jul 1829
HUNGERFORD, Levi - appraised a stray taken up by Samuel Turley.                14 Apr 1830
HURT, Berry - see Isaac Campbell.
JACKMAN, Porter - appraised a stray taken up by Zaccheus Barnett.               7 Jul 1830
JACKSON, C. F. - Pemberton Bridges' property in New Franklin sold to
               satisfy a claim of Jackson and Wm. & David Lamme.               13 Oct 1830
```

JACKSON, Elbridge - "two likely Negroes for sale."                                  6 Feb 1830
    John - Richmond Twp, Howard Co.; took up a red steer ae 3y                      16 Jan 1830
        appraised at $5 by George Eaton & Alfred Morrison.
    Richard - Bonne Femme Twp, Howard Co.; took up a bay horse ae 4y
        appraised at $20 by Lowri Adams & Charles Littrell.                         14 Jul 1830
            John Crawford JP.
JOHNSTON, W. H. - Abraham Barnes offers to race his horse "Tecumseh"                 7 Apr 1830
        against Johnston's "Georgian."
JONES, David - Monitor? Twp, Cooper Co.; JP, stray taken by Wm. Allison.            14 Jul 1830
KELLY, Marshall - building superintendent, Marion Co., asks for bids on            11 Jul 1829
        a courthouse.
KEMBLE, William S. - appraised a stray taken up by Jacob Nave.                      19 May 1830
KIRKBRIDE, J. - see Mr. Camplin.
KIRKPATRICK, Thomas - Richmond Twp, Howard Co.; took up a red heifer ae 2y          19 Dec 1829
        appraised at $4.50 by John Feland & John Cherry.
KIRTLY, Sinclair - appraised a stray taken up by William Shields.                  19 Dec 1829
KNOX, Thomas - Howard Co.; took up a bright bay horse ae 4y appraised at            24 Nov 1830
        $35 by S. P. Marshall & R. S. Campbell. Geo. Chapman JP.
KRUPER, Henry - a slave of his sold to satisfy the claim of James                  15 Dec 1830
            Harrison & Co.
LAMME, David, William & Samuel - Wm. Sullins' land in Old Franklin                 13 Feb 1830
            sold to satisfy their claim.
    David & William - Pemberton Bridges' property in New Franklin                   13 Oct 1830
            sold to satisfy their claim.
LEGIT, Joseph - Chariton Twp, Howard Co.; took up a bright bay mare ae 4y
        appraised at $40 by Little West & Joseph Legit. (sic)                      17 Nov 1830
            Wm. B. Warren JP.
LESLEY, James - Silver Creek Twp, Randolph Co.; took up a sorrel filly
        ae 3y appraised at $40 by John W. Garshwiler & William                     16 Mar 1830
        Stanis. John Dysart JP.
LITTRELL, Charles - appraised a stray taken up by Richard Johnson.                 14 Jul 1830
McCLELLON, James - President of the Bonne Femme Academy.                            14 Nov 1829
McCOLLUM, Stephen - Prairie Twp, Chariton Co.; took up a bay mare ae 3y
        appraised at $20 by John Sizenly & Peter Haughn.                           18 Aug 1830
            Frederick Bradford JP.
McCOY, Isaac - advertises the sale of public property used in surveying
        and marking the Delaware lands: bridles, pack saddles,                      8 Dec 1830
        blankets, tents, horses, guns, etc. Fayette.
    Dr. R. - now located permanently in Fayette.                                    4 Jul 1829
    Rice - offers a liberal reward for a strayed gray pony, Fayette.               28 Apr 1830
McCULLOCK, Thomas - Franklin Twp, Howard Co.; took up a chestnut sorrel
        mare ae 4y appraised at $35 by Wm. Seybert & Francis                       14 Nov 1829
        Whitlock. N. Burckhartt JP.
McGEE, James - Salt River Twp, Ralls Co.; took up two fillies appraised            28 Apr 1830
        at $40 by James See & Samuel Turner. Peter Grant JP.
McKEE, Eleazer - Franklin Twp, Howard Co.; took up an iron gray mare
        ae 3-4y appraised at $30 by Moss Prewitt & Peter B.                        23 Jun 1830
        Harris. George Chapman JP.
McKEEHAN, John - his wife Nancy has left his bed and board.                         28 Jul 1830
McREYNOLDS, Joseph - appraised a stray taken up by George Davies.                   17 Mar 1830
        - defendant in a suit by Waddy T. Currin, mortgage                          24 Mar 1830
        foreclosure, Howard Co.
    Samuel P. - Miami Twp, Saline Co.; JP, stray taken up by                        17 Mar 1830
                George Davies.
    William - candidate for constable, Richmond Twp, Howard Co.                     7 Jul 1830
MACK, N. W. - advertises the Virginia Hotel, St. Charles.                           28 Feb 1829
MAIZE, George - murdered on 11 Apr 1824, Perry Co.; John Steward, charged           4 Jul 1829
        with the crime, escaped jail.
MALONE, Richard - appraised a stray taken up by George Davies.                      17 Mar 1830
MARS, Samuel - appraised a stray taken up by William Pearson.                       4 Jul 1829
MARSHALL, John T. - with William Buster, warns the public not to accept
                a note they gave Elias Rector, "conditions not                      5 Sep 1829
                complied with."
    S. P. - appraised a stray taken up by Thomas Knox.                             24 Nov 1830
MEANS, William B. - Moniteau Twp, Howard Co.; JP, stray taken up by                15 Dec 1830
                Elmore Thompson.
MELODY, G. H. C. - dissolves partnership with John D. Stothart.                     5 Sep 1829

        WM                        35

MILLER, Alexander S. - Cooper Cp.; took up a chestnut sorrel mare ae 7-8y
             appraised at $40 by George Cathey & Samuel Miller.    12 Sep 1829
                               William A. Miller JP.
    James - asks his debtors to pay.    12 Dec 1829
    John - Cooper Co.; JP, stray taken up by John H. Howe.    12 May 1830
MOBLEY, William - appraised a stray taken up by Pleasant Wilson.    23 Jun 1830
MONROE, W. W. - candidate for constable, Richmond Twp, Howard Co.    7 Jul 1830
MORGAN, James - Prairie Twp, Chariton Co.; took up two bay fillies
             appraised at $49 by Samuel Duesmore & James Parks.    7 Jul 1830
                          Frederick Bradford JP.
MORRIS, John W. - appraised a stray taken up by Elijah Sampson.    14 Nov 1829
MORRIS, Thomas - appraised a stray taken up by John Burch.    26 May 1830
MORRISON, Alfred W. - appraised a stray taken up by Elijah Sampson.    14 Nov 1829
           - " by John Jackson.    16 Jan 1830
MORROW, David - appraised a stray taken up by Elmore Thompson.    15 Dec 1830
MULHOLLAN, Edward - appraised a stray taken up by John Hartgrave.    17 Nov 1830
MUNSON, Alonzo - lost a silver watch between Chariton and Captain Head's
             home in Randolph Co.    23 Jun 1830
NANSON, John - dissolves partnership with __ Simpson, will continue at the
             New White House on the west side of the public square.    6 Feb 1830
NAVE, Jacob - Arrow Rock Twp, Saline Co.; took up a chestnut sorrel mare
             ae 5y appraised at $15 by James Nave & Wm. S. Kemble.    19 May 1830
                          William Becknell JP.
ODELL, Jeremiah E. - bankrupt, Howard Co.    17 Nov 1830
OWENS, James - proprietor of a copper-and-tin manufactory, Fayette.    16 Jan 1830
OWINGS, James - appraised a stray taken up by Henry Burnam.    21 Apr 1830
PARKS, James - appraised a stray taken up by James Morgan.    7 Jul 1830
PATRICK, Garrison - Richmond Twp, Howard Co.; took up a bay mare ae 3y
             appraised at $40 by Watts D. Ewing & Abram Black.    17 Nov 1830
                          John B. Clark JP.
    John D. - "Two likely Negroes" to be sold by his guardian,
                            John D. Thomas.    9 Jan 1830
    William - Sugar Creek Twp, Randolph Co.; took up a yellow bay
             horse ae 3y appraised at $40 by Abraham Gooding &    4 Jul 1829
             James Shadden. John Peeler JP.
PATTEN, Nancy - can accommodate five or six boarders, wants to hire a
             Negro woman.    7 Jul 1830
PEARSON, William - Columbia Twp, Boone Co.; took up a bay mare ae 4y
             appraised at $15 by Samuel Mars & Jack Hum. J.T. Wood JP.    4 Jul 1829
PEELER, John - Sugar Creek Twp, Randolph Co.; JP, stray taken up by
                            Wm. Patrick.    4 Jul 1829
PENDLETON, Mace - appraised a stray taken up by Pleasant Wilson.    23 Jun 1830
PERRY, Thomas - appraised a stray taken up by John Burch.    26 May 1830
PIPES, James - his wife Nancy (nee Johnson) has left his bed and board.    17 Mar 1830
PREWITT, Moss - appraised a stray taken up by Eleazer McKee.    23 Jun 1830
PURDIN, William - is building a mill; will buy flax seed.    11 Aug 1830
RAWLINGS, John - appraised a stray taken up by Zaccheus Barnett.    7 Jul 1830
           - " by John Adams.    8 Sep 1830
    Th. G. - Moniteau Twp, Howard Co.; JP, stray taken up by
                           Zaccheus Barnett.    7 Jul 1830
REED, James - sells Stephen Trigg Sr.'s land in Chariton Co.    3 Mar 1830
           - lost a pocketbook on the way from Columbia to Fayette.    20 Oct 1830
    John Sr. - Rocky Fork Twp, Boone Co.; took up a brown stallion
             ae 3y appraised at $20 by Charles Helm & Simeon Rouse.    29 Aug 1829
                          Samuel Riggs JP.
RENNICK, Robert A. - Fort Osage Twp, Jackson Co.; took up a sorrel horse
             ae 4y appraised at $35 by Jacob Gregg & Mark Foster.    4 Aug 1830
             John Cook Jr. (of Blue Twp, Jackson Co.), JP.
RICE, Charles - Spencer Twp, Ralls Co.; took up a bright bay horse ae 6y
             appraised at $36 by David Watoon & Charles Glasscock.    14 Jul 1830
                          Stephen Glasscock JP.
RIGGS, Samuel - Rocky Fork Twp, Boone Co.; JP, stray taken by John Reed Sr.    29 Aug 1829
ROBERTS, James - his property sold by the sheriff to satisfy a judgment
             by the Howard Co. Court - mare, colt, yearling cow beast.    5 Sep 1829
    John - Boone Co.; took up a bright sorrel mare ae 3y appraised
             at $18 by Washington Willis & Robert Angell. Y.E. Hicks JP.    9 Jan 1830
ROBINSON, A. M. - see Mr. Camplin.

ROGERS, Robert - Jefferson Twp, Saline Co.; took up a brown mare ae 10y
    appraised at $20 by Mat C. & Elijah Guinn.                       15 Dec 1830
                                Bartlett Guinn JP.
ROLLINS, Pleasant - runaway apprentice of John D. Thomas, Lafayette Co.
    Age 16-17. 1¢ reward offered.                             17 Nov 1830
ROUSE, Simeon - appraised a stray taken up by John Reed Sr.        29 Aug 1829
SAMPSON, Elijah - Richmond Twp, Howard Co.; took up a bay horse ae 12y
    appraised at $20 by Alfred W. Morrison & John W.          14 Nov 1829
    Morris. Birch JP.
SAMUEL, George W. - see Isaac Campbell.
SANDERS, L. M. - see Mr. Camplin.
SANFORD, John D. - his land sold to satisfy a claim of John D. White.    30 Jan 1830
SEARCY, Alexander - dissolves partnership with James Spencer.        1 Sep 1830
SEARS, John - his Fayette town property for sale as he wants to move
    to the country.                                      7 Apr 1830
SEBREE, Uriel - advertises the stallion "Young Pretender" and the jack
    "Matchless" at stud.                              28 Feb 1829
SEE, James - appraised a stray taken up by James McGee.          28 Apr 1830
SEYBERT, William - appraised a stray taken up by Thomas McCullock.    14 Nov 1829
SHADDEN, James - appraised a stray taken up by William Patrick.      4 Jul 1829
SHEPHERD, Joseph - see Isaac Campbell.
SHIELDS, William - Columbia Twp, Boone Co.; took up a strawberry roan mare
    ae 10y & a black mare ae 5y, appraised at $30 by         19 Dec 1829
    Sinclair Kirtly & Daniel Wilcox. W. Woodson JP.
SHIRLEY, J. A. - building he formerly occupied taken over by Chrisman & Co.  30 Jan 1830
SILVEY, Gabriel - candidate for coroner, Howard Co.              28 Jul 1830
SIMPSON, Mary & sons - Old Franklin; general merchandise. (Later
    also advertised a commission business.)               14 Apr 1830
SIZENLY, John - appraised a stray taken up by Stephen McCollum.      18 Aug 1830
SKELTON, Willis - appraised a stray taken up by Simeon Arteberry.     11 Jul 1829
SMITH, Peter - appraised a stray taken up by Baily Davis.          16 Jan 1830
SPENCER, James - dissolves partnership with Alexander Searcy.       1 Sep 1830
STANIS, William - appraised a stray taken up by James Lesley.      16 Mar 1830
STEELE, William - Clear Creek Twp, Cooper Co.; JP, stray taken up by
                         James Doleson.          15 Dec 1830
STEPHENS, Daniel H. - opens a House of Entertainment in Fayette.     4 Aug 1830
    William - appraised a stray taken up by William Allison.    14 Jul 1830
STERNE, Charles - see Isaac Campbell.
STEWARD, John W. - charged with the murder of George Maize 11 Apr 1824,
    escaped; notice by Perry CO. JP, Gov. Miller              4 Jul 1829
    offers a reward for his capture.
STEWART, Reuben - runaway apprentice of William Hughes, tannier & currier,
    3 miles west of Fayette, who offers 1¢ reward. He was    11 Jul 1829
    about 17, dark, black-haired, large for his age.
STOTHART, John D. - dissolves partnership with G. H. C. Melody.       5 Sep 1829
STROTHER, Thornton - "near Arrow Rock Ferry;" JP, stray taken up by
                         John Hartgrave.        17 Nov 1830
SULLINS, William - his land in Old Franklin sold to satisfy a claim of
    David, William & Samuel Lamme.                    13 Feb 1830
SWEARINGEN, William - appraised a stray taken up by Wm. Allison.    14 Jul 1830
TEETER, John B. - took up a barrel of rum in the Missouri R., Boone Co.,
    appraised at $27 by James Calaway.                31 Mar 1830
THARP, Owen - Clay Co.; offers a 25¢ reward for his runaway apprentice
    Joshua Frost, "upwards of 14" with light hair       18 Aug 1830
    and blue eyes.
    Squire B. - wants a journeyman shoemaker; 3 miles from Fayette.  10 Oct 1829
THOMAS, John D. - guardian of John D. Patrick, selling his Negroes.    9 Jan 1830
    - offers 1¢ reward for his runaway apprentice Pleasant    17 Nov 1830
    Rollins, age 16 or 17. Lafayette Co.
THOMPSON, Elmore - Moniteau Twp, Howard Co.; took up a black filly ae 3y
    appraised at $30 by David Morrow & John Cornelius.      15 Dec 1830
                         Wm. B. Means JP.
TOOLY, John - appraised a stray taken up by Jacob Baily.           8 Sep 1830
TRIGG, Stephen Sr. - his land in Chariton Co. sold by James Reed.    3 Mar 1830
TRUETT, William S. - see Mr. Camplin.
TURLEY, Samuel - Boonville Twp, Cooper Co.; took up a sorrel mare ae 11y
    appraised at $17 by Levi Hungerford & Joseph Cunningham.   14 Apr 1830
                         John Dade JP.

WM

TURNER, James - Chariton Twp, Howard Co.; JP, stray taken up by
                                      Jacob Baily.          8 Sep 1830
    John H. - see Isaac Campbell.
    Samuel - appraised a stray taken up by James McGee.        28 Apr 1830
VASSOR, Samuel H. - of Clay Co.; warns the public not to accept a note
        he gave Julius Watts of KY, which he has paid.       4 Jul 1829
VILEY, John - advertises the stallion "Young Tiger" at stud.    21 Mar 1829
WALKER, Andrew B. - James Burnett warns the public not to accept a note
        he gave Walker.                         23 Jun 1830
WALLER, Zachariah - sues Hickerson Burnam for $300 debt, Jackson Co.  20 Oct 1830
WARREN, William B. - Chariton Twp, Howard Co.; JP, strays taken up by
        John Burch  (26 May 1830) and by Joseph Legit.    17 Nov 1830
    - "a likely Negro woman for sale," Fayette.          26 May 1830
WATOON, David - appraised a stray taken up by Charles Rice.    14 Jul 1830
WEATHERS, Gideon - candidate for constable, Richmond Twp, Howard Co.  7 Jul 1830
WEST, Little - appraised a stray taken up by Joseph Legit.    17 Nov 1830
WHITE, John D. - land of John D. Sanford sold to satisfy White's claim.  30 Jan 1830
WHITLOCK, Francis - appraised a stray taken up by Thomas McCullock.  14 Nov 1829
WHITTENBURG, Jacob - Ralls Co.; took up a sorrel filly ae ly appraised
        at $10 by H. Fox & J.R. Abernathy. John Burton JP.    4 Jul 1829
WHITTEN, E. - asks those indebted to him for carding in 1826-27-28 to pay.  16 Jan 1830
WILCOX, Daniel P. - appraised a stray taken up by William Shields.  29 Dec 1829
WILLOBY, John - appraised a stray taken up by Simeon Arteberry.  11 Jul 1829
WILLS, Washington - appraised a stray taken up by John Roberts.  9 Jan 1830
WILSON, Pleasant - Richmond Twp, Howard Co.; took up a chestnut sorrel
        horse ae 8-9y appraised at $25 by Mace Pendleton    23 Jun 1830
        and Wm. Mobley.  John B. Clark JP.
    William G. - a tailor in Fayette at 2nd-Main.         7 Apr 1830
WISDOM, David - appraised a stray taken up by Baily Davis.    16 Jan 1830
WISWALL, Noah - bankrupt, Clay Co.                  18 Aug 1830
WOOD, Jesse T. - see Mr. Camplin.
WOODS, Stephen - land of Benjamin Hargrove in Howard Co. sold to satisfy
                                   Woods' claim.      30 Jan 1830
WOOLERY, Abraham - appraised a stray taken up by James Doleson.  15 Dec 1830
YORK, James - his wife Bythia has left his bed and board.    25 Apr 1829

-/-

## A LIST OF LETTERS

REMAINING in the Post Office at Mar-maduke, in Saline county, Mo, on the 30th day of September, 1828, which if not taken out by the last day of December next will be sent to the General Post Office as dead letters.

Mrs Mary Becknell | William Head.

PEYTON NOWLIN, P. M.

1

WM

AND, J. - appraised a stray taken up by William Prior.     23 Jul 1831
ANDERSON, John - notifies Amon English that he will run his horse
       Pioneer against Inglish's Sir Archie.     4 Jun 1831
ATHERTON, Cornelius - Richard Webb, charged with his murder, broke
       jail at New Madrid.     17 Dec 1831
BABER, Hiram H. - JP, Jefferson Twp Cole Co., stray taken up by
       Thomas Chandler.     17 Sep 1831
BAKER, Sylvester - JP, Loutre Twp Montgomery Co., stray taken up by
       Aaron Groom(s).     18 Jun 1831
    Thomas F. - appraised a stray taken up by Thomas Hornbuckle.     26 Nov 1831
BARRY, John K. - 9 Mile Prairie Twp Callaway Co., JP, stray taken up
       by Robert J. Boyd.     20 Apr 1831
BASS, Isaac - appraised a stray taken up by Reuben Burnet.     14 May 1831
BATES, James - appraised a stray taken up by Thomas G. Childers.     2 Jul 1831
BOARD, John - appraised a stray taken up by Robert J. Boyd.     20 Apr 1831
BENTON, Henry - Meramec Twp Crawford Co., took up a dark chestnut
       sorrel mare ae 8y appraised at $33 by James Custer
       & William Clinton. Jonathan Clinton JP.     4 Jun 1831
BOYD, Robert J. - 9 Mile Prairie Twp Callaway Co., took up a dark bay
       filly appraised at $12 by John Board & Conrad Nuvsom.
       John K. Barry JP.     20 Apr 1831
BRADFORD, William - JP, Skaggs Twp Crawford Co., stray taken up by
       Thomas Cook.     20 Apr 1831
BREED, Israel - received a merchant's license, Cole Co.     26 Nov 1831
BROCKMAN, John - appraised a stray taken up by Reuben Burnet.     14 May 1831
BROOKS, James - Callaway Co., took up a black horse ae 5y appraised at
       $37.50 by John Link & William Henderson. H. Sheley JP.     20 Apr 1831
BROOKSHIRE, William L. - Jefferson Twp Cole Co., took up a sorrel
       horse ae 10-12y appraised at $30 by John &
       Robert Clendenen & Moses Philips. J.F. Royston, JP.
       Same day, appraised a stray taken up by
       Benjamin Webb.     18 Jun 1831
       Appraised a stray taken up by Uel B. Ramsay.     5 Nov 1831
BROWN, John - appraised a stray taken up by John Vest.     18 Jun 1831
    Josiah - appraised a stray taken up by Edward Carter.     23 Jul 1831
BUMPASS, William - JP, Clarke Twp Gasconade Co., stray taken up by
       George Tacket.     20 Apr 1831
    " stray taken up by Hugh Craig.     6 Aug 1831
BURNET, Reuben - Clark Twp Cole Co., took up a gray horse ae 15y
       appraised at $10 by Isaac Bass & John Brockman.
       George Greenway JP.     14 May 1831
CARTER, Edward - Clark Twp Cole Co., took up a roan mare ae 10y
       appraised at $17 by Levi W. Laughlin & Josiah Brown.
       John Greenup JP.     23 Jul 1831
CARY, John - Moniteau Twp Cooper Co., took up a bay horse ae 11y
       appraised at $12 by Levi & Jeriah Wood. David Jones JP.     17 Dec 1831
CHANDLER, Thomas - Jefferson Twp Cole Co., took up a bay mare ae 13-14y
       appraised by Moses Eads & John Stewart. Hiram H. Baber JP   17 Sep 1831
CHILDERS, Thomas G. - "on St. John's" in Franklin Co., took up a
       sorrel mare ae 3y appraised at $25 by James Bates
       & Eli Valentine. Jesse McDonald JP.     2 Jul 1831
CLENDENEN, John & Robert - appraised a stray taken up by Wm. Brookshire.     18 Jun 1831
CLINTON, Jonathan - JP, Meremeck Twp Crawford Co., stray taken up
       by Henry Benton.     4 Jun 1831
    William - appraised a stray taken up by Henry Benton.     "
COLGAN, Daniel - licensed to sell merchandise in Cole Co.; on the same
       day asks his debtors to pay.     26 Nov 1831
COOK, Thomas - Skaggs Twp Crawford Co., took up a brown horse ae 7y
       appraised at $25 by John Hunt & Wilson Lenox.
       William Bradford JP.     20 Apr 1831
COPPEGE, Henson - appraised a stray taken up by John Vest.     18 Jun 1831
    William P. - Skaggs Twp Crawford Co., stray taken up by John Vest.     "
    " stray taken up by David Lenox. JP/     6 Aug 1831
COUNTS, Joseph - appraised a stray taken up by Aaron Groom(s).     18 Jun 1831
          (cont.)
    JEF

COUNTS, Joseph - Loutre Twp Montgomery Co., took up a pale chestnut
   sorrel horse appraised at $25 by Aaron Groom(s) &
   Joseph McFarland. Sylvester Baker JP.                          17 Sep 1831
CRAIG, Hugh - Gray Twp Gasconade Co., took up a brown horse ae 8 y
   appraised at $25 by Ephraim Perkins & William Pointer.
   William Bumpass Jp.                                             6 Aug 1831
CUSTER, James - appraised a stray taken up by Henry Benton.        4 Jun 1831
DAVIS, Robert - JP, Callaway Co., stray taken up by Thomas Hornbuckle.   26 Nov 1831
DULEY, William H. - appraised a stray taken up by William Kidwell.      26 Nov 1831
EADS, Moses - appraised a stray taken up by Thomas Chandler.       17 Sep 1831
FERGUSON, Moses and Thomas - appraised a stray taken up by John Reed.    26 Nov 1831
   N.B. - appraised a stray taken up by Thomas Hornbuckle.        26 Nov 1831
GLASCOE, James - appraised a stray taken up by James Williams.     13 Aug 1831
GREENUP, John - JP, Clark Twp Cole So., stray taken up by Hiram Messersmith.  20 Apr 1831
   " stray taken up by Edward Carter.                             23 Jul 1831
GREENWAY, George - JP, Clark Twp Cole Co., stray taken up by Reuben Burnet.  14 May 1831
GROOM(S), Aaron - Loutre Twp Montgomery Co., took up a dark chestnut
   sorrel mare ae 10-11 appraised at $35 by Jacob Groom
   & Joseph Counts. Sylvester Baker JP.                           18 Jun 1831
   Appraised a stray taken up by Joseph Counts.                   17 Sep 1831
HALL, William - Callaway Co., took up a dark bay mare ae 12y appraised
   at $16 by Van Sheley & William Henderson. H. Sheley JP         20 Apr 1831
HEATHERLY, Hugh - appraised a stray taken up by George Tacket.     20 Apr 1831
   - his wife Isabel has left his bed and board.                   8 Oct 1831
HENDERSON, William - appraised a stray taken up by William Hall.   20 Apr 1831
   - " by James Brooks.                                           "
HOGUE, Hezekiah - appraised a stray taken up by Samuel D. Reaves.   6 Aug 1831
HOLT, James - appraised a stray taken up by Francis McDonald.      20 Apr 1831
HOOPS, David - JP, Gray Twp Gasconade Co., stray taken up by James Williams. 13 Aug 1831
HORNBUCKLE, Alfred - Fulton Twp Callaway Co., took up a brown horse
   ae 4y appraised at $45 by John G. Kelso & Lewis
   Overton. Thomas G. Jones JP.                                   20 Apr 1831
   Thomas - Callaway Co., took up an iron gray horse ae 5y
   appraised at $35 by N.B. Ferguson & Thomas F.
   Baker. Robert Davis JP.                                        26 Nov 1831
HUFFMAN, John G. - appraised a stray taken up by William Prior.    23 Jul 1831
HUNT, John - appraised a stray taken up by Thomas Cook.            20 Apr 1831
INGLISH, Amon - notifies John Anderson that he will race his horse
   Sir Archie against Anderson's horse Pioneer.                    4 Jun 1831
JONES, David - Moniteau Twp Cooper Co., JP, stray taken up by
   Samuel D. Reaves.                                               6 Aug 1831
   " stray taken up by John Cary.                                 17 Dec 1831
   Thomas G. - JP, Fulton Twp Callaway Co., stray taken up by
   Alfred Hornbuckle.                                             20 Apr 1831
KELSO, John G. - appraised a stray taken up by Alfred Hornbuckle.  20 Apr 1831
KIDWELL, William - Cedar Twp Callaway Co., took up a black horse ae 6y
   appraised at $13 by William H. Duley & William P.
   Scott. B.A. Ramsay JP.                                         26 Nov 1831
LAUGHLIN, Levi W. - appraised a stray taken up by Edward Carter.   23 Jul 1831
LENOX, David - "on the Little Piney," Skaggs Twp Crawford Co., took up
   a bay horse, no appraisers shown, valued at $35.
   William Coppege JP.                                             6 Aug 1831
   Wilson - appraised a stray taken up by Thomas Cook.            20 Apr 1831
LINK, John - appraised a stray taken up by James Brooks.           20 Apr 1831
McCLANAHAN, Job - Saline Twp Cooper Co., took up a yellow bay mare
   ae 2y appraised at $35 by Joshua McClanahan &
   Elijah Mullins. Elijah Randolph JP.                            20 Apr 1831
McDONALD, Francis - Callaway Co., took up a dark brown horse ae 7y
   appraised at $30 by John McDonald & James Holt.
   Horace Sheley JP.                                              20 Apr 1831
   Jesse -- JP, Franklin Co., stray taken up by Thomas G. Childers.  2 Jul 1831
McFARLAND, Joseph - appraised a stray taken up by Joseph Counts.   17 Sep 1831
McKENZIE, Daniel & William - licensed as merchants, Cole Co.       26 Nov 1831
McWILLIAMS, James - appraised a stray taken up by James Williams.  13 Aug 1831
MACOY, Joseph C. - appraised a stray taken up by Hiram Messersmith.  20 Apr 1831
MARGROVE, A. - Clark Twp Gasconade Co., JP, stray taken up by Wm. Prior.  23 Jul 1831
MARTIN, Shelby - appraised a stray taken up by Hiram Messersmith.  20 Apr 1831

   JEF                                      40

MESSERSMITH, Hiram - Clark Twp Cole Co., took up a mare and colt
            appraised at $65 by Joseph C. Macoy & Shelby Martin.
            John Greenup JP.                                          20 Apr 1831
MULLINS, Elijah - appraised a stray taken up by Job McClanahan.            "
NUVSOM, Conrad - appraised a stray taken up by Robert J. Boyd.             "
NEIL, Henry - JP., Cote Sans Dessein Twp Callaway Co., stray taken up
            by John Reed.                                             26 Nov 1831
OVERTON, Lewis - appraised a stray taken up by Alfred Hornbuckle.     20 Apr 1831
PERKINS, Ephraim - appraised a stray taken up by Hugh Craig.          6 Aug 1831
PHILIPS, Moses - appraised a stray taken up by Wm. L. Brookshire.     18 Jun 1831
            " taken up by Uel B. Ramsay.                              5 Nov 1831
POINTER, Ephraim - appraised a stray taken up by Hugh Craig.          6 Aug 1831
PONTON, Joel - appraised a stray taken up by Samuel D. Reaves.        6 Aug 1831
PRIOR, William - Clark Twp Cole Co., took up a dark bay mare ae 4y
            appraised at $30 by J. And & John G. Huffman.
            A. Margrave JP.                                           23 Jul 1831
RAMSAY, B.A. - JP, Cedar Twp Callaway Co., stray taken up by
            William Kidwell.                                          26 Nov 1831
    Uel B. - Jefferson Twp Cole Co., took up a brown bay horse ae 4y
            appraised at $35 by Moses Philips & Wm. L. Brookshire.
            J. F. Royston JP.                                         5 Nov 1831
RANDOLPH, Elijah - JP, Saline Twp Cooper Co., stray taken up by
            Job McClanahan.                                           20 Apr 1831
REAVES, Samuel D. - Moniteau Twp Cooper Co., took up a bay horse ae 7y
            appraised at $40 by Joel Ponton & Hezekiah Hogue.
            David Jones JP.                                           6 Aug 1831
REED, John - Cote sans Dessein Twp Callaway Co., took up a sorrel mare
            ae 7-8y appraised at $35 by Moses & Thomas Ferguson.
            Henry Neil JP.                                            26 Nov 1831
ROYSTON, J.F. - JP, Jefferson Twp Cole Co., stray taken up by
            William L. Brookshire.                                    18 Jun 1831
            " by Uel B. Ramsay.                                       5 Nov 1831
SALMOUS, Jacob - charged with the murder of Thomas Wilson, broke jail at
            St. Charles. Governor offers $200 reward. "Ordinary height"
            with heavy eyebrows, smooth face, high forehead. Ca 30.
            Probably going to Canada or Texas.                        8 Oct 1831
SCOTT, William P. - appraised a stray taken up by Wm. Kidwell.        26 Nov 1831
SHELEY, Horace - JP, Callaway Co., stray taken up by Francis McDonald. 20 Apr 1831
    Van - appraised a stray taken up by Wm. Hall.                         "
SHELTON, David - appraised a stray taken up by George Tacket.             "
STEWART, John - appraised a stray taken up by Thomas Chandler.        17 Sep 1831
TACKET, George - Clarke Twp Gasconade Co., took up a sorrel mare ae 5y
            appraised at $20 by Hugh Heatherly & David Shelton.
            William Bumpass JP.                                       20 Apr 1831
VALENTINE, Eli - appraised a stray taken up by Thomas G. Childers.    2 Jul 1831
VEST, John - Skaggs Twp Crawford Co., took up a black horse ae 5y
            appraised at $17 by Henson Coppege & John Brown. Wm. Coppege JP 18 Jun 1831
WEBB, Benjamin - Jefferson Twp Cole Co., took up a dark chestnut sorrel
            mare ae 12-13y appraised at $30 by George Wilson &
            William L. Brookshire. J.F. Royston JP.                   18 Jun 1831
    Richard - charged with the murder of Cornelius Atherton, broke jail
            at New Madrid. Governor offers $100 reward. Ae 50, brown
            hair, sandy beard, "stout built," about 5'10" tall.
            "Professes to be a preacher of the Gospel, works sometimes
            at the chair business, calls himself a doctor." Will
            probably go to the upper part of the state, or Alabama.   17 Dec 1831
WILLIAMS, James - Gray Twp Gasconade Co., took up a bay horse ae 5-6y
            appraised at $35 by James Glascoe & James McWilliams.
            David Hoops JP.                                           13 Aug 1831
WILSON, George - appraised a stray taken up by Benjamin Webb.         18 Jan 1831
    Thomas - Jacob Salmous charged with his murder, broke jail.       8 Oct 1831
WOOD, Levi & Jeriah - appraised a stray taken up by John Cary.        17 Dec 1831

                              ⨍

THE <u>INDEPENDENT PATRIOT</u>

ABERNATHY, Battie and J. - appraised a stray taken up by Isidore Moore.    31 May 1823
AKIN, John - bankrupt, Cape Girardeau.    15 Nov 1823
ANDERSON, Fergus -  defendant, with Benjamin Gilley, in an injunction
     suit by Thomas C. Powell, New Madrid.    10 Jan 1824
   Jane - offers a "handsome award" for the return of a bay horse
     stolen from her residence on Brazo Creek.    15 May 1824
   Samuel - offers 5¢ reward for his runaway apprentice Doke H.
     Caps, age 18. Anderson was a cabinet-maker.    8 Mar 1823
ANTHONY, Samuel - plaintiff in a mortgage-foreclosure suit vs William
     and Elizabeth Clark, Wayne Co.    3 Apr 1823
   William - Castor Twp, Madison Co.; JP, stray taken up by
     John Kimbrel.    31 Jul 1824
   - "   by Elisha Spiva.    24 Jun 1826
ARMOUR, D. - JP, stray taken up by Nathan Nations.    29 Nov 1823
   - ", Byrd Twp, Cape Girardeau Co., by Harmon Lincecum.    4 Mar 1826
   David - asks debtors of late firm David, Juden D. & E. H.
     Armour to pay their debts.    8 Mar 1823
   - sues the family of John P. Wright, mortgage foreclosure.    4 Oct 1823
   Solomon H. - assignee of David Armour, sues Maximilian Horrell,
     attachment of 334 acres on Cain Creek, Byrd Twp,    20 Sep 1823
     in the Cape Girardeau Circuit Court.
ASHABRANNER, Wiben - appraised a stray taken up by John May.    4 Oct 1824
ASHERBRANNER, William - appraised a stray taken up by John Matthews Jr.    25 Jun 1825
BAILEY, John - appraised a stray taken up by Mikel Smith.    6 Sep 1823
BALES, James - warns the public not to accept a note for $150 which he
     gave to John H. Lockert; it was "fraudulently obtained."    3 Jun 1826
BENNETT, Joseph & Mm. (sic) - appraised a stray taken up by John Kimbrel.    31 Jul 1824
BESS, Peter - appraised a stray taken up by John D. Wilson.    29 Apr 1826
   - "   by John Landers.    21 Oct 1826
BETTIS, Elijah - appraised a stray taken up by Daniel Shipman.    24 Jun 1826
   Overton - warns the public not to accept a note for $92 which
     he gave Matthew Hubble of Wayne Co.    28 Jul 1823
BIRD, G. A. - dissolves law partnership with J. Payne Jr.    19 Apr 1823
BISHER, Albert - appraised a stray taken up by Jonathan Wilson.    6 Mar 1824
* BOLIN, William - Lorance Twp, Cape Girardeau Co.; took up a brown bay mare
     ae 8y appraised at $20 by John Fraffer, Samuel Hews, &    4 Mar 1826
     Jacob Clark. Barnet Snider JP.
BROWN, John - Tywappity Bottom, Scott Co.; offers a liberal award for
     two strayed horses.    12 Jun 1824
BYRD, John - appraised a stray taken up by Sarah Hays.    8 Mar 1823
* BLISS, Pliny -  Townsend Nichols and Jacob Littleton warn the public not
     to accept a note given them by Bliss and Elick Powell;    8 Feb 1823
     it was "fraudulently obtained."
* BOLDUC, Pierre - appraised a stray taken up by Jonathan Wilson.    6 Mar 1824
BUIS, Jonathan - Byrd Twp, Cape Girardeau Co.; took up a roan mare
     appraised at $6 by John B. Young & Wm. Lanphor. D. Armour JP. 25 Mar'26
BULLITT, George - of Jackson, offers a liberal reward for a runaway Negro.    10 Sep 1825
BURNES, Peter - appraised a stray taken up by John Matthews Jr.    25 Jun 1825
BURNHAM, Benjamin - appraised a stray taken up by Samuel P. Harris.    5 Jun 1824
BUTCHER, Benjamin - summoned by the State to answer the petition of
     Theodise Butcher by her next friend Charles Griffard,    21 Aug 1824
     Ste. Genevieve.
CAPS, Doke H. - runaway apprentice of Samuel Anderson, cabinet-maker;
     Caps was 18 years old.    8 Mar 1823
CARTER, David - appraised a stray taken up by Isaac E. Kelly.    11 Dec 1824
CATO, Lewis - Jefferson Twp (? county?), JP, stray taken up by John May.    4 Oct 1824
CLARK, Jacob - appraised a stray taken up by William Bolin.    4 Mar 1826
   John B. - appraised a stray taken up by Boling Sublett.    6 Dec 1826
   William & wife Elizabeth - defendants in a mortgage-foreclosure
     suit by Samuel Anthony, Wayne Co.    3 Apr 1823
CONELL, Charles M. - appraised a stray taken up by Jacob Houts.    29 Jul 1826
CONROD, Ephraim R. - defendant, mortgage-foreclosure suit by the State,
     Cape Girardeau.    17 Jan 1824
COSTNER, Andrew - appraised a stray taken up by Michael Smith.    29 Apr 1826

INP

42

CRACROFT, Charles - assignee of John Cracroft, sues Charles C. Jackson
       for $600 debt and $600 damages, attachment levied on     27 Sep 1823
       a bay mare and 1/3 of a tract of land in Byrd Twp.;
       Cape Girardeau Circuit Court.
       William - appraised a stray taken up by Peter Crites.     8 Mar 1823
CREATH, William Esq. - agent for Johnson Ranney during his absence.     4 Oct 1824
CRITZE, Peter - at his plantation in Cape Girardeau; took up a sorrel mare
       ae 3y appraised at $20 by L. J. DeLashmutt, Wm. P. Lacy,     8 Mar 1823
       and Wm. Cracroft. Peter R. Garrett JP.
CROSS, Harriet - sues Joseph Cross for divorce by her next friend Harvey     6 Sep 1823
       Lane, Ste. Genevieve.
       John - property of Edmund Rutter sold to satisfy a claim by Cross     22 Feb 1823
       and Wm. Gardner.
CUPPLES, Samuel - dissolved partnership with Theodore Jones.     8 Mar 1823
       - papers authorizing settlement by debtors of late firm     22 Nov 1823
       are in the hands of Peter R. Garrett.
DAVIS, Joseph B. - Gilbert Peyton will not pay a note for $72 which he
       gave to Davis for the hire of a Negro boy, since Davis     19 Feb 1825
       took the boy away before his time was half up.
DEAKINS, William - defendant with Francis Hutson & Edward Robertson in a     30 Aug 1823
       suit by James Tanner, New Madrid Circuit Court.
DeLASHMUTT, L. J. - appraised a stray taken up by Peter Critze.     8 Mar 1823
DOLTON, John - appraised a stray taken up by Elisha Spiva.     24 Jun 1826
DONNOHUE, John - defendant in a mortgage-foreclosue suit by the U.S.,     25 Sep 1824
       Perry Co.
       - defendant in a mortgage-foreclosure suit by Henry Keil,     16 Apr 1825
       Ste. Genevieve.
DOUGHERTE, Ralph - surviving partner of Frisel & Daugherty, asks payment     6 Sep 1823
       of debts; Frisel has died.
DOUGLASS, Henry - warns the public not to accept a note for $225 which he     23 Aug 1823
       gave William Hickman; it was "fraudulently obtained."
DOWTY, James - bankrupt.     1 Nov 1826
DUBREUIL, A. - appraised a stray taken up by Jonathan Wilson.     6 Mar 1824
DUNN, John - his wife Elizabeth has left his bed and board.     1 Nov 1823
EAKER, John - appraised a stray taken up by John D. Wilson.     29 Apr 1826
EDMONDS, J. - Medad Randol takes over his "stand" at Bainbridge.     20 Dec 1823
ELLIS, A. P. - took up a Negro man who is now in prison for safekeeping;     31 May 1823
       owner to claim and pay reasonable charges.
ERWIN, Louis - German Twp, Cape Girardeau Co.; took up a mare ae 12-13y
       appraised at $30 by Wm. King, Isaac Gregory, & Burrel     16 Aug 1823
       Revelle. William Johnson JP.
EVANS, James - plaintiff in a suit for debt vs John Stump, Cape Girardeau;     5 Mar 1825
       action by Wm. Hickman for use of Evans.
       Owen - took up a Negro woman who said she belonged to Sarah Wood;     25 Sep 1824
       she was placed in the hands of John Layton, Esq., and is
       being held in the Perry Co. jail.
FOSTER, Robert - runaway apprentice of G. M. Scribbs; ae 19½, about     11 Jun 1825
       5'8 or ;0" tall.
FRAFFER, John - appraised a stray taken up by Wm. Bolin.     4 Mar 1826
FRICKE, George - agent for Charles Seavers.     25 Dec 1824
FULTON, Hugh - defendant in a mortgage-foreclosure suit by John     17 Jul 1824
       McFarland, Madison Co.
GANTT, E. S. - those wishing to buy Negroes advertised by Jonathan Guest     8 Mar 1823
       should apply at Gantt's.
       William S. - bankrupt, Cape Girardeau.     15 Nov 1823
GARNER, William - property of Edmund Rutter sold to satisfy a claim of     22 Feb 1823
       Garner & John Cross.
GARRETT, J. T. - offers a Spanish claim tract of 640 acres for sale,     8 Nov 1826
       four miles below Greenville, Wayne Co.
       Peter R., Esq. - attorney acting for Samuel Cupples.     22 Nov 1823
       Westly - Liberty Twp, Madison Co.; JP, stray taken up by     5 Mar 1825
       Ephraim Stout.
GILILAND, Hiram - appraised a stray taken up by Sarah Hayes.     8 Mar 1823
GILLEY, Benjamin - defendant with Fergus Anderson, in an injunction     10 Jan 1824
       suit by Thomas C. Powell, New Madrid.
GLASSCOCK, Charnal - bankrupt.     9 Aug 1823
GOALD, Thomas H. - his wife Odeal has left his bed and board.     9 Aug 1823

    INP

GOCLA, Thomas H. - defendant, suit for debt by Daniel F. Steinbeck, New Madrid. — 18 Dec 1824

GREGORY, Isaac - appraised a stray taken up by Lewis Erwin. — 16 Aug 1823

GRIFFARD, Charles - next friend of Theodise Butcher in her divorce suit, Ste. Genevieve. — 21 Aug 1824

GRIGGS, Thomas - east fork of the St. Francois R., Madison Co.; took up a sorrel horse ae 8y appraised at $30 by Mathias P. Ringer and Nicholas Tomure. Tom Moseley JP. — 5 Aug 1826

GUEST, Jonathan - offers two valuable Negroes for sale, with two children; apply at Dr. E. S. Gantt's. — 8 Mar 1823

HARRIS, Samuel P. - Liberty Twp, St. Francois Co.; took up an iron gray mare ae 5y appraised at $45 and a bay horse ae 3y, $30, by Benjamin Burnham & Isaac Murphy. John D. Piers JP. — 5 June 1824

HARRISON, William Henry - defendant, suit in chancery by James Logan, Cape Girardeau. — 4 Oct 1823

HAYDEN, Dr. B. - "will attend in Jackson on all who may think proper to come, that are afflicted with cancer, scrophula, and white-swelling." — 11 Dec 1824

HAYS, Sarah - on Indian Creek, Cape Girardeau Co.; took up a white horse ae 9-10y with a 50¢ bell, leather collar and single buckle, appraised at $25 by Ezekiel Seely, Hiram Gililand, and John Byrd. James Russell JP. — 8 Mar 1823

HENDRICKS, John - appraised a stray taken up by Nathan Nations. — 29 Nov 1823

HERRICK, Ezekiel B. - plaintiff vs Joseph Soilbildos, Madison Co. — 30 Aug 1823

HEWS, Samuel - appraised a stray taken up by William Bolin. — 4 Mar 1826

Teral - his wife Petty has left his bed and board. — 5 Feb 1825

HICKMAN, William - Henry Douglass warns the public not to accept a note for $225 he gave Hickman, "fraudulently obtained." — 23 Aug 1823

- sues John Stump for debt, to the use of James Evans. — 5 Mar 1825

- defendant, mortgage-foreclosure suit by the State. — 4 Mar 1826

HILER, David - bankrupt, Cape Girardeau. — 8 Nov 1826

HOGH, Levi - St. Francois Twp (county?), took up a mare ae 3y appraised at $20 by Lott Joiner & Curtis Wood. Ezekiel Rubottom JP. — 4 Mar 1826

HOLMES, John - on Bear Creek, St. Francois Twp, Wayne Co.; took up a black horse ae 5y appraised at $22.50 by John Varris & David Rees. A. Wheeler JP. — 11 Jun 1825

- St. Francois Twp, Wayne Co.; JP, stray taken up by John Landers. — 21 Oct 1826

HOPE, Robert Y. - with Mathew Smith, warns the public not to accept a note given them by Hugh Sparkman of Hickman Co., KY, "fraudulently obtained." — 22 Nov 1826

HORRELL, Maximilian - defendant, suit by Solomon H. Armour (assignee of David), attachment of 334 acres on Cain Creek, Byrd Twp.; Cape Girardeau Circuit Court. — 20 Sep 1823

HOUTS, C. G. - next friend of Mary A. Stidger in her divorce suit, New Madrid. — 15 Jan 1825

Jacob - Moreland Twp, Scott Co., adjoining the town of Benton; took up a sorrel mare ae 3y appraised at $40 By Charles M. Conell & Wm. Myers. Daniel Payne JP. — 29 Jul 1826

HUBBLE, Mathew - Overton Bettis warns the public not to accept a note for $92 which he gave Hubble, of Wayne Co. — 28 Jul 1823

HUFSTETLER, Henry - appraised a stray taken up by John D. Wilson. — 29 Apr 1826

HUGHES, Christian - appraised a stray taken up by Michael Smith. — 29 Apr 1826

HUTSON, Francis - with Edward Robertson & William Deakins, defendants in a suit by James Tanner, New Madrid Circuit Court. — 30 Aug 1823

JACKSON, Charles C. - defendant, suit for $600 debt and $600 damages by Charles Cracroft, assignee of John Cracroft; attachment levied on a bay mare and 1/3 of a tract of land in Byrd Twp, Cape Girardeau Co. (Cape Girardeau Circuit Court) — 27 Sep 1823

- plaintiff vs John P. Wright, mort gage-foreclosure, Cape Girardeau. — 4 Oct 1823

JOHNSON, John - Apple Creek Twp, Cape Girardeau Co.; JP, stray taken up by William P. Lacy. — 5 Aug 1826

William - German Twp, Cape Girardeau Co.; JP, stray taken up by Lewis Erwin. — 16 Aug 1823

JOINER, Lott - appraised a stray taken up by Levi Hogh. — 4 Mar 1826

INP

44

JONES, Theodore - dissolves partnership with Samuel Cupples.    8 Mar 1823
KEIL, Henry - plaintiff vs John Donnohue, mortgage-foreclosure suit,    16 Apr 1825
                                        Ste. Genevieve.
KELLY, Isaac E. - Kelly Twp, Wayne Co.; took up a sorrel mare ae 8y
            appraised at $20 by David Carter & James Kelly.    11 Dec 1824
                                        Charles Sweased JP.
KEYS, John - bankrupt, Wayne Co.    20 Dec 1823
KIMBREL, John - Caster Twp, Madison Co.; took up a bay horse ae 13y
            appraised (amount not shown) by Joseph & Mm. (Madame?)    31 Jul 1824
            Bennett. William Anthony JP.
KING, William - appraised a stray taken up by Lewis Erwin.    16 Aug 1823
LACY, William P. - appraised a stray taken up by Peter Critze.    8 Mar 1823
        - "    by Nathan Nations.    29 Nov 1823
        - Apple Creek Twp, Cape Girardeau Co.; took up 15 head of
            hogs appraised at $28 by James C. Wilson & James    5 Aug 1826
            Stephenson.  John Johnson JP.
LANDERS, John - St. Francois Twp (county?), took up a chestnut sorrel
            horse ae 7y appraised at $35 by Oliver Lo gan and Peter    21 Oct 1826
            Bess.  John Holms JP.
LANPHOR, William - appraised a stray taken up by Jonathan Buis.    25 Mar 1826
LAYTON, John - Perry Co.; JP, stray taken up by Isidore Moore.    31 May 1823
LIGGITT, Henry - appraised a stray taken up by William Welch Jr.    6 May 1826
LINCECUM, Harmon - Byrd Twp, Cape Girardeau Co.; took up a brown bay gelding
            ae 5y appraised at $12 by Andrew Martin & John L. Miller.    4 Mar 1826
                                        D. Armour JP.
LINCOLN, Joseph - appraised a stray taken up by Michael Smith.    29 Apr 1826
LITTLETON, Jacob - with Townsend Nichols, warns the public not to accept a
            note given them by Pliny Bliss and Elick Powell,    8 Feb 1823
            "fraudulently obtained."
LOCKERT, John H. - a stonecutter, 8 miles north of Jackson.    29 Apr 1826
        - James S. Bales warns the public not to accept a note
            he gave Lockert for $150, "fraudulently obtained."    3 Jun 1826
LOCKHART, Samuel - a saddler, wants apprentices.    19 Apr 1823
        - offers 6¼¢ reward for runaway apprentice Vardy Ramsey,
            ae 19, about 5' tall, at Jackson.    8 Nov 1826
LOGAN, James - plaintiff vs William Henry Harrison, suit in chancery,    4 Oct 1823
                                        Cape Girardeau.
        Oliver - appraised a stray taken up by John Landers.    21 Oct 1826
McARTHUR, J. - St. Michael's Twp, Madison Co.; JP, stray taken up by    25 Jun 1825
            John Matthews Jr.
McBRIDE, Ro- - Randol Twp (county?); JP, stray taken up by Boling Sublett.    6 Dec 1826
McCABE, John G. W. - defendant, mortgage-foreclosure suit by the State.    28 Feb 1824
McCLAIN, John - bankrupt.    21 Oct 1826
McFARLAND, John M. - plaintiff, mortgage-foreclosure suit against Hugh    17 Jul 1824
            Fulton, Madison Co.
MACOMB, William - appraised a stray taken up by Daniel Shipman.    24 Jun 1826
MANSFIELD, James S. - Nicholas Whitelaw warns the public not to accept a
            note for $110 which he gave Mansfield.    6 Dec 1826
MARTIN, Andrew - appraised a stray taken up by Harmon Lincecum.    4 Mar 1826
MASSIE, James - offers red chaff wheat·for sale at the plantation known
            as Bond's place, 62½¢ per bu. or, in 20-bushel or larger    11 Sep 1824
            quantities, 50¢ per bushel.
MASTERS, Littleton - appraised a stray taken up by John May.    4 Oct 1824
MATTHEWS, John Jr. - St. Michael's Twp, Madison Co.; took up a sorrel horse
            appraised at $25 by John T. Vaughan, Wm. Asherbranner,    25 Jun 1825
            and Peter Burnes.  J. McArthur JP.
MAULSEY, Lemuel H. - Sheriff of New Madrid Co., publishes a notice of the    25 Mar 1826
            capture of a runaway slave.
MAY, John - Jefferson Twp (county?), took up a sorrel horse ae 10 appraised    4 Oct 1824
            at $30 by Wiben Ashabranner & Littleton Masters. Lewis Cato JP.
MENEFEE, Jonas S. - defendant, mortgage-foreclosure suit by the State,    17 Jan 1824
                                        Cape Girardeau.
MILLARD, Josiah - defendant, injunction suit by Thomas Oliver,    15 May 1824
                                        Ste. Genevieve.
MILLER, Jacob V. - sues Mary Ann Miller for divorce, Madison Co.; charges    29 Apr 1826
            that she deserted him.
        John L. - appraised a stray taken up by Harmon Lincecum.    4 Mar 1826

            INP
                                    45

MOORE, Isidore - on Apple Creek in Perry Co.; took up several head of
    hogs appraised at $20.25 by J. & Battie Abernathy           31 May 1823
    and Francis Narce. John Layton JP.
MOSELEY, Tom - Madison Co.; JP, stray taken up by Thomas Griggs.      5 Aug 1826
MURPHY, Isaac - appraised a stray taken up by Samuel P. Harris.       5 Jun 1824
    William - sues Richard Murphy; chancery, St. Francois Co.      6 Mar 1824
MYERS, William - appraised a stray taken up by Jacob Houts.        29 Jul 1826
NARCE, Francis - appraised a stray taken up by Isidore Moore.       31 May 1823
NATIONS, Nathan - "on his plantation" took up a mare appraised at $25 by
    John Hendrick, Austin Young, & Wm. P. Lacy; D. Armour JP.   29 Nov 1823
NICHOLS, Townsend - with Jacob Littleton, warns the public not to accept a   8 Feb 1823
    note given them by Pliny Bliss and Elick Powell which
    was "fraudulently obtained."
OLIVER, Thomas - JP, stray taken up by Jonathan Wilson.         6 Mar 1824
PAYNE, Daniel - Moreland Twp, Scott Co.; JP, stray taken up by Jacob Houts.  29 Jul 1826
    J. Jr. - dissolves law partnership with G. A. Bird.       19 Apr 1823
PEYTON, Gilbert W. - will not pay a note for $72 he gave Joseph B. Davis
    for the hire of a Negro boy, as Davis has taken the     19 Feb 1825
    boy away "before his time was half up."
PIERS, John D. - Liberty Twp, St. Francois Co.; JP, stray taken up by
    Samuel P. Harris.                 5 Jun 1824
POWELL, Elick - with Pliny Bliss, "fraudulently obtained" a note they had   8 Feb 1823
    given Townsend Nichols and Jacob Littleton.
    Thomas C. - plaintiff vs Fergus Anderson & Benjamin Gilley,    10 Jan 1824
    injunction, New Madrid.
QUARLES, Runstall - plaintiff vs James Whiteside, chancery, Cape Girardeau.  28 Feb 1824
RAMSEY, Andrew - plaintiff (for use of David Armour), mortgage foreclosure   4 Oct 1823
    suit vs John P. Wright et al.
    Vardy - runaway apprentice of Samuel Lockhart, saddler, Jackson;
    ae 19, about 5' tall, light complexion. 6¼¢ reward.     8 Nov 1826
RANDOL, Medad - opens a House of Entertainment in Bainbridge at the    20 Dec 1823
    "stand" formerly occupied by J. Edmonds.
RANNEY, Johnson - appoints Wm. Creath as his agent during his absence   4 Oct 1824
    from Jackson.
REES, David - appraised a stray taken up by John Holmes.        11 Jun 1825
REVELLE, Burrel - appraised a stray taken up by Lewis Erwin.      16 Aug 1823
RHODES, Jacob - Lorance Twp, Cape Girardeau Co.; JP, stray taken up by   29 Apr 1826
    Michael Smith.
RINGER, Mathias - appraised a stray taken up by Thomas Griggs.     5 Aug 1826
RISHER, John - plaintiff vs George Roush, chancery, Cape Girardeau.   28 Feb 1824
ROBERTSON, Edward - defendant (with Francis Hutson and Wm. Deakens) in a  30 Aug 1823
    suit by James Tanner, New Madrid Circuit Court.
ROBINSON, William - plaintiff vs John Rogers, damages, Cape Girardeau.   4 Mar 1826
ROGERS, John - defendant, damage suit by Wm. Robinson, Cape Girardeau.   4 Mar 1826
ROUSH, George - defendant, suit in chancery by John Risher, Cape G.   28 Feb 1824
RUBOTTOM, Ezekiel - St. Francois Twp, Cape Girardeau Co.; JP, stray     4 Mar 1826
    taken up by Levi Hogh.
RUNYEANS, Benjamin - appraised a stray taken up by John Tinnin.     6 May 1826
RUSSELL, James - wants immediate payment of money owed him or he will put  8 Feb 1823
    debts in the hands of a proper officer for collection.
    - Cape Girardeau Co.; JP, stray taken up by Sarah Hays.    8 Mar 1823
RUTTER, Edmund - his property sold to satisfy claims of John Cross and   22 Feb 1823
    William Garner.
    - sues Bartlet Sims for debt, Madison Co.           3 Apr 1824
SCRIBBS, G. M. - offers 6¼¢ reward for runaway apprentice Robert Foster.  11 Jun 1825
SEAVERS, Charles - being Gideon asks his debtors to pay or       25 Dec 1824
    he will "resort to coercive measures."
SEELY, Ezekiel - appraised a stray taken up by Sarah Hays.      8 Mar 1823
SHARP, Anthony - appraised a stray taken up by Ephraim Stout.     5 Mar 1825
SHELL, Benjamin - guardian of Benjamin Whitener, intends to make a   21 Oct 1824
    final settlement, Cape Girardeau.
    - JP, stray taken up by John Tinnin.            6 May 1826
SHEPPARD, William - bankrupt.                   28 Jul 1823
SHIPMAN, Daniel - Wayne Co.; took up a sorrel mare appraised at $10 by   24 Jun 1826
    Elijah Bettis & Wm. Macomb. A. Wheeler JP.
SIMS, Bartlet - defendant, suit for debt by Edmund Rutter, Madison Co.   3 Apr 1824

SMITH, Archibald R. - runaway apprentice of Philip Young, Jackson; ae 18.    1 Nov 1826
    Bernet - German Twp, Cape Girardeau Co.; JP, stray taken up by     6 Sep 1823
                Mikel Smith.
    John - appraised a stray taken up by Ephraim Stout.     5 Mar 1825
    Mathew - with Robert Y. Hope, warns the public not to accept a note    22 Nov 1826
      given them by Hugh Sparkman of Hickman Co., KY, which
      was "fraudulently obtained."
    Mikel     - German Twp, Cape Girardeau Co.; took up a sorrel horse
    (Michael)    ae 3y appraised at $30 by John Snider & John Bailey.     6 Sep 1823
           Bernet Smith JP.
       - Lorance Twp, Cape Girardeau Co.; took up a bay horse
       ae 6y appraised at $15 by Christian Hughes, Joseph    29 Apr 1826
       Lincoln, & Andrew Costner. Jacob Rhodes JP.
SNIDER, Barnet - Lorance Twp, Cape Girardeau Co.; JP, stray taken up by     4 Mar 1826
              William Bolin.
    John - appraised a stray taken up by Mikel Smith.     6 Sep 1823
SOILBILDOS, Joseph - defendant in a suit by Ezekiel Herrick, Madison Co.    30 Aug 1823
SPIVA, Elisha - Castor Twp, Madison Co.; took up an iron gray horse
       appraised at $35 by John Dolton, Wm. Underwood, & Henry    24 Jun 1826
       Tucker. William Anthony JP.
STEINBECK, Daniel F. - plaintiff in a suit for debt against Thomas H.    18 Dec 1824
       Gocla, New Madrid.
STEPHENSON, James - appraised a stray taken up by Wm. P. Lacy.     5 Aug 1826
STIDGER, Mary A. - sues William B. Stidger for divorce, by next friend    15 Jan 1825
       C. G. Houts, New Madrid.
STORY, William - opens a new store in Bainbridge.    25 Mar 1826
STOUGHTER, Samuel, M.D. - tenders his services to the citizens of    22 May 1824
             Cape Girardeau.
STOUT, Ephraim - Liberty Twp, Madison Co.; took up a mare ae 4y appraised
       at $60 by John Sutton, John Smith, and Anthony Sharp.     5 Mar 1825
          Westly Garrett JP.
STROTHER, George F. - sues John Donnohue (for the use of the U.S.),    25 Sep 1824
           mortgage foreclosure, Perry Co.
STROUP, Samuel P. - bankrupt, Greenville.     6 Dec 1826
STUMP, John - defendant in a suit by William Hickman for the use of     5 Mar 1825
       James Evans, debt, Cape Girardeau.
       - appraised a stray taken up by Boling Sublett.     6 Dec 1826
SUBLETT, Boling - Randol Twp, Cape Girardeau Co.; took up a bay horse
       ae 9y appraised at $35 by John R. Clark & John Stump.     6 Dec 1826
          Ro-- McBride JP.
SUTTON, John - appraised a stray taken up by Ephraim Stout.     5 Mar 1825
SWAYNE, Sherard G. - bankrupt, Wayne Co.     4 Oct 1823
SWEASED, Charles - Kelly Twp, Wayne Co.; JP, stray taken up by Isaac Kelly.    11 Dec 1824
TANNER, James - plaintiff vs Francis Hutson, Edward Robertson, and    30 Aug 1823
       William Deakins, New Madrid Circuit Court.
TENNILLE, George - defendant in a mortgage foreclosure suit by Robert G.    17 Jan 1824
       Watson, Cape Girardeau.
THOMAS, Claiborne J. - advertises wool carding, 10¢ per pound.    31 May 1823
THOMPSON, John - advertises a cotton gin now in operation on his farm.    19 Apr 1823
TINNIN, John - took up a brown mare ae 6y appraised at $25 by Wm. Wilson     6 May 1826
       and Benjamin Runyeans. Benjamin Shell JP.
TOMURE, Nicholas - appraised a stray taken up by Thomas Griggs.     5 Aug 1826
TUCKER, Henry - appraised a stray taken up by Elisha Spiva.    24 Jun 1826
UNDERWOOD, William - appraised a stray taken up by Elisha Spiva.    24 Jun 1826
VARRIS, John - appraised a stray taken up by John Holmes.    11 Jun 1825
VAUGHAN, John T. - appraised a stray taken up by John Matthews Jr.    25 Jun 1825
WATSON, Robert C. - plaintiff vs George Tennille, mortgage foreclosure,    17 Jan 1824
          Cape Girardeau.
WELCH, William Jr. - took up a dark bay horse ae 14y appraised at $13 by     6 May 1826
       Morris Young & Henry Liggitt.
WHEELER, A. - St. Francois Twp, Wayne Co.; JP, stray taken up by    11 Jun 1825
                 John Holmes.
      - " by Daniel Shipman.    24 Jun 1826
WHITELAW, Nicholas - warns the public not to accept a note for $110 which     6 Dec 1826
       he gave James S. Mansfield.
WHITENER, Benjamin - his guardian, Benjamin Shell, intends to make final    21 Oct 1824
       settlement of the guardianship.

INP         47

WHITESIDE, James - defendant, suit in chancery, Cape Girardeau, by
Runstall Quarles.                                                 28 Feb 1824
WILLIAMS, James - JP, stray taken up by John D. Wilson.                  29 Apr 1826
James C. - appraised a stray taken up by Wm. P. Lacy.               5 Aug 1826
WILSON, John D. - took up a black mare ae lly appraised at $15 by Peter
Bess, John Eaker, and Henry Hufstetler.                           29 Apr 1826
James Williams JP.
WILSON, Jonathan - "on the road from Ste. Genevieve to Mine-a-Breton,"
took up a stud colt appraised at $14 by Pierre Bolduc,             6 Mar 1823
A. Dubreuil, & Albert Bisher. Thomas Oliver JP.
William - appraised a stray taken up by John Tinnin.               6 May 1826
WINDES, Samuel - notified by the State to appear before the Circuit Court
of St. Francois Co. to answer the complaint of                     1 Nov 1823
Katherine Windes.
WOOD, Curtis - appraised a stray taken up by Levi Hogh.                  4 Mar 1826
Sarah - named as the owner of a Negro woman taken up by Owen Evans.  25 Sep 1824
WRIGHT, John P. - defendant in a mortgage-foreclosure suit by Charles C.  4 Oct 1823
Jackson, Cape Girardeau.
John P., Sarah, Alexander, Allison, Betsey, Sarah, Nancy, Maria,
Jane, & Emily - defendants in a suit by Andrew Ramsey             4 Oct 1823
(for use of David Armour) to foreclose a mortgage.
YOUNG, Austin - appraised a stray taken up by Nathan Nations.           29 Nov 1823
John B. - appraised a stray taken up by Jonathan Buis.             25 Mar 1826
Morris - appraised a stray taken up by William Welch Jr.            6 May 1826
Philip - of Jackson; warns the public not to harbor his runaway     1 Nov 1826
apprentice Archibald R. Smith. Offers 6¼¢ reward.

—⊢—

INP

48

ADAMS, Burwell B. - appraised a stray taken up by Russel Brown. 19 Apr 1823
ARNOLD, James Jr. - leaving St. Louis, asks debtors to pay. 10 Nov 1823
BALDRIDGE, John - see Joseph Norman.
BENTON, Abraham - Calvy Twp, Franklin Co.; took up a chestnut sorrel horse
    appraised at $40 by Delafiel Ramsey & Neuman Powers. 19 Apr 1824
        Thomas Clark JP.
BERRY, Thomas - sues Samuel Livermore for damages. 13 Dec 1823
BOBB, John - Isaac Letcher advertises for brick wood at a brickyard 12 Jul 1823
    formerly belonging to Bobb.
BOND, Thomas - appraised a stray taken up by Garland Hording. 23 Aug 1823
BROWN, Russel - Boles Twp, Franklin Co.; took up a black mare ae 5-6y
    appraised at $27 by Ambrose Ranson & Burwell B. Adams. 19 Apr 1823
        Henry Brown JP.
BRYANT, David - Joachim Twp, Jefferson Co.; JP, stray taken up by 12 Jul 1823
        Joshua Herrington.
BUTLER, Edward - Plattin Twp, Jefferson Co.; took up a brown mare ae 9y
    appraised at $30 by Wm. Staples, James Dwitt, & Joseph 29 Mar 1824
    Kinds. Samuel McMullin JP.
CAIN, Daniel - appraised a stray taken up by Patrick Malone. 23 Aug 1823
CALDWELL, Kinkead - Franklin Co.; his wife Mary has left his bed and board. 11 Dec 1824
CHAMBERS, Thomas - appraised a stray taken up by Sarah Kennedy. 11 Dec 1824
CHARLESS, Joseph - advertises boarding and stabling. 25 Jan 1823
CHRISTMAN, William - a hatter, advertises "waterproof hats." 25 Jan 1823
CLARK, Thomas - appraised a stray taken up by Abraham Benton. 19 Apr 1824
CODE, John - see Joseph Norman. 23 Aug 1823
CODGE, William - appraised a stray taken up by Martin Witerwitch. 25 Jan 1823
COHEN, Thomas - advertises clocks and watches "in the former post office." 31 May 1823
COLBURN, Jesse - has taken the livery stable formerly occupied by Price 3 May 1823
    and Pitzer; also advertises as a farrier.
COLE, Jacob - appraised a stray taken up by Capt. John Morgan. 19 Apr 1823
COLLIER, George - two suits for mortgage-foreclosue in Lincoln Co.; one 1 Feb 1823
    against Zadock Woods, one against James & Martin Woods.
COLLINS, Roger - bankrupt, St. Louis. 10 May 1823
CONNER, Jeremiah - offers "several parcels of valuable land" for sale. 1 Feb 1823
CORNELIUS, James - the store he lately occupied now in use by 15 Dec 1824
    Caleb Jones & Co.
COWHERD, William - renewing a certificate for 1/4 section of land in 27 Jan 1824
    Callaway Co.; certificate accidentally burned in his shop.
CRIPPEN, Elijah - see Joseph Norman.
CROSS, John - selling his estate in Cape Girardeau Co. and other parcels. 19 Apr 1823
DABBIN, Victoire vs Pierre, divorce, by next friend Bte. Morain. 13 Dec 1823
DAVIDSON, E. - has taken the "well-known brick stable on the hill," also 31 May 1823
    advertises as a farrier.
DEANE, William - asks his debtors to pay. 14 Jun 1824
DESHLER, David - store at #10 N. Main, St. Louis; dry goods, groceries, 26 Apr 1824
    Queensware, hardware, etc.
DETANDEBARATZ, M. - offers various goods, wholesale and retail. 31 May 1823
DOGGET, Jesse - appraised a stray taken up by Martin Witerwitch. 25 Jan 1823
    - " by Patrick Malone; signed with an "x." 23 Aug 1823
DWITT, James - appraised a stray taken up by Edward Butler. 29 Mar 1824
EARLS, J. D. - wants coach or wagon makers. 18 Oct 1823
ELLIOTT, Mrs. Mary Lewis - advertises her Female Academy. 19 Apr 1823
ELLIS, Samuel - surgeon-dentist, St. Louis; at Col. Mitchell's Hotel or 16 Feb 1824
    "at their place of residence if persons wish."
EVENS, T. D. - a tailor, moved to 14 N. Main, St. Louis. 25 Jan 1823
EVERHART, George - warns the public not to accept a note he gave Alfred
    McCarthy of New Orleans, now in the hands of H. C. 23 Aug 1823
    Simms (probably Simmons), "extorted from me by threats."
FOREMAN, S. W. - with R. McCloud, proposes to publish the Missouri 25 Oct 1823
    Gazette in St. Charles.
FOSTER, Sarah vs Dabney, divorce, Washington Co. 21 Jun 1824
FREVIER, Louis - defendant in a damage suit by Reubin Kilby. 13 Dec 1823
FRY, Jacob - leaving Missouri, offers his personal property for sale: 13 Dec 1823
    livestock, slave woman and child, etc.
FRYER, George - appraised a stray taken up by Louis Rogers. 13 Mar 1824

ENQ

GASKINS, John - see Joseph Norman.

GILHULY, Bernard - advertises "cheap goods."  19 Apr 1823

GORDON, John C. - Trustee of the City of Jefferson.  19 Apr 1823

GOREY, Patrick - offers $5 reward for bay horse strayed or stolen.  1 Feb 1823

GOWEN, Mrs. - will take a "few genteel boarders on moderate terms" in the
    north part of a house opposite Hawken's shop.  20 Nov 1824

GRIFFIN, G. W. - advertises a "soda water fountain."  7 Jun 1823

GRIMSLEY, Thornton - dissolves partnership with Stark; advertises patent
    spring saddles and other merchandise.  25 Jan 1823

GUNN, Calvin - sues Robert McCloud, mortgage foreclosure, St. Charles.  23 Aug 1823

HALL, Sergeant - attorney at law, St. Louis, on 2nd St. in the building
    formerly occupied by H. Cozens.  15 Dec 1824

HASKINS, Thomas S. - asks debtors to pay.  15 Feb 1823

HENRY, William - bankrupt, St. Louis.  18 Oct 1823

    - defendant, suit for debt by Charles Mitchell, St. Charles.  13 Dec 1823

HERRINGTON, Joshua - Joachim Twp, Jefferson Co.; took up a brown mare ae 4y
    appraised at $30 and a dun horse, $35, by J. Warren &  12 Jul 1823
    Wm. Herrington.  David Bryant JP.

HOFFA, John - advertises perfumes, etc., 27 N. Main, St. Louis.  1 Dec 1823

HOFFMAN, H. L. - asks for return of his lost books.  1 Feb 1823

HOPE, Adam - Trustee of the City of Jefferson.  19 Apr 1823

HORDING, Garland - Calvy Twp, Franklin Co.; took up a black mare ae 11-12y
    appraised at $35 by Thomas Johns & Thomas Bond.  23 Aug 1823
    Jonathan Potts JP.

HORINE, Benjamin - Richwoods; offers 6¼¢ reward for runaway apprentice
    Peter Low; about 18, dark, "tolerably well grown."  27 Nov 1824

HOUSE, Joseph - appraised a stray taken up by Sarah Kennedy.  11 Dec 1824

HUME, John - a runaway Negro woman owned by Samuel Shy is said to be
    living at Hume's residence.  18 Oct 1823

HUNT, Ezra - a lawyer in St. Charles, partner of Wm. Smith.  19 Apr 1823

JACOBY, John and Jane - St. Charles; their house sold by John Yates, Trustee. 18 Oct 1823

JOHNS, Thomas - appraised a stray taken up by Joseph Robnett.  10 May 1823

    - " by Garland Hording.  23 Aug 1823

JONES, Caleb & Co. - general merchandise, at the store lately occupied
    by James Cornelius, St. Louis.  15 Dec 1824

JOURNEY, James - Elkhorn Twp, Montgomery Co.; JP, stray taken up by
    Richard Wright.  15 Feb 1823

    - " stray by Sarah Kennedy.  11 Dec 1824

KENNEDY, Sarah - Elkhorn Twp, Montgomery Co.; took up a bay mare ae 2y
    appraised at $20 by Thomas Chambers & Joseph House.  11 Dec 1824
    James Journey JP.

KILBY, Reubin - sues Louis Frevier for damages, St. Louis.  13 Dec 1823

KINDS, Joseph - appraised a stray taken up by Edward Butler.  29 Mar 1824

LACROZE, J. J. & Co. - closing business in St. Louis, asks debtors to pay.  19 Apr 1823

LANE, W. - Gray Twp, Gasconade Co.; took up two strays, appraiser and
    JP not shown.  1 Dec 1823

LASLY, Alexander - appraised a stray taken up by Joseph Robnett.  10 May 1823

LEBEAU, John B. - a gunsmith "on the river bank below Mr. Landreville's,"
    St. Louis.  13 Mar 1824

LEDUKE, Morris - his wife Nelly has left his bed and board.  10 Nov 1823

LEE, Mrs. - advertises a boarding house in the "agreeable mansion"
    lately occupied by George Pitzer.  12 Jul 1823

LETCHER, Isaac A. - wants to buy 100 cords of brick wood at the brickyard
    formerly owned by John Bobb, St. Louis.  12 Jul 1823

LEWIS, J. & Co. - tailors, St. Louis.  1 Feb 1823

LIGGETT, Joseph - offers 6¢ reward for runaway apprentice Laton G. Moore.  14 Jun 1823

    Joseph C & Co. - tinware & copperware, St. Louis.  19 Apr 1823

LIPPINCOTT, S. - bankrupt, St. Louis.  1 Feb 1823

LIVERMORE, Samuel - defendant in a damage suit by Thomas Berry, St. Louis.  13 Dec 1823

LOW, Peter - runaway apprentice of Benjamin Horine, Richwoods; age about 18,
    dark, "tolerably well grown."  27 Nov 1824

McCLOUD, R. - with S. W. Foreman, proposes to publish the Missouri _Gazette_
    in St. Charles.  18 Oct 1823

    Robert - defendant in a mortgage foreclosure suit by Calvin
    Gunn, St. Charles.  23 Aug 1823

McDONALD, Susannah - sues Benjamin McDonald for divorce, Franklin Co., by
    next friend John Sullin.  7 Jun 1824

ENQ

50

McKENNA, Owen & Bridget - trust sale of their land in Callaway Co. by Horatio Cozens, Trustee. — 24 May 1824

McKENNEY, Samuel T. - St. Charles; warns the public not to harbor or trust his runaway apprentice Frederick I. Massey, or he will prosecute. — 7 Jun 1823

McMULLIN, Samuel - Plattin Twp, Jefferson Co.; JP, stray taken up by Edward Butler. — 29 Mar 1824

MALONE, Patrick - St. Ferdinand Twp, St. Louis Co.; took up a strawberry roan horse ae 10y appraised at $25 by Daniel Cain & Jesse Doggett. Thomas Whiteside JP. — 23 Aug 1823

MARTIN, Dr. John B. - new in St. Louis, "lately from Virginia." — 12 Jul 1823

Moses - offers his property in St. Louis Co. for sale; 151 acres with house and outhouses. — 17 Nov 1823

MASSIE, David - advertises the Mansion House, St. Louis. — 25 Jan 1823

MASSY, Frederick I. - runaway apprentice of Samuel T. McKenney, St. Charles. — 7 Jun 1823

MILLAGEN, R. (Richard) - tailor in St. Louis, offers "latest fashions." — 25 Jan 1823

- offers $20 reward for his runaway apprentice John Hanna and 1¢ reward for B. Star; Millagen stated that he was Star's guardian. — 19 Apr 1823

MITCHELL, Charles - sues Wm. Henry for debt, St. Charles. — 13 Dec 1823

Samuel - now in charge of the Missouri Hotel, St. Louis, due to the death of Dr. Mitchell. — 18 Oct 1823

William - appraised a stray taken up by Louis Rogers. — 13 Mar 1824

MORGAN, Capt. John - Bowles Twp, Franklin Co.; took up a bay mare ae 7-8y appraised at $39 by Wm. H. Murray & Jacob Cole. — 19 Apr 1823

MURPHY, Dennis - River des Peres, St. Louis; took up a bright bay mare ae 4y appraised at $25 by James Hanlost & Daniel Murphy. Th. Douglass JP. — 27 Apr 1824

MURRAY, William H. - appraised a stray taken up by Capt. John Morgan. — 19 Apr 1823

NIEL, Francis - advertises the St. Louis College. — 19 Apr 1823

NORMAN, Joseph - absconded from the Gasconade Saw Mill with $200. Notice signed by John Baldridge, John Code, John Gaskins, and Elijah Crippen. — 23 Aug 1823

OLDENBURG, Lewis - takes charge of the Mansion House livery stable. — 20 Nov 1824

- proposes a stagecoach line to St. Charles. — 27 Nov 1824

ORR, William - transfers his interest in the Enquirer to Duff Green. — 3 Jan 1824

PARMELE, Sylvanus - asks his debtors to pay. — 12 Jul 1823

PERRY, W. M. & J. - Potosi; advertise dry goods, groceries, hardware, etc. "new goods from Philadelphia and New Orleans." — 31 May 1823

PITZER, George - the "agreeable mansion" he lately occupied is now the site of Mrs. Lee's boarding house. — 12 Jul 1823

POTTS, Jonathan - Calvy Twp, Franklin Co.; JP, stray taken up by Joseph Robnett. — 10 May 1823

- " by Garland Hording. — 23 Aug 1823

POWERS, Neuman - appraised a stray taken up by Abraham Benton. — 19 Apr 1824

PRITCHETT, Jesse - appraised a stray taken up by Louis Rogers. — 13 Mar 1824

RAMBO, Jacob - at the lead mines, Washington Co.; offers a $50 reward for runaway Negro Tom. — 24 May 1824

RAMSEY, Delafiel - appraised a stray taken up by Abraham Benton. — 19 Apr 1824

RAMSY, Josiah Jr. - Trustee of the City of Jefferson. — 19 Apr 1823

RANKEN, Robert - offers two stores for sale or rent. — 25 Jan 1823

- advertises "fresh importations" from Philadelphia - fabrics, clothing, groceries, whiskey, tobacco. — 1 Feb 1823

RANSON, Ambrose - appraised a stray taken up by Russel Brown. — 19 Apr 1823

REED, James & Co. - "new store" in St. Louis: whiskey, salt, bacon, dry goods, groceries, hardware, etc. — 20 Nov 1824

ROBERTS, Michael - his wife Ann has left his bed and board. — 1 Feb 1823

ROBNETT, Joseph - Calvy Twp, Franklin Co.; took up a sorrel horse ae 10y appraised at $30 by Thomas Johns & Alexander Lasly. Jonathan Potts JP. — 10 May 1823

ROGERS, Louis - Calvy Twp, Franklin Co.; took up a black horse ae 7y appraised at $25 by Jesse Pritchett, Wm. Mitchell, and George Fryer. Samuel Short JP. — 13 Mar 1824

SAMUEL, Giles M. - storage and commission business, Franklin. — 12 Jul 1823

SAVAGE, W. H. - offers dry goods, groceries, salt, iron, lead, shot, etc.; will take beeswax in payment. St. Louis. — 15 Feb 1823

ENQ

SHORT, Samuel - Calvy Twp, Franklin Co.; JP, stray taken up by Louis Rogers. 13 Mar 1824

SHY, Samuel - St. Charles; offers a $10 reward for a runaway Negro woman Gin, said to be living at John Hume's. 18 Oct 1823

SIMMONS, H. C. - St. Louis; dissolves partnership with A. Shackford, will continue the auction business. 1 Feb 1823

SMITH, J. J. Jr. - St. Louis; sells drugs, medicines, paints, groceries. 1 Feb 1823

    William O. - a lawyer in St. Charles, partner of Ezra Hunt. 19 Apr 1823

STAPLES, William - appraised a stray taken up by Edward Butler. 29 Mar 1824

STEBBINS, S. - St. Louis; "fashionable boot and shoe factory." 14 Jun 1824

STEEL, John - St. Louis; hats for sale "next door to Mrs. Paddock." 19 Apr 1823

STINE, J. R. - advertises a boarding house on Main St., St. Louis. 23 Aug 1823

TALIAFERRO, Lawrence - of "Oak Hill" in Pike Co., offers a valuable farm for sale. 19 Apr 1823

TIFFANY, C. & Co. - "European and East Indian goods" for sale, St. Louis. 3 May 1823

    Comfort & Osmond - dissolve partnership. 29 Mar 1824

WALTER, W. & Co. - copper and tin manufactory on N. Main, St. Louis. 23 Aug 1823

WARREN, J. - appraised a stray taken up by Joshua Herrington. 12 Jul 1823

WHEELER, Asa - dissolves partnership with Daniel D. Page. 31 May 1823

WHITESIDE, Thomas - St. Ferdinand Twp, St. Louis Co.; JP, stray taken up by Patrick Malone. 23 Aug 1823

WITERWITCH, Martin - St. Ferdinand Twp, St. Louis Co.; took up a gray mare ae 10y appraised at $25 by Wm. Codge & Jesse Dogget. 25 Jan 1823

WOODS, James and Martin - defendants, suit by George Collier (mortgage foreclosure), Lincoln Co. 1 Feb 1823

    Zadock - defendant, mortgage foreclosure suit by George Collier, Lincoln Co. 1 Feb 1823

WRIGHT, Richard - Elkhorn Twp, Montgomery Co.; took up a sorrel mare ae 3y appraised at $25 and a black mare ae 2y at $15, appraisers not named. James Journey JP. 15 Feb 1823

YATES, John - St. Charles; trustee in the house of John and Jane Jacoby at its sale. 18 Oct 1823

COMMISSIONER'S SALE

WILL be sold, at Public Sale, on the 10th day of November next, for cash in hand, before the Court House door in the Town of Fayette, Four likely

*Negroes,*

named as follows—Will, Little Lucy, Anthony, and Clement, the property of Stephen Trigg, and to be sold by virtue of a decree of the Circuit Court of Howard county, sitting as a court of chancery, made at March term, 1828, in favor of George Tompkins for use of Gaw's minor being against said Trigg.

. The sale will take place between the hours of 10 o'clock, A. M. and 3 o'clock, P. M. of said day.

DAVID PREWITT,
Commissioner.

.October 10, 1828 12 2w

ALLEN, George - appraised a stray taken up by Henry A.H. Russell.  31 Oct 1829
ANDERSON, William H. - St. John's Twp, Franklin Co.; took up a black mare
    in foal, ae 7y, appraised at $30 by Joseph  13 Apr 1829
    Jamison (only).  W. Bray JP.
ARMSTRONG, Eliza - student in the St. Louis Female Academy.  23 Jun 1831
    James A. - advertises the "West Indian Fruit and Cordial and  21 Apr 1831
    Confectionary Store," opposite Scott & Rule, St. L.
    Thomas - Bedford Twp, Lincoln Co.; JP, stray taken up by  2 Dec 1830
    Jeremiah Beck.
    W. - Bourbon Twp, Callaway Co.; JP, stray taken up by Thomas West. 31 Mar 1831
ATKINSON, Dr. H. - a dentist, St. Louis.  24 Oct 1829
BABER, Thomas H. - Boeuf Twp, Franklin Co.; JP, stray taken up by  19 Jan 1832
    Benjamin Brown.
BAILEY, James - bankrupt, St. Louis.  16 Feb 1832
BALDWIN, John H. - dissolves partnership with James P. Slencer.  17 Oct 1830
    - "chair manufactory" one door north of Laurel St., St. Louis. 1 Sep 1831
    Virginia - student in the St. Louis Female Academy.  23 Jun 1831
BARADA, P. D. - appraised a stray taken up by John Wright.  3 Feb 1831
BARNETT, Thomas - partner of James T. Ivers, copper and tin, on Main St.  7 Nov 1829
    in St. Louis.
BARRADA, Ant. - appraised a stray taken up by Abraham Ringer.  19 Jan 1832
BARRY, James - Bonhomme Twp, St. Louis Co.; took up a black mare appraised  27 Jan 1831
    at $15 by Rolla F. Rose & James McKnight. H. Sappington JP.
BATCHELOR, William C. - "The Retreat. . ." fruit, ice cream, cakes,  29 Jul 1830
    segars, nuts, olives, etc. St. Louis.
BECK, Jeremiah - Bedford Twp, Lincoln Co.; took up a gray mare ae 3y  2 Dec 1830
    appraised at $25 by Joseph W. Gibson & Isaac Litton.
    Thomas Armstrong JP.
BELL, Isaac & Samuel - sue Philip R. Thompson for $1000 damages, St. Louis. 23 Sep 1830
BERGER, Peter or Pierre - bankrupt, St. Louis 24 Feb and 13 Oct, 1831.
BERRY, Rosanna - bankrupt, St. Louis.  20 Feb 1830
BIGELOW, Moses - Femme Osage Twp, St. Charles Co.; JP, stray taken up  31 Oct 1829
    by Henry A. H. Russell.
BISSELL, James - St. Ferdinand Twp, St. Louis Co.; took up a bay filly  9 Dec 1830
    ae 2y appraised at $10 by Henry W. Carter & James
    Patterson. Benjamin B. Ray JP.
BLAND, Isaac - offers lots for sale in Canton (with E. White &  20 Feb 1830
    Robert St. Clair).
BOGERT, Ruliff - a stonecutter in St. Louis, Churct St. between Elm  31 Apr 1829
    and Myrtle.
BOGGS, Joseph - Jefferson City, offers $50 reward for runaway Negro.  24 Jun 1830
BOLTON, R. E. - house and sign painter, St. Louis, moved to Main St.  22 Jul 1830
BORCHARD, Samuel - Gasconade Co.; JP, stray taken up by James Renfro.  15 Dec 1831
BRADBURY, H. P. - offers the "Post Meridian" for sale, in the vicinity  8 Aug 1829
    of the steamboat landing, St. Louis.
BRAY, W. - St. John's Twp, Franklin Co.; JP, stray taken up by  13 Apr 1829
    Wm. H. Anderson.
BRICE, J. C. & Co. - St. Louis; "Lotteries about to be drawn. . .  20 Jan 1831
    opposite Deaver's Emporium of Fashion."
BROWN, George F. - bankrupt, St. Louis.  19 May 1831
    Benjamin - Boeuf Twp, Franklin Co.; took up a bay horse ae 6y  19 Jan 1832
    appraised at $50 by Wm. Wyat & Caleb Nix.  Thos. Baber JP.
    Henry J. - appraised a stray taken up by Samuel Staples.  29 Dec 1831
BRUCE, Amos J. - appraised a stray taken up by Augustus Jones.  10 Nov 1831
BRYAN, John - opens a new livery stable near the Land Office, St. Louis.  3 Jun 1830
BUCHANAN, Andrew - partner of George Sproule in a new commission house  6 Feb 1830
    in St. Louis, formerly of Florence, AL.
BUFORD, Francis K. - Fulton Twp, Callaway Co.; JP, stray taken up by  20 May 1830
    John Meredith.
BUMPASS, William - Bowleware Twp, Gasconade Co.; JP, stray taken up  24 May 1832
    by Owen Shockley.
BURK, John - Saverton Twp, Ralls Co.; took up a bright bay horse ae 9y  18 Aug 1831
    appraised by James M. Creason & Ptolemy Wilson.
    Hosea Northbut JP.
CALL, Dr. George W. - physician, surgeon, St. Louis; at Major Hopkins'  4 Jul 1829
    Boarding House.

BEA

CAMPBELL, G. - appraised a stray taken up by John Wright.     3 Feb 1831
CARPER, Dr. William - office in St. Louis, one door above George     14 Jul 1831
         Kennerly's store.
CARR, Cornelia and Virginia - students in the St. Louis Female Academy.     23 Jun 1831
CARTER, Miss H. - partner of Mrs. R. S. Johnson, milliners and mantua-     21 Jan 1830
         makers in St. Louis, lower Main St.; formerly of
         Lexington & Danville, KY.
CARTER, Henry W. - appraised a stray taken up by James Bissell.     9 Dec 1830
CHENIE, Athalia - student in the St. Louis Female Academy.     23 Jun 1831
CHRISTY, Edward - St. Louis Co.; took up a yellow bay mare ae 12y
         appraised at $40 by Isham L. Moore & James McReynolds.     14 Apr 1831
                 J.V. Garnier JP.
CLARK, John - appraised a stray taken up by Henry Evans.     11 Nov 1830
CLAYTON, James - defendant in a trespass suit by Henry Pinkley,     25 Aug 1831
         Washington Co.
COHEN, Adaline, Amanda, & Sarah - students in the St. Louis Female Academy.     23 Jun 1831
     Alexander - his wife Susan has left his bed and board.     12 Jan 1832
         - bankrupt, St. Louis.     9 Feb 1832
COLBURN, Jesse - offers $50 reward for a runaway Negro, Elizabeth, ae _ca_ 24,     16 Dec 1830
         he had bought from Wm. H. Edgar of Fayette.
     Margaret & Sophia - students in the St. Louis Female Academy.     23 Jun 1831
COLEMAN, Benjamin - Merrimac Twp, Franklin Co.; took up a bay horse ae 8y
         appraised at $23 by Aaron Cook & John Wickerham.     9 Dec 1830
                 John Stewart JP.
COLLIER, Thomas W. - appraised a stray taken up by Thomas West.     31 Mar 1831
COLLINS, A., M., Wm. B., and Frederick dissolve partnership; A. & M. will     13 May 1830
         continue the business.
CONNER, Armstrong - appraised a stray taken up by Isaac Roberts.     5 Jan 1832
CONWAY, William - dissolves partnership with John Rice at Old Mines.     15 Apr 1830
COOK, Aaron -appraised a stray taken up by Benjamin Coleman.     9 Dec 1830
COONSE, Jacob - of Crawford Co.; accused of slandering George W. Gibson.     20 Feb 1830
COWEN, Rachel - student in the St. Louis Female Academy.     23 Jun 1831
COWHERD, William - appraised a stray taken up by John Meredith.     20 May 1830
COX, Robert - Joachim Twp, Jefferson Co.; took up a bay mare & bay filly
         appraised at $35 by Aaron Henry & Thomas Skillett.     13 Oct 1831
                 G. Hammond JP.
CREASON, James M. - appraised a stray taken up by John Burk.     18 Aug 1831
CROW, Lewis - bankrupt, St. Charles.     13 Jan 1831
DAVIS, Rev. John - superintendent of the St. Louis Female Academy.     23 Jun 1831
DEAN, John - says that Dr. Nelson, of St. Louis, not only failed to cure     17 Feb 1831
         him but actually made his condition worse.
DELANNA, Augustin - St. Ferdinand Twp, St. Louis Co.; took up a dark bay
         horse ae 12y appraised by Gilbert & Phineas James.     13 Apr 1829
         Amount not shown. Hugh O'Neil JP.
DOANE, Frances- student in the St. Louis Female Academy.     23 Jun 1831
DOUGHERTY, Sarah B. - offers land for sale in Pike Co., and a house and     17 Jun 1830
         lot in Florissant.
DOUGLASS, Mary - student in the St. Louis Female Academy.     23 Jun 1831
DOWNING, Samuel - Bonhomme Twp, St. Louis Co.; took up a dark bay horse
         ae 5y appraised by Harris & William Downing; amount     4 Nov 1830
         not shown. Hartly Sappington JP.
DRENON, William - Merrimac Twp, Franklin Co.; took up a brown horse ae 15y
         appraised at $25 by Jonathan Drenon & Samuel Wilson.     7 Apr 1831
                 John Stewart JP.
DUGAL, Xavier - his house and lot sold to satisfy a claim of Alexander Fryer.11 Nov 1829
DUNCAN, Caroline - student in the St. Louis Female Academy.     23 Jun 1831
     David - "new cheap store" -- drygoods, groceries, etc. Main St.     21 Oct 1829
DYER, Martha - student in the St. Louis Female Academy.     23 Jun 1831
EDGAR, Lewis - plaintiff vs Abraham Wilcox, attachment, Washington Co.     30 Aug 1832
     William H. - Fayette; former owner of Jesse Colburn's runaway slave.     16 Dec 1830
EDWARDS, William - St. Charles; broke jail, allegedly stole from the post     17 Feb 1831
         office. About 20, slender.
ELLINGTON, William - appraised a stray taken up by John Putnam.     28 Apr 1831
ELLIOTT, Benjamin - appraised a stray taken up by David Parker.     4 Jul 1829
EVANS, Henry - Bedford Twp, Lincoln Co.; took up a gray filly ae 3y
         appraised at $20 by John Clark & Joseph House.     11 Nov 1830
                 Charles Wheeler JP.

        BEA

FAIR, Adaline - see Thomas Hobbs.
FERGUSON, Fergus - St. Louis Co.; JP, stray taken up by Lewis E. Martin.   23 Dec 1830
FLEMING, Arthur - saddle, harness, and trunk maker, has returned to
      St. Louis. Now at 76 S. Main.   22 Jul 1830
FLEMMING, James - appraised a stray taken up by Rinshun Roertson.   24 Nov 1831
FLOUGHERTY, Felix W. - appraised a stray taken up by Wm. Skinner Jr.   28 Oct 1830
     - Elkhorn Twp, Montgomery Co.; took up a brown colt
     appraised at $6 by Neil McCan & Wm. Skinner Jr.   28 Oct 1830
                      Benoni McClure JP.
FORRESTER, Stephen - his son found "a small amount of money" on a street   4 Aug 1831
     in St. Louis.
FORSYTH, Thomas - his house and lot on Main St. for rent.   13 Apr 1829
FOSTER, Judge William P. - father of Virginia Wetherill, who has left her   17 Oct 1829
     husband and is living at her father's home.
FRYER, Alexander - the house and lot of Xavier Dugal sold to satisfy a   11 Nov 1829
     claim of Fryer.
FUGATE, Burr - appraised a stray taken up by John Putnam.   28 Apr 1831
GALLAUDET, C. - opens a bookkeeping school in St. Louis; tuition, $15   9 Sep 1829
     for three months.
GARDNER, Johnson - forbids the cutting of timber on his farm, 8 or 9   4 Mar 1830
     miles out on the St. Charles road.
GIBSON, George W. - says that Jacob Coonse of Crawford Co. has been   20 Feb 1830
     slandering him . . . says he stole horses and a
     pistol, etc.
     Joseph W. - appraised a stray taken up by Jeremiah Beck.   2 Dec 1830
GILL, C. - advertises "a large and convenient boarding house," on   17 Oct 1829
     Elm St., St. Louis.
GILLET, Philo - St. Charles Twp, St. Charles Co.; JP, stray taken up by   27 Jun 1829
                        Wiatt Woodruff.
     - " by Evin Lamasters.   10 Jun 1830
     Leonard and/or Leonard F., appraised the stray by Lamasters.   10 Jun 1830
GLOVER, Robert - appraised a stray taken up by Thomas West.   31 Mar 1831
GOODYEAR, Wooster - "gentlemen's boot and ladies' fancy shoe store,"   24 Jun 1830
     and manufactory, St. Louis.
GREENE, R. - Troy, Lincoln Co.; took up two horses appraised at $80 by   16 Jun 1831
     John B. Stone & Jordan Sallee. Charles Wheeler JP.
GRIFFIN, Zachariah - appraised a stray taken up by Thomas Haile.   19 Jan 1832
GROBE, David - appraised a stray taken up by Lewis Martin.   23 Dec 1830
HAILE, Thomas - Perry Twp, St. Francois Co.; took up a brown horse ae 6y   19 Jan 1832
     appraised at $65 by James S. Ray & Zachariah Griffin.
                      George McGahan JP.
HAMILTON, Abby & Eliza - students in the St. Louis Female Academy.   23 Jun 1831
     Richard - his wife Josette has left his bed and board.   20 Jan 1831
HAMMOND, G. - Joachim Twp, Jefferson Co.; JP, stray taken up   28 Jul 1831
               by Landon Williams.
HARDEN, Joseph - runaway apprentice of Harlow Spencer, a cabinet maker   17 Oct 1830
     in St. Louis. Age 17.
HARRODS, P. D. - appraised a stray taken up by Abraham Ringer.   19 Jan 1832
HAWKINS, John R. - appraised a stray taken up by John McCune.   16 Jun 1831
HEMPSTEAD, Cornelia - student in the St. Louis Female Academy.   23 Jun 1831
HENRY, Aaron - appraised a stray taken up by Robert Cox.   13 Oct 1831
HINES, Wiley - Monroe Twp, Lincoln Co.; took up a bay mare ae 3y appraised   1 Jul 1830
     at $29 by Simon Stephens & A. C. Inman. Freeland Rese JP.
HOBBS, Thomas - "new boot and shoe factory," on Main St., St. Louis; has   4 Jul 1829
     "an extensive assortment of square-toed boots" for sale.
     - his wife Adaline, nee Fair, has left his bed and board.
HOGAN, William - appraised a stray taken up by Samuel Staples.   29 Dec 1831
HOPKINS, Ely & Co. - St. Louis; auction sale of looking glasses, fire   23 Sep 1830
     brasses, Brittania ware, etc.
HORINE, Michael - bankrupt, Potosi.   21 Jan 1830
HOUGH, Mary - student in the St. Louis Female Academy.   23 Jun 1831
HOUSE, Joseph - appraised a stray taken by Henry Evans; signed "x."   11 Nov 1830
HUDSON, J. H. - bankrupt, St. Louis.   1 Mar 1832
HUGHES, James - Charrette Twp, Montgomery Co.; JP, stray taken up by   15 Jul 1830
                  Duglass Wyatt.
HUNT, Julia & Theodosia - students in the St. Louis Female Academy.   23 Jun 1831

BEA

55

```
HUTCHINSON, L. - dissolves partnership with Seraphinus Vangeyt.          11 Nov 1830
HUTTON, E. P. - "old made new. . " cleaning and dyeing, St. Louis.        9 Dec 1830
IMBODEN, David - Belleview Twp, Washington Co.; $25 reward for runaway Negro. 13 Jan '30
INMAN, A. C. - appraised a stray taken up by Wiley Hines.                 1 Jul 1830
IVERS, James T. - partner of Thomas Barnett, copper and tinware, St. Louis. 7 Nov 1829
JAMES, Gilbert & Phineas - appraised a stray taken up by Augustin Delanna. 13 Apr 1829
JAMISON, H. M. - appraised a stray taken up by John Warfield.            27 May 1830
     Joseph - appraised a stray taken up by Wm. H. Anderson.             13 Apr 1829
JENKINS, James - executed for the murder of his wife Sinah.              30 Sep 1830
JOHNSON, John M. - "caution to printers," St. Louis; with Wm. D. Waddell,
     says the St. Louis Times has not paid for their work,               30 Sep 1830
     cautions printers not to work there "as long as
     T. J. Miller has any connection with it."
     Mary, Rosella, & Susan - students in the St. Louis Female Academy.  23 Jun 1831
     Mrs. R. J. - partner of Miss H. Carter, milliners and mantua-
     makers, St. Louis, lower Main St.; formerly of                     21 Jan 1830
     Lexington and Danville, KY.
     William H. - appraised a stray taken up by Evin Lamasters.          10 Jun 1830
JONES, Augustus - Belleview Twp, Washington Co.; took up a mule ae 10-15y
     appraised at $20 by Amos J. Bruce, Wm. Shields, and                 10 Nov 1831
     Robert Setton. George Masters JP.
JUDSON, J. P. - advertises a "coffee house and victualing room," upper
     part of the chequered building at Water & Vine, St. Louis.          23 Sep 1829
KEMPER, John F. - denies that the St. Louis Brass Foundry equipment is to
     be sold, as A. Mead has advertised.                                 8 Dec 1831
KENNERLY, Mary - student in the St. Louis Female Academy.                23 Jun 1831
KIMBALL, Dudley - bankrupt, St. Louis.                                   27 Jun 1829
KINCAID, Samuel - dissolves partnership with Wm. D. Lewis.               12 May 1830
KING, Ann - student in the St. Louis Female Academy.                     23 Jun 1831
     Michael - wholesale and retail leather store, boot and shoe factory,
     Main St. opposite Kenney's saddle shop, St. Louis. Will             1 Apr 1830
     take apprentices.
LAMASTERS, Evin - St. Charles Twp, St. Charles Co.; took up a bright bay
     mare ae 4y appraised at $35 by Wm. H. Johnson and                   10 Jun 1830
     Leonard F. Gillet. Philo Gillet JP.
LANDON, Laben - St. Louis Co.; took up a brown mare and a bright sorrel
     mare appraised at $65 by Daniel Quick & Elijah Owen.                5 May 1831
LANE, Sarah - student in the St. Louis Female Academy.                   23 Jun 1831
LEWIS, William D. - dissolves partnership with Samuel Kincaid.           12 May 1830
LITTON, Isaac - appraised a stray taken up by Jeremiah Beck.             2 Dec 1830
LONG, Amelia & Julia - students in the St. Louis Female Academy.         23 Jun 1831
     Mathias - says that Dr. Nelson of St. Louis cured his wife's
     rheumatism "after Virginia doctors had failed."                    17 Mar 1831
LOPER, James - his lot sold to satisfy a claim of Thomas Biddle.         11 Nov 1829
McCAN, Neil - appraised a stray taken up by Wm. Skinner Jr.              28 Oct 1830
McCARTAN, Amanda - student in the St. Louis Female Academy.              23 Jun 1831
McCAUSLAND, William Jr. - oppers $20 reward for runaway Negro Ben.       14 Jul 1831
McCLURE, Benoni - Elkhorn Twp, Montgomery Co.; JP, stray taken up by
     Wm. Skinner Jr.                                                     28 Oct 1830
McCORMICK, Isaac - appraised a stray taken up by Philip Martin.          17 Mar 1831
McCOY, Joseph - offers 160 head of young cattle for sale.                23 Jun 1831
McCREERY, Robert - appraised a stray taken up by Landon Williams.        28 Jul 1831
McCUNE, John - Cuivre Twp, Pike Co.; took up a blood bay horse ae 12y
     appraised at $35 by John Montgomery & John R. Hawkins.             16 Jun 1831
     L. Rogers JP.
McGAHAN, George - Perry Twp, St. Francois Co.; JP, stray taken up
     by Thomas Haile.                                                    19 Jan 1832
McGEARY, John - offers $30 reward for six strayed horses.                30 Jun 1831
McKEE, Mary A. - student in the St. Louis Female Academy.                23 Jun 1831
McKNIGHT, James - appraised a stray taken up by James Barry.             27 Jan 1831
McNEIL, William S. - his wife Emeline has left his bed and board.        2 Feb 1832
McREYNOLDS, James - appraised a stray taken up by Edward Christy.        14 Apr 1831
MACK, N. W. - offers $200 reward for detection and conviction of the
     person who set fire to his stable on 24 May.                        10 Jun 1830
     - offers his tavern for lease.                                      4 Aug 1831
MANSFIELD, Isaac - advertises the New Harmony & Nashoba Gazette or
     The Free Enquirer.                                                  13 Apr 1829

                    BEA
                          56
```

MARTIN, Lewis E. - St. Louis Co.; took up a sorrel horse ae 15y appraised
    at $15 by David Grobe & A. Martin, Jr.                       23 Dec 1830
                                Fergus Ferguson JP.
    - appraised a stray taken up by Ellzey H. Rose.           20 Jan 1831
    Philip - St. John's Twp, Franklin Co.; took up two colts appraised
    at $35 by Nathan Richardson & Isaac McCormick.        17 Mar 1831
                                  Wm. G. Owens JP.
MASON, Benjamin - appraised a stray taken up by John Warfield.      27 May 1830
MASTERS, George - Belleview Twp, Washington Co.; JP, stray taken up    10 Nov 1831
                                by Augustus Jones.
MEREDITH, John - Fulton Twp, Callaway Co.; took up two fillies appraised
    at $35 by Wm. Miller Jr. & Wm. Cowherd. Francis Buford JP.    20 May 1830
MILLER, Robert - appraised a stray taken up by Wiatt Woodruff.      27 Jun 1829
    T. J. - named in a "caution to printers" by Wm. D. Waddell and
    John M. Johnson, who said the St. Louis *Times* had not        30 Sep 1830
    paid them for their work.
    William Jr. - appraised a stray taken up by John Meredith.      20 May 1830
MOFFITT, N. - took over the Virginia Hotel, St. Charles.           20 Oct 1831
MONTGOMERY, John - appraised a stray taken up by John McCune.      16 Jun 1831
MOORE, Isham L. - appraised a stray taken up by Edward Christy.      14 Apr 1831
    John - boot and shoe maker, St. Louis, Main St.           23 Sep 1829
MORGAN, Luther - offers $20 reward for runaway mulatto Claiborne.    22 Sep 1831
MOSS, Mark - appraised a stray taken up by Landon Williams.        28 Jul 1831
MUSICK, Reuben - appraised a stray taken up by John Putman.        21 Jul 1831
NELSON, Dr. - of St. Louis; John Dean says the doctor didn't cure him but  17 Feb 1831
    actually made his condition worse.
    - Mathias Long responds that the doctor cured his wife's    17 Mar 1831
    rheumatism "after Virginia doctors failed."
NEVIS, Tilman - defendant suit by Peter Smyth, Washington Co.    30 Aug 1832
NICHOLS, M. - Monroe Twp, Lincoln Co.; JP, stray taken up by Rinchun Roertson. 24 Nov'31
NIX, Caleb - appraised a stray taken up by Benjamin Brown.        19 Jan 1832
NORTHBUT, Hosea - Saverton Twp, Ralls Co.; JP, stray taken by John Burk. 18 Aug 1831
O'FALLON, Ellen - student in the St. Louis Female Academy.        23 Jun 1831
O'NEIL, Hugh - St. Ferdinand Twp, St. Louis Co.; JP, stray taken up    13 Apr 1829
                            by Augustin Delanna.
OWEN, Elijah - appraised a stray taken up by Laben Landon.        5 May 1831
PADDOCK, Mrs. - St. Louis; boarding house on Mechanic's Row, opposite  7 Nov 1829
    Pilkington's boot and shoe factory.
PALEN, Sophia - student in the St. Louis Female Academy.         23 Jun 1831
PARKER, David - Union Twp, Washington Co.; took up a dark bay mare and a
    yellow bay colt, appraised at $30 by John Trimble &        4 Jul 1829
    Benjamin Elliott. Alex Starbuck JP.
PATTERSON, James - appraised a stray taken up by James Bissell.     9 Dec 1830
PERRY, Angeline - student in the St. Louis Female Academy.       23 Jun 1831
PILKINGTON, R. C. - boot and shoe factory, St. Louis, on Mechanic's   7 Nov 1829
    Row, opposite Mrs. Paddock's boarding house.
PINKLEY, Henry - plaintiff vs James Clayton, trespass, Washington Co.  25 Aug 1831
POPE, Henry C. - attorney and counselor-at-law, St. Louis.        30 Jan 1830
PRICE, Harriet - student in the St. Louis Female Academy.        23 Jun 1831
PUTMAN or  John - St. Louis Co.; took up a bay mare and a sorrel horse
PUTNAM,        appraised at $50 by Burr Fugate & Wm. Ellington.    28 Apr 1831
                            A. J. Whiteside JP.
    - St. Ferdinand Twp, St. Louis Co.; took up a bay mare
    ae 7y appraised at $10 by Reuben Musick & D. St. Vrain.   21 Jul 1831
                            B. B. Ray JP.
QUICK, Daniel - appraised a stray taken up by Laben Landon.       5 May 1831
RAINEY, Nathan - appraised a stray taken up by Ellzey H. Rose.    20 Jan 1831
RANKIN, James - "an invalid pensioner," lost his pension papers and   4 Mar 1830
    land patent.
RAY, Benjamin B. - St. Ferdinand Twp, St. Louis Co.; JP, strays taken up
    by James Bissell (9 Dec 1830) & Ellzey H. Rose.        20 Jan 1831
    James S. - appraised a stray taken up by Thomas Haile.       19 Jan 1832
REED, Strother - bankrupt, St. Louis.                      24 Feb 1831
RENFRO, James - Gasconade Co.; took up a bay mare ae 3y appraised at $30  15 Dec 1831
    by B. D. Yates & Uriah Shockley. Samuel Borchard JP.
RESE, Freeland W. - Monroe Twp, Lincoln Co.; JP, stray taken by Wiley Hines. 1 Jul 1830

      BEA

RICE, John - dissolves partnership with William Conway, Old Mines.    15 Apr 1830
RICHARDS, D. B. - wants to hire "a smart and active black man who
                 speaks French."    27 Jun 1829
RICHARDSON, Nathan - appraised a stray taken up by Philip Martin.    17 Mar 1831
RIDGELY, Mary J. and Sarah - students in the St. Louis Female Academy.    23 Jun 1831
RINGER, Abraham - St. Louis Co.; took up two mares, ae 6y & 10y,
            appraised at $32 by Ant. Barrada & P. D. Harrods.    19 Jan 1832
                                  J. R. Stine JP.
ROBERTS, Isaac - Joachim Twp, Jefferson Co.; took up a bay mare ae 4y
            appraised at $12 by Armstrong Connor & Linus Roberts.    5 Jan 1832
                           Chauncey Smith JP.
ROERTSON, Rinshun - Monroe Twp, Lincoln Co.; took up a bay filly appraised    24 Nov 1832
            at $15 by James Flemmirg & James Simpson. M. Nichols JP.
ROGERS, L. - Cuivre Twp, Pike Co.; JP, stray taken up by John McCune.    16 Jun 1831
ROSE, Ellzey H. - St. Ferdinand Twp, St. Louis Co.; took up a gray mare
            ae 4y appraised at $18 by Louis Martin & Nathan Rainey.    20 Jan 1831
                          Benj. B. Ray JP.
    Rolla F. - appraised a stray taken up by James Barry.    27 Jan 1831
RUSSELL, Henry A. H. - Femme Osage Twp, St. Charles Co.; took up a horse
            ae 7y appraised at $30 by Darling Smith & George    31 Oct 1829
            Allen. Moses Bigelow JP.
St. CLAIR, Robert - lots for sale in Canton (with E. White & Isaac Bland).    20 Feb 1830
St. LEGER, Dr. Josh - offers a $20 reward for a lost gold watch.    19 Aug 1830
St. VRAIN, D. - appraised a stray taken up by John Putman.    21 Jul 1831
SALLEE, Jordan - appraised a stray taken up by R. Greene.    16 Jun 1831
SALMOUS, Jacob - accused murderer of Thomas Wilson, broke jail in
            St. Charles. Age about 50, ordinary height, smooth face,    6 Oct 1831
            high forehead, heavy eyebrows; might go to CA or TX.
SAUNDERS, Mary & Grace - students in the St. Louis Female Academy.    23 Jun 1831
SETTON, Robert - appraised a stray taken up by Augustus Jones.    10 Nov 1831
SHACKFORD, Charlotte - student in the St. Louis Female Academy.    23 Jun 1831
SHARP, Dr. L. A. - doctor in St. Louis, office on Pine St. "one door
            east of Dr. Call."    11 Aug 1831
SHEPARD, Elizabeth & Sarah - students in the St. Louis Female Academy.    23 Jun 1831
SHIELDS, William - appraised a stray taken up by Augustus Jones.    10 Nov 1831
SHOCKLEY, Owen - Bowleware Twp, Gasconade Co.; took up a brown mare ae 12y
            appraised at $35 by Joel Starkey & John J. Wyatt.    24 May 1832
                         Wm. Bumpass JP.
    Uriah - appraised a stray taken up by James Renfro.    15 Dec 1831
SIMPSON, James - appraised a stray taken up by Rinshun Roertson.    24 Nov 1831
SKILLETT, Thomas - appraised a stray taken up by Robert Cox.    13 Oct 1831
SKINNER, William Jr. - Elkhorn Twp, Montgomery Co.; took up a brown mare
            and black colt appraised at $21 by Neil McCan &    28 Oct 1830
            Felix Flougherty. Benoni McClure JP.
SMART, Glover - Callaway Co.; his wife Louisiana has left his bed and board. 24 Mar 1831
SMITH, Chauncey - Plattin Twp, Jefferson Co.; JP, stray taken up
                     by Samuel Staples.    29 Dec 1831
    Darling - appraised a stray taken up by Henry A. H. Russell.    31 Oct 1829
    Henry - Bonhomme Twp, St. Louis Co.; JP, stray taken up by    27 May 1830
                        John Warfield.
    John - of Shibboleth, Washington Co.; offers $100 reward for a    26 Jul 1832
                       runaway slave.
    Laurena - student in the St. Louis Female Academy.    23 Jun 1831
SMYTH, Peter - plaintiff, attachment suit vs Tilman Nevis, Washington Co.    30 Aug 1832
SPALDING, Margaret - student in the St. Louis Female Academy.    23 Jun 1831
SPENCER, Harlow - a cabinet maker in St. Louis, advertises for his
            runaway apprentice Joseph Harden.    17 Oct 1830
    James S. - dissolves partnership with John H. Baldwin.    17 Oct 1830
SPROULE, George - partner of Andrew Buchanan in a new commission house
            in St. Louis; formerly of Florenca, AL.    6 Feb 1830
STAPLES, Samuel - Plattin Twp, Jefferson Co.; took up a bay mare ae 3y
            appraised at $20 by Wm. Hogan & Henry J. Brown.    29 Dec 1831
                         Chauncey Smith JP.
STARBUCK, Alex - Union Twp, Washington Co.; JP, stray taken up by    4 Jul 1829
                     David Parker.
STARKEY, Joel - appraised a stray taken up by Owen Shockley.    24 May 1832

STEAVERS, William - defendant in a $300 damage suit by Thomas and
    William Townsend, St. Louis.                                 5 Sep 1829
STEPHENS, Simon - appraised a stray taken up by Wiley Hines.      1 Jul 1830
STEWART, John - Merrimac Twp, Franklin Co.; JP, strays taken up by
    Benjamin Coleman (9 Dec 1830) and William Drenon.        7 Apr 1831
STIFF, Edward - St. Louis; advertises "electric waterproof hat manufactory"
    on Main St., wants two journeymen.                 20 Feb 1830
STINE, Jacob R. - St. Louis Twp, St. Louis Co.; JP, stray taken by G. Campbell. 3 Feb'31
STONE, John B. - appraised a stray taken up by R. Greene.     16 Jun 1831
TANNER, Allen C. - Montgomery Co.; forbids cutting of timber on his land.  15 Aug 1829
TEISON, Caroline - student in the St. Louis Female Academy.     23 Jun 1831
THOMAS, Mary - student in the St. Louis Female Academy.       23 Jun 1831
THOMPSON, Philip R. - defendant in a suit by Samuel and Isaac Bell for
    $1000 damages, St. Louis.                    23 Sep 1830
TOWNSEND, Thomas and William - plaintifs vs William Steavers, $300 damages. 5 Sep 1829
    Thomas - bankrupt, St. Louis.                  16 Jan 1830
TRIMBLE, John - appraised a stray taken up by David Parker.     4 Jul 1829
VANGEYT, Seraphinus - dissolves partnership with L. Hutchinson.    11 Nov 1830
VAN SWEARINGEN, J. - Jefferson Barracks; has lost a large white pointer dog. 4 Mar 1830
VON PHUL, Maria - student in the St. Louis Female Academy.     23 Jun 1831
WADDELL, James & Co. - St. Louis; "cheap and fashionable clothing."   13 Apr 1829
    - moved to Chouteau's brick house on Main St.      24 Oct 1829
    James & Samuel - $10 reward for a strayed or stolen horse.  20 May 1830
    William B. - a printer; with John M. Johnson cautions other
        printers to have no connection with the St. Louis    30 Sep 1830
        Times "as long as T.J. Miller has any connection with
        it;" they were not paid for their work.
WARFIELD, John - Bonhomme Twp, St. Louis Co.; took up a strawberry roan
    horse ae 4y appraised at $52.50 by H.M. Jamison and    27 May 1830
    Benjamin F. Mason. Henry Smith JP.
WEST, Thomas - Bourbon Twp, Callaway Co.; took up a bay horse appraised
    at $10 by Robert Glover & Thomas W. Collier. W. Armstrong JP. 31 May 1831
WETHERILL, John - his wife Virginia has left him and is staying with
    her father, Judge William F. Foster.             17 Oct 1829
WHEELER, Charles - Bedford Twp, Lincoln Co.; JP, strays taken up by
    Henry Evans (11 Nov 1830) and by R. Greene at Troy.   16 Jun 1831
WHITE, E. - lots for sale in Canton (with Robert St. Clair & Isaac Bland). 20 Feb 1830
    Isaac D. - "will prepare a Jackson dinner. . . a plentiful repast
        will be spread." St. Louis, 1/2m from town, west of   27 Jun 1829
        the city burial ground.
WHITESIDE, A. J. - St. Louis Co.; JP, stray taken up by John Putnam.  28 Apr 1831
WICKERHAM, John - appraised a stray taken up by Benjamin Coleman.   9 Dec 1830
WIGGINS, Adaline & Julia - students in the St. Louis Female Academy.
WILCOX, Abraham - defendant, attachment suit by Lewis Edgar, Washington Co. 30 Aug 1832
WILKINSON, R. J. - St. Louis; advertises the Mechanic's Coffee House at
    Main & Laurel.                          13 Apr 1829
WILLIAMS, Landon - Joachim Twp, Jefferson Co.; took up a chestnut sorrel
    horse ae 6-7y appraised at $40 and a bay horse ae 6-7,  28 Jul 1831
    $25 by Robert McCreery & Mark Moss. G. Hammond JP.
WILLSON, J. G. - will teach "short hand write," St. Louis.      21 Jan 1830
WILSON, Ptolemy - appraised a stray taken up by John Burk.     18 Aug 1831
    Samuel - appraised a stray taken up by William Drenon.   7 Apr 1831
    Thomas - his accused murderer, Jacob Salmous, broke jail in
        St. Charles.                        6 Oct 1831
WOLFE, H. M. - of Manchester, serves motice that no debtors should pay 1¢
    without his order as his account books have been fraudulently 11 Oct 1832
    obtained by others "with no power to collect."
WOLFORD, Henry - bankrupt, Washington Co.              20 Feb 1830
WOODRUFF, Wiatt P. - St. Charles Twp, St. Charles Co.; took up a sorrel
    mare appraised at $30 by Robert Miller and Leonard F.  27 Jun 1829
    Gillet. Philo Gillet JP.
WOOLFOLK, Dr. John - St. Louis; between Church & Main; "formerly of KY." 7 Nov 1829
WRIGHT, J. J. - the Hibernian Relief Society having been dissolved, he
    wants to form a St. Louis Charitable Society; there will  25 Jul 1829
    be a meeting at Shamrock Hall.

WRIGHT, John - St. Louis Twp, St. Louis Co.; took up a bay horse ae 5y
            appraised at $25 by P. D. Barada & G. Campbell. Stine JP.    3 Feb 1831
WYAT, William - appraised a stray taken up by Benjamin Brown.           19 Jan 1832
WYATT, Duglass - Charrette Twp, Montgomery Co.; took up a dark bay mare and
            yearling colt, appraised at $21.   James Hughes JP.         15 Jul 1830
            (appraisers not shown)
       John J. - appraised a stray taken up by Owen Shockley.           24 May 1832
YATES, B. D. - appraised a stray taken up by James Renfro.             15 Dec 1831

BEA

THE MISSOURI REPUBLICAN

ABBAY, A. D. - City Constable, St. Louis, issues notices about  19 Apr 1831
    keeping the city clean.
ABBOTT, John C. - with George Hood, sues Isaac G. Gardner for $300.  13 Sep 1831
ADAMS, Burwell B., appraised a stray taken up by Cain J. Brown.  9 Jul 1823
    John - defendant in a suit by John Darby for $150, debt
    and damages.  21 Aug 1832
    Phineas - appraised a stray taken up by Reuben Harrison.  24 Feb 1829
    William - Bonhomme Twp, St. Louis Co.; took up a bay mare
    appraised at $12 by John Raynold & Daniel Moore.  23 Dec 1828
    A. P. Harris JP.
AERTSEN, Robert B. - with Romulus Riggs, sues John J. Daley for $1621.23.  10 May 1831
ALBERT, Jacob - appraised a stray taken up by James Phillips.  19 Jun 1832
ALEXANDER, Hiram - dissolves partnership with Thompson Ficklin at
    Caledonia, Washington Co.  10 Feb 1829
    Martin - appraised a stray taken up by Henry Robust.  26 Jun 1832
ALFREY, James - appraised a stray taken up by John Freeman.  5 Jan 1830
ALKIRE, Solomon - Femme Osage Twp, St. Charles Co.; took up a black mare
    ae 3y appraised at $20 by Cyrus Carter, Abraham Shobe,  27 Dec 1831
    & Nicholas Fisher. Th. Hopkins JP.
ALLEN, Archibald - 9-Mile-Prairie, Callaway Co.; JP, stray taken up by
    Felix Brown.  15 Sep 1829
    Benjamin - Hurricane Twp., Lincoln Co.; JP, stray taken up by
    Jonathan Cottle.  9 Aug 1827
    - " by Philemon Plummer.  26 Aug 1828
    Cecelia - action in the Legislature to remove disabilities she  25 Jan 1831
    incurred as a result of her divorce from Samuel W.
    Francis - appraised a stray taken up by Andrew Tilford.  1 Jun 1830
    George - Femme Osage Twp, St. Charles Co.; took up a black mare
    ae 7y appraised at $35 by Joseph Lynn & Henry A. H.  29 Jun 1830
    Russell. Moses Bigelow JP.
    George - his wife Elizabeth has left his bed and board.  23 Feb 1826
    Levi B. - Palmyra; wants two or three journeymen saddlers.  5 May 1829
    William N. - appraised a stray taken up by Betsey Parry.  22 Mar 1831
ALLEY, W. E. - appraised a stray taken up by Joseph Snell.  14 Jun 1831
ALLISON, Andrew - appraised a stray taken up by John Crow.  29 Jun 1830
    Robert H. - Buffalo Twp, Pike Co.; took up two mares appraised
    at $25 by E. D. Emerson & Robert Burbridge.  15 Feb 1831
    Willis Mitchell JP.
    Welch - Buffalo Twp, Pike Co.; took up a sorrel mare ae 3y
    appraised at $30 by John Burnett & William Gilbert.  14 Dec 1826
    Michael J. Noyes JP.
AMES, William H. - bankrupt, St. Louis.  16 Feb 1824
ANDERSON, James D. - appraised a stray taken up by John Bently.  2 Mar 1830
    John - Perce Twp, Boone Co.; JP, stray taken up by Elijah Stevens.  6 Jul 1826
    Bowles Twp, Franklin Co.; took up a bay horse ae 9y
    appraised at $50 by Henry Brown & Robert Burns.  19 Jul 1827
    Thomas Henry JP.
    Pressly - appraised a stray taken up by Reuben Pew.  29 Dec 1829
    Roland - appraised a stray taken up by Thomas Spalding.  2 Nov 1830
    Sampson - Joachim Twp, Jefferson Co.; took up a dark bay mare
    ae 7y appraised by John Wilson & James F. Northcraft.  17 Nov 1829
    William Millen JP.
    William - appraised a stray taken up by Eli Clay.  2 Mar 1830
    - Fabius Twp, Marion Co.; took up a black horse ae 7y
    appraised at $50 by John Gash & John Parmer.  12 Oct 1830
    William Gash JP.
ANDREWS, John - appraised a stray taken up by Jesse Colburn.  3 May 1827
    - candidate for Coroner, St. Louis Co.  12 Jun 1832
    John and Elizabeth - petition for divorce in the Legislature.  25 Jan 1831
    Selleck B. - defendant, suit for $150 by Eli Mintonge.  13 Sep 1831
    Thomas - dissolves partnership with Joseph Liggett.  17 Mar 1829
    - offers $10 reward for runaway apprentice Michael McGuire.  16 Oct 1832
    Thomas and William - will continue the copper- and tin-manufactory  14 Sep 1826
    of Joseph Liggett, having bought his stock.

MOR
61

ANGEVINE, Jonathan - with Robert Stewart, proposes to publish the
    Missouri Courier in Palmyra.                 3 Apr 1832
APLING, Thomas - appraised a stray taken up by Samuel King.     13 Jul 1830
ARBUCKLE, Hugh - Bowles Twp, Franklin Co.; JP, stray taken up by
    George Barnes.                              25 May 1826
ARMSTRONG, Eulalie - sues John Armstrong for divorce in the St. Louis
    Circuit Court.                              28 Apr 1829
    James - appraised a stray taken up by Giles Sullivan.     3 Aug 1830
ARTHUR, William - Meramec Twp, Franklin Co.; took up a chestnut sorrel
    mare with a large bell, appraised at $30 by Thomas       26 Aug 1828
    Blair, William Mitchell, & David Blankenship.
    Samuel Conn JP.
ARNOLD, B. & T. - Water St., St. Louis; offer sweet Malaga wine for
    sale, want to buy three Negro men and a girl house      30 Aug 1831
    servant.
    Nancy - executed a note to Thomas Philips, with John Mosely;
    Mosely has sued Philips.                     2 Oct 1832
ARNSPIGUR, David - appraised a stray taken up by Isaac Wiatt.   13 Dec 1831
ASHBROOK, G. - Belleview Twp, Washington Co.; JP, stray taken up by
    Robert B. Maxwell.                       30 Aug 1824
ATCHISON, Pierce - appraised a stray taken up by Joseph Spalding.   8 Feb 1827
ATWOOD, William - appraised a stray taken up by John Stuart.    22 Dec 1825
AUDRAIN, James - Cuivre Twp, St. Charles Co.; JP, stray taken up by
    Moors B. Banks.                        2 Mar 1830
AULL, Robert - Liberty, Clay Co.; dissolved partnership with Samuel Ringo.   8 Feb 1831
AUSTIN, Moses B. - Joachim Twp, Jefferson Co.; took up a sorrel horse
    ae 7y appraised at $35 by David Beard & William      9 Nov 1826
    Ogle. G. Hammond JP.
AWBRAY, Rowland - took up a bay mare ae 12-4y appraised at $14 by Ira
    Millington & Montgomery Perry. W. C. Pettus JP.     15 Nov 1831
AYRES, B. Warren - now the proprietor of the Green Tree Tavern.   5 Jan 1830
BABER, Edward - appraised a stray taken up by Elmsly Fount.    28 Jun 1831
    Thomas - appraised a stray taken up by David Martin.    10 Jan 1832
    - " by Absalom Holloway.                        15 May 1832
BACON, James - appraised a stray taken up by Nicholas Long.    30 Nov 1830
    John P. - appraised a stray taken up by William Long.    17 Jan 1828
    Ludwell - offers $20 reward for two runaway Negroes.    10 May 1831
    Nathaniel - appraised a stray taken up by James Boyer.    17 May 1831
BADGER, J. B. - announces dental services, St. Louis.       9 Feb 1824
BAILEY, James & Co. - auctioneers.                 3 Nov 1829
    - offer miscellaneous "new goods."          30 Nov 1830
BAILY, J. M. - St. Louis Twp, St. Louis Co.; took up a bay mare ae 8y
    appraised at $20 by Peter Fine & John Finegan.      24 Jun 1828
BAIRD, Samuel - appraised a stray taken up by William Wiley.    24 Jun 1828
BAKER, Edward - will teach a course at the St. Louis Philanthropic
    School; will take 120 scholars at $6 per year plus $1 for   24 May 1827
    books. Payment to be 62½¢ per month until the $7 is paid.
    Subjects: reading, writing, arithmetic, geography, grammar.
    Esau - appraised a stray taken up by Aaron Groom.      6 Jul 1830
    Ovesey - appraised a stray taken up by John Hearst.     14 Apr 1829
    Robert - appraised a stray taken up by Robert McClelland.   12 Jan 1830
    Sylvester - Loutre Twp, Montgomery Co.; JP, stray taken up by
    Green B. Bush.                         15 Jun 1830
    Thomas H. - Boeff Twp, Franklin Co.; JP, stray taken up by
    Eli Valentine.                       17 Jan 1832
BALDRIDGE, Malachi - appraised a stray taken up by George Chapman.  15 Jun 1826
BALDWIN, John H. - former owner of a lot bought by Pamela Hayden.   6 Mar 1832
BALL, Abner - St. Ferdinand; took up a dark chestnut sorrel mare ae 6y
    appraised at $35 by John Massey & Henry Gimblin.     14 Jun 1831
    A. J. Whiteside JP.
    Jeremiah - St. Ferdinand; took up a sorrel filly ae 3y appraised
    at $25 by James Carter & Peter Ellington. O'Neill JP.   23 Dec 1828
BANISTER, Benjamin - will not be responsible for the debts of his wife
    Elizabeth whom he believes "somewhat deranged."    17 Jun 1828
BANKS, Moors B. - Cuivre Twp, St. Charles Co.; took up two young mares
    appraised at $45 by Francis Day & Benjamin Comegys.   2 Mar 1830
    James H. Audrain JP.

        MOR

BARADA, Isidore - appraised a stray taken up by John Richardson.     18 Nov 1828
    Louis - St. Louis Twp, St. Louis Co.; took up a sorrel horse ae 3y
    appraised at $28 by Joseph Guion & Louis Constant.     21 Oct 1828
    J. R. Stine JP
BARADAN, Sylvester - at Shabonsin, St. Charles Twp, St. Charles Co., took
    up a white mare ae 8-9y appraised at $25 by Etienne     2 Apr 1823
    Kennel & Toussaint Brunel. John Slater JP.
BARBIER, A. - opens a new store "in the house of General Clark," offering
    dry goods, jewelry, wine, coffee, cheese, etc.     17 Jul 1832
BARKER, Perrine - defendant in a suit for $100 by Samuel Simpson, in the
    Pike Co. Circuit Court.     21 Feb 1832
BARNES, Aquilla & James - appraised a stray taken up by Elijah Stevens.     6 Jul 1826
    George - Bowles Twp, Franklin Co.; took up a small brown mare
    ae 9y appraised at $12 by Benjamin Hodges & John Bell.     25 May 1826
    Hugh Arbuckle JP.
BARNETT, Enoch - appraised a stray taken up by William Ralls.     1 Feb 1831
    Thomas - dissolved partnership with J. T. Ivers.     8 Nov 1831
    - in St. Louis Circuit Court, sues Archy Kasson & William
    Leavenworth for $300 damages; sues John W. Merritt &     21 Aug 1832
    William Bagley for $500.
BARNEY, John - appraised a stray taken up by Elijah Weaver.     17 Jul 1832
BARNSBACK, George - Perry Twp, St. Francois Co.; took up a bay horse
    ae 5y appraised at $25 by Sam McIlroye & Luke     24 Jan 1828
    Flemming. Michael Gara JP.
BARRY, Robert - advertises a new dry goods store opposite Henry Shaw's
    hardware store.     8 Apr 1828
BARTLETT, Phineas - offers 10¢ reward for his runaway apprentice Thomas
    Fry (a carpenter) ae 17 or 18, stout, clumsy,     24 Aug 1830
    with light hair and blue eyes.
    William - appraised a stray taken up by Henry Hendricks.     10 Feb 1829
BARTOLE, Joseph - runaway apprentice of Edward Herrington, wagonmaker.     15 Mar 1831
BASCOM, Hiram - partner of A. L. Watwood, clocks and watches, on Main St.
    in St. Louis.     11 Jan 1831
BASKET, Thomas - appraised a stray taken up by Thomas Sterman.     31 Jul 1832
BATCHELOR, William C. - defendant in a suit for $300 by Henry Underhill.     4 Oct 1831
BATES, Elias - dissolves partnership with John W. Honey, Herculaneum.     22 Mar 1831
    Joseph - dissolves partnership with Stewart McKee & Robert
    Cathcart in the Union Steam Mill.     4 Sep 1832
BATTERSON, Morris - obtained a merchant's license, St. Louis.     29 May 1832
BAUGH, Benjamin - appraised a stray taken up by John Naylor.     19 Jan 1830
    Joseph - appraised a stray taken up by George Chapman.     15 Jun 1826
    J. - asks his debtors to pay by 1 February.     3 Jan 1828
    - merchant tailor, advertises new goods from Philadelphia.     16 Nov 1830
    - asks his debtors to pay.     19 Apr 1831
    Matthew - broke jail, accused of arson. Is about 5'6" tall, ae
    18-20, dark hair and eyes, "bad countenance."     2 Oct 1832
BAXTER, Green B. - Bonhomme Twp, St. Louis Co.; took up a bay horse ae 7y
    appraised at $20 and a bay mare ae 3y appraised at $20     21 Sep 1826
    by John Johnson & Thomas Murry. Hartley Lanham JP.
    - appraised a stray taken up by William Long.     17 Jan 1828
    - took up a gray horse ae 6-7y appraised at $28 by     9 Dec 1828
    Capt. Joseph Conway & Alexander Smith.
BAY, Robert - appraised a stray taken up by James Caldwell.     6 Aug 1823
    Samuel - St. Louis Co.; took up a sorrel mare ae 3y appraised at
    $27.50 by James & Thomas Withinton. Fergus Ferguson JP.     30 Mar 1830
BEAR, Joseph - plaintiff in a suit in chancery in the Washington Circuit
    Court, vs John Corder.     8 Jan 1823
BEARD, David - appraised a stray taken up by Moses B. Austin.     23 Nov 1826
    W. A. - dissolves partnership with John Salmon.     18 Nov 1828
    - dissolves partnership with John Lee.     19 May 1829
BEASLEY, Noah - Buffalo Twp, Pike Co.; took up a sorrel horse ae 12y
    appraised at $20 by A. Stewart & John D. Callet.     24 May 1831
    M. J. Noyes JP.
BEAUCHAMP, Joseph D. - appraised a stray taken up by Robert Quarles Jr.     22 Jan 1823

MOR

BEAVIS, Prudence - Joachim Twp, Jefferson Co.; took up a sorrel mare
        ae 12y appraised at $20 by Moses B. Austin & Willard        1 Mar 1831
        Frissell. G. Hammond JP.
BEEBEE, Elisha S. - dissolves partnership with David Gay.          19 Mar 1823
BELKNAP, O. A. - Concord Twp, Washington Co.; JP, stray taken up by
                        Magness Tullock.                           13 Apr 1827
        - again by Tullock (17 May 1827); stray by Joseph
        Neill Sr (31 May 1831) and by Washington Edgar.            31 Jul 1832
BELL, John - appraised a stray taken up by George Barnes.          25 May 1826
        - " by Jacob Presley.                                      15 Nov 1831
        Thomas C. - defendant in a suit for $300 by David Miller in the
                        Pike Co. Circuit Court.                    21 Feb 1832
BENJAMIN, Joseph - two houses for sale in the South Ward, St. Louis. 19 Oct 1830
        Joseph and Pamela - their town lot in St. Louis sold as the
                        result of a claim against them by P. Bartlett. 6 Mar 1832
        (Other transactions, same issue, show that
        she was formerly Pamela Hayden.)
BENNETT, Benjamin - Bonhomme Twp, Manchester Road, offers a farm for
        sale, 162 acres, 55 cultivated, "abundant timber."         2 Oct 1832
        - Bonhomme; took up a red cow ae 10-11 years with a        4 Mar 1828
        calf, appraised at $8; a red-and-white cow ae 7-8 y,
        with a calf, appraised at $8; a red-and-white steer
        ae 5y, $8; red-and-white heifer, 2y, $3, all appraised
        by Richard Lowe & Hugh M. Jamison. Thomas Mason JP.
BENNING, James - appraised a stray taken up by Thomas J. Elliott.  4 Jan 1831
BENT, Charles - offers $10 reward for a horse escaped from Ragsdale's
                        livery stable.                             25 Dec 1832
BENTLY, John - Prairie Twp, Montgomery Co.; took up three steers appraised
        at $23 by James Smith, James D. Anderson. John Dutton JP.  2 Mar 1830
BENTON, Signor - her husband Thomas states that she has left his bed and
        board and "no man shall employ her to do midwifery         2 Feb 1826
        without settling with me for it."
BROWN, Caleb E. - appraised a stray taken up by Levi McMurtry.     31 Jul 1832
BERTHELOT, Joseph - appraised a stray taken up by Sebastian Willot. 14 Feb 1832
BERTRAND, Simon - Jacques Martel states that Bertrand "fraudulently
        obtained" a note from him.                                 15 Jan 1823
BESSER, John S. - succeeded Emanuel Block as postmaster at Troy.   17 Nov 1829
BEST, John - Loutre Twp, Montgomery Co.; took up a mare and horse
        appraised at $50 by Wm. J. & D. I. Talbot. A. G. Irvine JP. 2 Jun 1829
BETTICK, Thomas - appraised a stray taken up by Henry Reed.        23 Feb 1826
BIDSTRUP, Herman Emil - announces the organization of the town of
                        Danesburg, 25 miles southwest of Boonville, one 12 Apr 1831
                        mile west of Lamine River, in Cooper Co.
BIGELOW, Moses - Femme Osage Twp, Ct. Charles Co.; JP, strays taken up
        by Adam Cluck (2 Jun 1829), by Eli Clay (2 Mar 1830)
        and by Elijah Bryan.                                       11 Sep 1832
BIGGERS, James & Clark - appraised a stray taken up by David Logan. 15 Nov 1824
BILLS, W. M. - appraised a stray taken up by George Lockland.      27 Nov 1832
BIRD, Antoine - appraised a stray taken up by Pleasant Stewart.    14 Jul 1829
        G. A. - opens a law office opposite Horse Boat Landing on the
                        third street from the river, St. Louis.    11 Oct 1827
BITTICK, Simeon - appraised a stray taken up by Henry Votaw.       3 Jul 1832
BIVENS, Francis J. - appraised a stray taken up by Benjamin Sharp. 24 May 1827
BLACK, David W. - appraised a stray taken up by Luman Ruggie.      11 Jul 1825
        Isaac - Bourbon Twp, Callaway Co.; JP, stray taken up by
                        Robert McClelland.                         12 Jan 1830
        J. R. - "late of Kentucky," forms Hart, Black & Co., druggists,
                        with John & William Hart.                  19 Apr 1831
        William - appraised a stray taken up by John P. Webb.      20 Jul 1830
BLACKWELL, Jeremiah - Breton Twp, Washington Co.; took up a deep bay
                        horse ae 4y appraised at $30 by Cornelius Burnett 6 Jul 1826
                        & Marshal Parks. Henry Shurlds JP.
        Zachariah - appraised a stray taken up by George Reid.     5 May 1829
BLAIN, A. C. - appraised a stray taken up by George Reid.          "
        - " by James C. Curry.                                     2 Jun 1829
BLAIR, Thomas - appraised a stray taken up by William Arthur.      26 Aug 1828
BLANCHARD, Roswell - William Bonnet warns the public not to accept a
                        note he gave Blanchard.                    26 Jul 1827

        MOR

                        64

BLAND, James - appraised a stray taken up by Scudder Smith.  9 Oct 1832
BLANKENSHIP, David - appraised a stray taken up by William Arthur.  26 Aug 1828
BLANN, James - Charrette Twp, Montgomery Co.; took up a dark sorrel
    horse appraised at $50.  James Hughes JP.  4 Aug 1829
BLANTON, Isaac - Calumet Twp, Pike Co.; took up a dun mare ae 5y
    appraised at $20 by John R. Clifford & Ervin Guyer.  14 Jul 1829
    Thomas McQueen JP.
BLEDSOE, Moses O. - took over the Missouri Hotel, St. Louis.  13 Jan 1829
BLISS, Neziah - defendant in a mortgage foreclosure suit by Martin
    Thomas, St. Louis.  25 Aug 1829
BLIZE, Abner - Bonhomme Twp, St. Louis Co.; took up a bay horse ae 7-8y
    appraised at $28 by Levi Defoe & Alexander Smith. Smith JP.  12 Jun 1832
BLOCK, Emanuel - removed as postmaster at Troy, Lincoln Co.; John S.
    Besser succeeds him.  17 Nov 1829
    Levi & Simon - dissolve partnership.  13 Jun 1825
BLOOD, Sullivan - appraised a stray taken up by Coonrod Cashman.  12 Feb 1823
    - leaving the city for three or four months, appoints
    Otis Reynolds Deputy Constable. (St. Louis)  21 May 1823
BLUE, John - appraised a stray taken up by John Ellington.  13 Nov 1832
BLUNT, P. D. - appraised a stray taken up by James H. Griffin.  9 Sep 1828
BOARMAN, Alexander - named accessory in the shooting of Charles Rouse
    at New London.  29 Dec 1829
BOBB, John - President of the St. Louis Mechanics' Benevolent Assn.
    announces a meeting at the house of Peter Ferguson.  2 Mar 1826
BOGGS, Robert W. - appraised a stray taken up by William W. Smith.  24 Jan 1832
    - " by John Hawkins.  13 Nov 1832
BOICE, John P. - appraised a stray taken up by Walter Dorsett.  19 Jul 1831
    - " by George Lockland.  27 Nov 1832
BONNET, William - warns the public not to accept notes he gave, one to
 .   John Hight for $1000 and one to Roswell Blanchard for  26 Jul 1827
    $451 "and some cents" at Fever River lead mines.
BOODEN, Joseph - bankrupt, St. Louis.  23 Feb 1830
BOON, Willis W. - with John Chapman, accused by William Wallace of the
    seduction of Wallace's daughter. Boon was about 6' tall,  25 Jul 1825
    fair; had a wife and children; also had a quantity of
    counterfeit money.
BOONE, John - appraised a stray taken up by James Brumfield.  31 May 1827
    Samuel - 9-Mile-Prairie Twp, Callaway Co.; took up a chestnut
    sorrel mare ae 7y appraised at $35 by Turner Crump &  8 Dec 1829
    Boone Hayes. Enoch Fruit JP.
BORING, J. - appraised a stray taken up by James Smith.  16 May 1825
BOSTWICK, John - defendant in a suit for $404.00½ by Seth W. Nye.  16 Jul 1823
BOWLES, Augustus - dissolved partnership with William P. Maddox.  10 Aug 1830
    Caleb - Bonhomme Twp, St. Louis Co.; JP, strays taken up by
    Joseph Longwith (23 Feb 1826), James Longwith  26 Apr 1827
    and Jabez Ferris.  18 Jan 1831
    William - appraised a stray taken up by Harris Spears.  17 Jun 1828
BOWNDS, William - Belleview Twp, Washington Co.; took up a sorrel mare
    ae 6y appraised at $30 by Samuel W. Rayburn &  19 Mar 1823
    Benjamin Imboden. J. N. Rayburn JP.
BOYCE, Parthenia - by next friend William W. Lewis sues James Boyce for
    divorce in Marion Co. Court.  10 Mar 1829
    Richard - Spencer Twp, Ralls Co.; JP, stray taken up by Wm. Mills.  2 Dec 1828
BOYD, John - dissolves partnership with Thomas Graham Jr; Graham
    will continue the business.  6 Nov 1832
    Thomas - appraised a stray taken up by Samuel Whitworth.  23 Feb 1826
BOYDSTON, William et al - defendants in a suit by Lemuel Hewitt in
    Chancery, Washington Co.  27 Sep 1824
BOYER, Godfrey - shot in the head while sitting in his room at Valle's
    Mines on 14 January; J. R. Valle offers a reward for  7 Feb 1828
    the capture of the assassin or assassins.
    James - Bonhomme Twp, St. Louis Co.; took up a yellow bay horse
    ae 5y appraised at $40 by Nathaniel Bacon & Andrew  17 May 1831
    Hamilton Jr., and a dun horse ae 7y appraised at $27 by
    Ninian Hamilton & Michael Roberts. H. McCullough JP.
    John - opens a dancing school at Mrs. Deroin's on 3rd St.,
    St. Louis.  12 Oct 1830

MOR  65

BOYERS, James - Bonhomme Twp, St. Louis Co.; took up three stray horses
    appraised at $52.50 by John Johnson & James Cundiff.      22 Dec 1829
    Henry Smith JP.
BOZARTH, Squire - appraised a stray taken up by Jacob Weaver.       7 Jul 1829
BRACKENRIDGE, John - Bonhomme Twp, St. Louis Co.; took up an iron gray
    horse ae 9-10y appraised at $45 by Alton Link &      11 May 1830
    Jonathan St. Clair. McCullough JP.
    - appraised a stray taken up by John Miller.      1 Mar 1831
BRADBURY, H. P. - opens the "Post Meridian" saloon in St. Louis.      28 Oct 1828
    - proposes to open a reading room at the saloon, to
    include newspapers and other reading material.      2 Dec 1828
BRADSHAW, William - Dent's Settlement, Pendleton Twp, St. Francois Co.;
    JP, stray taken up by John Carter.      13 Nov 1832
BRAINARD, Oliver - plaintiff in a mortgage foreclosure suit vs Henry
    Jones, St. Louis.      8 Mar 1824
BRANSON, Joseph C. - of Lansdell & Branson, quits business in St. Louis.      27 May 1828
BRANSTUTTER, Henry - Cuivre Twp, Pike Co.; took up a brown mare ae 4y
    appraised at $27 by John & Elijah Purdom.      10 Jan 1832
    Harrison Hendrick JP.
BRANT, J. B. - opens a market house in St. Louis with Wm. K. Rule.      26 Jun 1832
BRAY, John - St. Ferdinand Twp, St. Louis Co.; took up a stud horse
    ae 7y appraised at $25, a brown mare ae 10y, with colt, $30,      3 Jun 1828
    a black mare ae 3y, $12, by Dockweed Munroe & Daniel
    Sullivan. Hugh O'Neil JP.
    - took up a bay mare ae 13y appraised at $35 by Joshua Norton
    and James L. Halliday. O'Neill JP.      10 Jun 1828
BRAZEAU, Nicholas - his wife Archange has left his bed and board.      15 Feb 1827
BRECKENRIDGE, James - sues John B. Gilley for $10,000 damages in
    the St. Louis Circuit Court.      25 Jan 1827
    Palmer - Washington Co.; took up a two-year-old filly
    appraised at $28 by Nathaniel Hickey & Abel      13 Sep 1827
    Sparks. Airs Hudspeth JP.
BREDEN, J. W. - offers cider vinegar for sale.      18 Nov 1828
BREEDING, John - appraised a stray taken up by William Roark.      17 Nov 1829
BRETON, Dr. G. - St. Louis; "practitioner of medicine," botanist, etc.      18 Nov 1828
BREWER, John - broke jail in St. Louis, Sheriff R. Simpson offers $200
    reward. He was about 40, was under sentence for perjury.      26 Oct 1826
BREWSTER, Ulysses B. - offers "fancy goods" - boots, shoes, clothing,      8 Nov 1831
    groceries at Main and Chestnut, St. Louis.      30 Oct 1832
    (originally shown only as U. B.)
BRIAN, Benjamin B. - appraised a stray taken up by Reuben Pew.      28 Jun 1831
BRICKEY, Jeremiah - Breton Twp, Washington Co.; took up a brindle cow
    and calf, a red steer, a brindle heifer, a black      5 Apr 1827
    heifer, a red-and-white ox, total appraisal $31.50 by
    Aquilla Wilson & John Mussett. John Brickey JP.
    John - Breton Twp, Washington Co., see above.
    - offers $50 reward for runaway Negro Edmund, at Potosi.      11 Sep 1832
    - JP, stray taken up by John Hawkins.      13 Nov 1832
BRINDLEY, Michael - appraised a stray taken up by Joshua Herrington.      29 Mar 1827
BROCK, Joshua - appraised a stray taken up by Scudder Smith.      23 Jun 1829
    Thomas - appraised a stray taken up by James Hewitt.      5 Jul 1827
BROOKS, Edward - advertises wholesale and retail drugs, Main St., St. Louis.      3 Jan 1832
    Samuel S. - bankrupt, St. Louis.      23 Feb 1830
BROTHERTON, John - St. Ferdinand Twp, St. Louis Co.; took up a black
    horse ae 8y appraised at $75 and a bright bay ae 8y,      30 Nov 1826
    $65, by Lockwood Munroe & John Watt. Hugh O'Neil JP.
BROWN, Cain J. - Bowles Twp, Franklin Co., took up a sorrel mare ae 4y
    appraised by Russel Brown & Burwell B. Adams. H. Brown JP.      9 Jul 1823
    - appraised a stray taken up by Samuel Downing.      14 Jul 1829
    - " by Isaac Wiatt.      13 Dec 1831
    Caleb - St. Louis Co.; took up a gray horse ae 7y appraised at $15
    by Samuel T. McKenney & Oliver DuBois. J.V. Garnier JP.      9 Sep 1828
    - bankrupt, St. Louis.      27 Jan 1829
    Elisha - appraised a stray taken up by Eleazer Clay.      6 Mar 1832
    Felix - 9-Mile-Prairie, Callaway Co.; took up a brown horse ae 3y
    appraised at $35 by John Robinson & Joel Palmer.      15 Sep 1829
    Archibald Allen JP.

BROWN, George F. - his wife Raney has left his bed and board.                           28 Apr 1829
    Henry - Bowles Twp, Franklin Co.; JP, stray taken up by Cain Brown.            9 Jul 1823
       - appraised a stray taken up by John Anderson.                             19 Jul 1827
       - advertises as a "veterinary surgeon and operative farrier."          10 Feb 1829
    J. C. - St. Louis Co.; JP, stray taken up by Chukesberry Redmound.              17 Mar 1829
    James - with Daniel C. Ross, defendant in a suit by Washington
       West, St. Louis.                                                         10 Dec 1823
    James Jr. - Rock Twp, Franklin Co.; took up a mare ae 7-8y appraised
       at $15 by James McDonald & John Sullins Jr.                              6 May 1828
       Jesse McDonald JP.
    John B. - appraised a stray taken up by Hannah Morris.                     11 Jan 1831
    John J. - appraised a stray taken up by Isaac Hall.                         1 Sep 1829
    John P. - runaway apprentice of Jacob Fahsnacht. Age about 18,
       height 5' 7 or 8".                                                        8 Feb 1831
    Joseph - Prairie Twp, Montgomery Co.; took up a light gray horse
       ae 10y appraised at $50 by Levi Fine & Walker Hopkins.                   19 Jan 1830
       Philip Glover JP.
       - appraised a stray taken up by George Westover.                         19 Jun 1832
    Margaret - by next friend William Kerr, sues Henry S. Brown for
       divorce in the Pike Co. Circuit Court.                                   18 Oct 1831
       - receives a judgment against Henry S. and his land
       is sold as a result.                                                      3 Jul 1832
    Russell - Franklin Co.; took up a brown mare ae 4y appraised at
       $25 by Cain J. Brown & Burrel Adams. Henry Brown JP.                     19 Apr 1824
       - appraised a stray taken up by Jacob Cole.                              29 Nov 1827
    William - appraised a stray taken up by Andrew Cobb.                       29 Jul 1828
       - " by Osias Heatherly.                                                  26 May 1829
       - " by Thomas Sterman.                                                   31 Jul 1832
BROWNE, Dr. Joseph - has a new supply of medicines and drugs which he
       will sell for cash.                                                      19 Jul 1824
BROWNEJOHN, W. R. - opens a dancing academy in St. Louis.                    15 Apr 1828
BROWNER, Vincent - appraised a stray taken up by John Hume.                    2 Sep 1828
BRUCE, Amos J. - appraised a stray taken up by Joseph Haigh.                    8 Feb 1827
BRUMFIELD, James - Femme Osage Twp, St. Charles Co.; took up a sorrel
       horse ae 6-7y appraised at $33-1/3 by John Boone &                      31 May 1827
       Andrew Stapp. Archibald Shobe JP.
       -appraised a stray taken up by James Silvey.                             25 Sep 1832
BRUNEL, Toussaint - appraised a stray taken up by Sylvester Baradan.           2 Apr 1823
BRYAN, Elijah - appraised a stray taken up by Adam Cluck.                       2 Jun 1829
       - Femme Osage Twp, St. Charles Co.; took up a sorrel mare
       ae 4y appraised at $25 by James McClenny & Benjamin                      11 Sep 1832
       Hancock. Moses Bigelow JP.
    James - appraised a stray taken up by Dugal Wyatt.                         12 Aug 1828
    Stephen - appraised a stray taken up by Hardy Merrill.                     27 May 1828
BUFORD, Francis K. - attorney and counselor-at-law, in Boone, Callaway,
       Lincoln, Pike, and Montgomery Cos.; office in Fulton.                    29 Sep 1829
    John - Black River Twp, Washington Co.; took up a mare and horse
       appraised at $40 by Jesse Lester & Mark Hughes.                           1 Jun 1830
       Daniel Lester JP.
BUMPASS, William - Gray Twp, Gasconade Co.; JP, stray taken up by
       Henry Reed.                                                              23 Feb 1826
BURBRIDGE, Benjamin - Louisiana, Pike Co.; advertises for a journeyman
       tanner and currier.                                                       6 Sep 1827
    Robert - appraised a stray taken up by Robert H. Allison.                  15 Feb 1831
BURCKHARTT, Joshua H. - Bonhomme, St. Louis Co., took up a bright bay
       mare ae 4y appraised at $20 by James McKnight &                         25 May 1826
       John Reynolds. A. P. Harris JP.
       - offers a 25 acre farm for rent, with good cabins
       and outhouses, 12 miles from St. Louis on the                           21 Dec 1826
       road to St. Charles.
BURGESS, Edmund - Grand Glaize, Joachim Twp, Jefferson Co.; took up a bay
       horse ae 7y appraised at $17.50 by David McMeans &                      30 Jun 1829
       John Wilson. Wm. McMillan JP.
    George - sues James Cotter for debt and damages of $231.                    8 May 1832
BURGET, Nancy - next friend of Ann Chesley who is suing Alexander Chesley
       for divorce in Perry Co.                                                 18 May 1830
BURK, David - bankrupt, St. Louis.                                           15 Jun 1830

    MOR        67

BURNETT, Cornelius - appraised a stray taken up by Jeremiah Blackwell.          6 Jul 1826
    John - appraised a stray taken up by Welch Allison.                        14 Dec 1826
    Joseph - appraised a stray taken up by John Hall.                          25 Jan 1831
BURNHARD, Benjamin - appraised a stray taken up by David Jones.                16 Feb 1830
BURNS, Robert - appraised strays taken up by Robert Chunning and by
                                                        John Anderson.         19 Jul 1827
    Uriah - Franklin Co.; took up two horses appraised at $30 each by
            Jesse Eueloe & John Wilson.  Thomas Henry JP.                      13 Jul 1830
          - advertises "a bundle of clothes" found by the little
            daughter of Widow Reeves in Merrimack Twp, Franklin Co.             9 Aug 1831
    William - "at his plantation on Dardenne Creek" took up a dark bay
            mare ae 4y appraised at $35 by Stephen Isler,  George S.           15 Dec 1829
            Spencer, & Lewallen Turnbough.  Robert Spencer JP.
BURROS, George R. - appraised a stray taken up by Eli Valentine.                1 Sep 1829
    Thomas - appraised a stray taken up by Scudder Smith.                      23 Jun 1829
BURROUGHS, John - defendant in a suit for $900 brought by Richard
                Tunis & George Cromwell.                                        4 Sep 1832
BURT, A. - will sell or rent the White Hall Tavern, Potosi.                    18 Jan 1831
    Andrew - dissolves partnership with Bernard Green at Mine-a-Breton
            and Mine-a-Valle, Jefferson Co. He will continue the              14 Sep 1826
            business at Mine-a-Valle.
    George W. - appraised a stray taken up by Levi McMurtry.                   31 Jul 1832
BURTON, Elliott - Union Twp, Ralls Co.; took up a bright bay mare
            appraised at $30 by Joel Noel & Richmond Saling.                   12 Aug 1828
            John Burton JP.
    John - see above.
    Squire - appraised a stray taken up by Zephaniah Robnett.                  23 Sep 1828
BURTS, Stephen - appraised a stray taken up by Alexander Emerson.              15 Aug 1825
BUSH, Green ,B. - Loutre Twp, Montgomery Co.; took up a dark bay mare
            ae 7-8y appraised at $35 by David Craid & Reid                     15 Jun 1830
            Culpepper.  Sylvester Baker JP.
BUTCHER, Moses - St. Charles Co.; took up a bright sorrel horse ae 7-8y
            appraised at $30 by Thomas & William Spalding.                     28 Jul 1829
            Robert Foster JP.
BUTTERWORTH, Alexander - Liberty Twp, Washington Co.; offers $10
                    reward for two horses, strayed or stolen.                  31 Jul 1832
BUZBY, William D. - advertises the "St. Louis French Burr Millstone
                            Manufactory."                                      17 Aug 1830
BYLER, Joseph - "7 miles south of Boonville, Cooper Co." offers a $25
            reward for a runaway Negro.                                        18 May 1826
BYRN, Thomas - defendant in a suit by Lewis Jacques for $300.                   6 Sep 1831
BYRNE, Michael - appraised a stray taken up by Jesse Colburn.                   3 May 1827
BYRNS, James - bankrupt, St. Louis.                                            13 Sep 1824
CADY, Dr. S. C. - "surgeon dentist, lately from New York," in St. Louis.       13 Oct 1829
CADWALLADER, Eli - appraised a stray taken up by Avington K. Wilson.            5 Jul 1831
    Rees - appraised a skiff taken up by Charles Geoger.                       25 May 1830
CALBERT, Charles N. - defendant in a suit for $150 damages by John
                Hollyman in the Marion Co. Circuit Court.                       7 Dec 1830
CALDWELL, Archibald - appraised a stray taken up by Michael Keeny.              3 Oct 1825
    Andrew - appraised a stray taken up by David Pursley.                       1 Mar 1831
    Green V. - keeper of the inn at New London where Charles B.
            Rouse was shot.                                                     29 Dec 1829
    James - Cainy Twp, Franklin Co.; took up a sorrel horse ae 14y
            appraised at $30 by Robert Baye & Elye Short.                       6 Aug 1823
            Samuel Short JP.   (possibly Calvy Twp?)
    John - St. John's Twp, Franklin Co.;  JP, stray taken up by
                                                        Robert Frazer.         22 Jun 1826
    Matthew - appraised a stray taken up by Isaiah Todd.                       19 Feb 1828
CALLAHAN, Beston - Charrette Twp, Montgomery Co.; JP, stray taken up by
                                                        Elmsly Fount.          28 Jun 1831
CALLET, John D. - appraised a stray taken up by Noah Beasley.                  24 May 1831
CALLWELL, John - St. John's Twp, Franklin Co.; JP, stray taken up by
                                                        Scudder Smith.         23 Jun 1829
CALVERT, John - appraised a stray taken up by William Keatley.                  9 Mar 1826
          -      "  by Austin Shelton.                                         27 Jul 1830
          - defendant in a suit for $200 by John F. Hamtramck.                 17 May 1831

        MOR               68

CAMPBELL, Dr. C. - dissolves partnership with Dr. J. Woolfolk.                      28 Aug 1832
    Joel - dissolves partnership with William R. Turpin in                          13 Apr 1830
        Louisiana, Pike Co.
    John P. - of Kickapoo Prairie, Crawford Co.; found a pocketbook                 15 May 1832
        with notes, etc. at the Trading House in Old
        Delaware Town, Crawford Co.
    Richard - defendant in a mortgage-foreclosure suit by Peter &                   17 Sep 1823
        Jesse Lindell in the Pike Co. Circuit Court.
    William - Belleview Twp, Washington Co.; took up a bay horse                     15 Mar 1831
        appraised at $40 by Green Patter & John L. Goforth.
        A. Goforth JP.
CANNON, Ephraim - "on the waters of Lost Creek," Hurricane Twp, Lincoln Co.,        16 Nov 1830
        took up a strawberry roan mare ae 2y appraised at $18
        by John A. L. McQueen & James Ragsdall. E.H. Powers JP.
CARDER, Jonathan - appraised a stray taken up by George King.                        7 Dec 1830
    -   "   by Justus Post.                                                         29 May 1832
    Lawrence - appraised strays taken up by Alexander Kinkead (20 Oct
        1829), Hugh Miller (31 Aug 1830), John M. Collins
        (15 Mar 1831) and Joseph Snell.                                             14 Jun 1831
CARLILE, Absalom - plaintiff vs James White, suit for $250 in the                    3 Jan 1832
        St. Louis Circuit Court.
CARMAN, John - plaintiff vs John L. Jones, suit for $500.                           13 Sep 1831
CARR, Mrs. Francis - her seminary for young ladies opened in St. Louis.             17 May 1824
CARREL, John - appraised a stray taken up by William R. McCortney.                  16 Jun 1829
(CARRELL) - defendant in a suit by Brown Cozzens for $300.                           2 Oct 1832
CARRICO, Benjamin - accused burglar, broke jail in St. Louis. He was                 2 Oct 1832
        about 25 or 30, light hair, blue eyes, "stout built,"
        with a "very surly look" and "fond of drink."
CARROLL, John B. - his wife Polly has left his bed and board.                        2 Mar 1830
CARTER, Christ - appraised a stray taken up by Littleton Davis.                     15 Feb 1831
    Cyrus - appraised a stray taken up by Solomon Alkire.                           27 Dec 1831
    James - appraised a stray taken up by Jeremiah Ball.                            23 Dec 1828
    John - Dent's Settlement, Pendleton Twp , St. Francois Co.; took                13 Nov 1832
        up a black mare ae 6y appraised at $30 by Hezekiah Horton &
        William Nicholson. William Bradshaw JP.
    Larking - Lewiston Twp, Montgomery Co.; JP, stray taken up by                   14 Jun 1831
                            Tilman Cullom.
CARVER, John - appraised a stray taken up by Enoch Spry.                             3 Nov 1829
CASEY, Andrew - Union Twp, Washington Co.; took up a strawberry roan horse          27 Jul 1830
        ae 6y appraised at $50 by John G. McCabe & Morgan Casey.
        John Trimble JP.
    John Jr. - Old Mines; offers $10 reward for Negro Joe.                          24 Aug 1830
CASHMAN, Coonrod - St. Louis Co.; took up a dark bay mare ae 17y appraised          12 Feb 1823
        at $25 by Daniel Freeman & Sullivan Blood. Moses Scott JP.
    - bankrupt.                                                                     28 Mar 1825
CASNER, George - defendant in a suit by Frederick Hyatt for $200.                    3 Jan 1832
    - defendant in a suit for $300 by Daniel & Asa Hough.                           10 Jan 1832
        (both suits in St. Louis)
CASSILLY, Philip - dissolves partnership with Henry Johnson; Cassilly will          31 Mar 1829
        continue the "Lafayette Hall & St. Louis Billiard Room."
CATHCART, John - with Edward Walsh, takes over the Union Steam Mill.                  4 Sep 1832
    Robert - dissolves partnership with Stewart McKee and Joseph                     4 Sep 1832
        Bates in the Union Steam Mill.
CATON, George W. - partner of Joseph Woods, tailor; will take apprentices.           4 Oct 1831
CAULK, Sarah - Bonhomme Twp, St. Louis Co.; took up a bay filly appraised           26 Jun 1832
        at $15 by Hugh Miller & Isaac Caulk.  Henry Smith JP.
    Thomas - appraised a stray taken up by Stephen Hancock.                         15 Apr 1828
CAVANAGH, Patrick and Dorothy his wife - former owners of a lot bought               6 Mar 1832
                            by Pamela Hayden.
CHAFFIN, Isaac - opens a liquor and commission store, "nearly opposite             22 Apr 1828
        Dr. Lane" in St. Louis.
CHAMBERS, A. - appraised a stray taken up by James Robinson.                         9 Sep 1828
    -   "   by John McIntire.                                                       19 Feb 1828
    Thomas - appraised a stray taken up by Sarah Kennedy.                           17 Aug 1826
        - Elkhorn Twp, Montgomery Co.; took up a roan horse ae 8y                   15 Jul 1828
        appraised at $45 by Abraham Kenneda & Joseph Liles.
                            Caleb Williams JP.

    MOR
                            69

CHAPMAN, George - Femme Osage Twp, St. Charles Co.; took up a yellow sorrel mare ae 6-7y appraised at $18 by Joseph Baugh & Malachi Baldridge. John Smith JP. — 15 Jun 1826

John - with Willis W. Boon, accused by William Wallace of the seduction of Wallace's daughter. John was 5'6" tall, dark; had a wife and several children, and a quantity of counterfeit money. — 25 Jul 1825

John - appraised a stray taken up by William Downing. — 3 Feb 1829

Robert - appraised a stray taken up by Ferdinand Hervin. — 18 Dec 1832

CHARLES, R. M. - offers "house, sign, ornamental and fancy painting" on Mullanphy's Row, Olive between Main-Church, St. Louis. — 4 Sep 1832

CHARTERS, Adam - appraised a stray taken up by Alexander McAllister. — 2 Jun 1829

CHESLEY, Ann - by next friend Nancy Burget, sues Alexander for divorce in the Perry Co. Court. He deserted her 6 years before. — 18 May 1830

CHITTENDEN, Lucius - obtained a merchant's license, St. Louis. — 29 May 1832

CHOISNE, L. - "manufacturer of perfumery, from Paris." — 26 Jul 1831

CHOUQUETTE, Antoine - will pay no bills but his own. — 29 Nov 1824

CHUNNING, Robert - Bowles Twp, Franklin Co.; took up a bay horse ae 5y appraised at $20 and a sorrel mare ae 3y, $25, & a bay "skewball" horse ae 6-7y, $25, all by Robert Burns & John Morris. Thomas Henry JP. — 19 Jul 1827

CLARE, Daniel - Union Twp, Lincoln Co.; took up a sorrel horse ae 12-13y appraised at $20 by James Gilmore & Thomas Foley. — 22 Jun 1830

CLARK, Carlton - advertises horse-shoeing and farriery work in part of Hawken's gun shop. — 14 Feb 1825

Harvey - appraised a stray taken up by Austin Willard. — 20 Mar 1832

John - defendant in a suit for $550 by Hardin Robirds. — 30 Aug 1831

    - " in a suit by Samuel Gray for $1000. — 1 May 1832

CLARKE, Dr. Frederick - Plattin Twp, Jefferson Co.; took up a sorrel mare ae 5y appraised at $55 by P. W. Hose & George Stam. J. W. Garraty JP. — 20 Nov 1829

CLAY, Eleazer - St. Francois Co.; took up a brown horse ae 15y appraised at $15 by Thomas Wilborn & Elisha Brown. James Wilburn JP. — 6 Mar 1832

Eli - Femme Osage Twp, St. Charles Co.; took up a mare ae 3y appraised at $20 by Darling Smith & William Anderson. Moses Bigelow JP. — 2 Mar 1830

George - Elkhorn Twp, Montgomery Co.; JP, stray taken up by Sarah Kennedy. — 17 Aug 1826

CLAYTON, R. - advertises for runaway apprentice Fealdon Phelps. — 10 Mar 1829

Ralph - sues Peter Haldeman for damages. — 30 May 1825

CLEVELAND, John - dissolves partnership with Nathaniel Potter. — 10 May 1824

CLIFFORD, John - appraised a stray taken up by Isaac Blanton. — 14 Jul 1829

CLINTON, Charles D. - St. Louis; offers $10 reward for black horse ae 5-6y strayed or stolen, formerly property of H. Raynerd. — 7 Dec 1826

CLUCK, Adam - Femme Osage Twp, St. Charles Co.; took up a sorrel horse ae 9y appraised at $30 by Elijah Bryan, John Mason, & Charles McLee Ferris. Moses Bigelow JP. — 2 Jun 1829

COBB, Andrew - Upper Loutre Twp, Montgomery Co.; took up a mare ae 8-9y appraised at $27 by William Brown & William McCormic. Joseph Howard JP. — 29 Jul 1828

COBBS, Waddy S. - Liberty Twp, Marion Co.; took up a black horse ae 13y appraised at $20 by Clement White & Andrew Muldoon. — 16 Dec 1828

COBLE, Andrew - appraised a stray taken up by James Davis. — 25 Jan 1831

CODMAN, Francis - advises that the auction of real estate he had advertised is unavoidably put off. — 19 Oct 1826

    - offers real estate for sale in St. Louis. — 27 May 1828

COLBURN, Jesse - "at his stable on the Hill" took up a sorrel horse ae 7y appraised at $35 by John Andrews & Michael Byrne. — 3 May 1827

COLE, Jacob - Bowles Twp, Franklin Co.; took up a bay horse ae 5y appraised at $30 by John Morris & Russell Brown. T. Henry JP. — 29 Nov 1827

Matthew - appraised a stray taken up by Charles R. Jeffries. — 21 Jul 1829

Nathan - offers $5 reward for the apprehension of "a black man" who stole some clothing. — 29 Nov 1824

Plato - Calvy Twp, Franklin Co.; took up a strawberry roan horse appraised at $35 by William King & Alexander Lasley. — 2 Dec 1828

William - appraised a stray taken up by Alexander Smith. — 27 May 1828

MOR

COLEMAN, James - offers his services as a Notary Public at the office of
    the Register & Receiver near the Mansion House, St. Louis.  1 Nov 1827
    Stephen O. - partner of Robert D. Sutton, cabinet makers, in the
      shop formerly occupied by William Reed.  3 Aug 1830
      - dissolve partnership.  20 Sep 1831
COLLARD, E. - appraised a stray taken up by Edward Yates.  22 Jun 1826
COLLIER, George - dissolves partnership with Peter & Joseph Powell.  12 Oct 1830
COLLIN, Owen - took up a bright bay horse on Gravois Road, appraised
    at $35. Sappington JP.  16 Jul 1823
COLLINS, Charles - opens a livery stable near the Missouri Hotel.  20 Jul 1830
    - Sues Oliver Dubois for $3000.  6 Sep 1831
    - Defendant in a suit by George W. Martin & Benjamin
      Green for $1200.  13 Sep 1831
    John M. - Bonhomme Twp, St. Louis Co.; took up an iron gray mare
      appraised at $10 by Alexander Smith & Lawrence Carder.  15 Mar 1831
      Henry Smith JP.
    Lawson - Boeuf Twp, Franklin Co.; took up a bay horse ae 5y
      appraised at $25 by Daniel & Richard Richardson.  20 Jul 1830
      Jesse McDonald JP.
    Owen - St. Louis Twp, St. Louis Co.; took up a bright bay horse
      ae 2y appraised at $10 by Granville Eads & Seaden Posey.  29 Dec 1829
    Smith - Trustee for John B. Davis, sells 80 acres of Davis'
      property at the house of Thomas N. Graves, Montgomery Co.  6 Sep 1831
    - still as Trustee, Davis "of unsound mind," sells land.  11 Sep 1832
COLVIN, John - appraised a stray taken up by George Reed.  31 Mar 1829
COLVINS, William - took up a black walnut canoe with four pounds of brown
    sugar, two pair of mens' shoes, a tin cup, and a dead  29 Oct 1823
    chicken, appraised at $5.50 by Cain J. Brown and
    Russell Brown.
COMEGYS, Benjamin - appraised a stray taken up by Moors B. Banks.  2 Mar 1830
CONN, Samuel - Meramec Twp, Franklin Co.; JP, strays taken up by Ann
    Frasier (19 Jul 1827), William Arthur (26 Aug 1828),
    Wm. R. Stewart (18 May 1830) and Ferry Harrison.  8 Feb 1831
CONIOR, Robert - Sandy Diggings near Herculaneum; offers $10 reward for
    a strayed or stolen bay horse.  7 Dec 1826
CONKLIN, James - opens a tailoring business at 24 Main St., St. Louis.  18 Jun 1823
    - wants four or five journeymen tailors.  21 Nov 1825
CONKLING, George S. - advertises cleaning and dyeing, St. Louis.  24 May 1831
CONSTANT, Louis - appraised a stray taken up by Louis Barada.  21 Oct 1828
CONWAY, Samuel - appraised a stray taken up by Gabriel Rush.  16 Feb 1830
COONS, David - obtained a license to sell groceries, St. Louis.  29 May 1832
    Mrs. S. - sets up a business on Main St., St. Louis - gilding and
      repairing of portraits, mirrors, frames.  19 May 1827
    William A. - sues John L. Jones for $300.  13 Sep 1831
COPELAND, Robinson - appraised a stray taken up by Thomas Jackson.  13 Sep 1827
CORDER, John - defendant in a suit in Chancery, Washington Co. Circuit
    Court; plaintiff, Joseph Bear.  8 Jan 1823
CORSON, Rev. L. H. - opens a "Classical English School" at $10 per
    quarter, St. Louis.  19 Apr 1831
    - offers a reward for a small bay mare strayed or
      stolen from Judge Carr's enclosure in October.  10 Jan 1832
COSHOW, William - Femme Osage Twp, St. Charles Co.; offers $15 reward
    for runaway Negro Abram Champ.  21 Jul 1829
    - took up a bay mare ae 15-20y appraised at $5 by James
      D. Moore & D. H. & Isaac Darst. Thomas Hopkins JP.  10 Jan 1832
COTNER, Coonrod, convicted of manslaughter, broke jail in Madison Co.;
    a $100 reward is offered. He was heavy,with dark eyes  30 Sep 1838
    and black hair and a long sharp nose; a German, spoke
    broken English.
COTTER, James - defendant in a suit for $231 debt and damages brought
    by George Burgess.  8 May 1832
COTTLE, Edward - appraised a stray taken up by Edward Yates.  22 Jun 1826
    - Monroe Twp, Lincoln Co.; took up a bright bay horse
      "rising 3 years" appraised at $25 by John Geiger  8 Apr 1828
    and John Cottle. C. K. Duncan JP.
    Jonathan - Hurricane Twp, Lincoln Co.; took up a black horse ae 18y
      appraised at $8 by John M. Hugh & Richard Ripley.  9 Aug 1827
      Benjamin Allen JP.
    MOR

71

COTTLE, Martial - next friend of Ardelia Woodbridge in her divorce suit.    30 Jun 1829
    Sherman - appraised a stray taken up by Allen Jameson.    30 Nov 1826
COULTER, John D. - attorney-at-law, St. Louis, "at the residence of
    Judge Peck on 3rd St."    25 Mar 1828
COUCH, Leonard - appraised a stray taken up by Samuel Graham.    11 Apr 1825
COUNTS, Joseph - appraised a stray taken up by Aaron Groom.    14 Jul 1829
COWAN, Richard D. - Wayne Co.; sues William Line for debt.    5 Sep 1825
COWIE, James - of the Green Tree Livery Stable; offers a "reasonable
    reward" for a horse strayed or stolen from the farm of    27 Dec 1824
    Wm. McCutcheon between St. Louis & Bonhomme.
    John & William - partnership dissolved by mutual consent.    22 Nov 1827
    John - obtains a grocer's license, St. Louis.    29 May 1832
    - offers "a tenement to rent" on Church St.    2 Oct 1832
COX, Caleb - advertises the same of prime sugar just received by boat.    7 May 1823
    Jesse - appraised a stray taken up by Joseph W. Sitton.    13 Jul 1826
    John - appraised a stray taken up by Elijah Marden.    21 Feb 1832
COZZENS, Brown - sues John Carrell for $300.    2 Oct 1832
CRAID, David - appraised a stray taken up by Green B. Bush.    15 Jun 1830
CRAIG, John - appraised a stray taken up by Daniel Peveler.    26 Jul 1827
    William Y. - appraised a stray taken up by James H. Griffin.    9 Sep 1828
CRANCH, Thomas - Clark Co.; took up two fillies appraised at
    $30 by Semor Davis & Stephen Jones. Silas M. Davis JP.    25 Dec 1832
CRAWFORD, William - store at #10 Market St., St. Louis; offers "foreign,
    domestic and fancy goods."    24 Jul 1832
CRESSWELL, Robert - appraised a stray taken up by Asa Griffith.    1 Jun 1830
CRIDER, Christopher - appraised a stray taken up by Magness Tullock.    13 Apr 1826
    Christopher and Thomas -    "         "    16 May 1827
CRISWELL, James - "on St. John's," Franklin Co.; took up a yellow bay
    filly ae 2y appraised at $15 by Lewis Williams and    23 Mar 1830
    William Murphy. Jesse McDonald JP.
CROMWELL, George - with Richard Tunis, sues John Burroughs for $900.    4 Sep 1832
CROSAIR, Simon - lost a pocketbook.    25 Mar 1828
CROSS, H. N. - advertises a new store at Market & Church Sts., St. Louis;
    dry goods, hardware, Queensware, groceries, etc.    17 Apr 1832
    - forms a partnership with L. B. Shaw; they have bought the
    stock of E. C. March.    9 May 1832
    John - Elkhorn Twp, Montgomery Co.; JP, stray taken up by
    Archibald Gibson.    20 Jan 1829
CROW, John - Cuivre Twp, Pike Co.; took up a bay horse ae 7y appraised
    at $22.50 by Thomas G. Keer, Greenberry D. Steel, & Andrew    29 Jun 1830
    Allison. Harrison Hendrick JP.
    Jonathan - offers a $50 reward for a chestnut sorrel horse ae 5y,
    stolen; a person named Lampkins suspected.    23 Mar 1824
CRUMP, Benjamin - Perry Twp, St. Francois Co.; took up a bay horse ae 8y
    appraised at $35 by Robert Guthrie & William Estes.    11 Apr 1825
    George McGahan JP.
    Turner - appraised a stray taken up by Samuel Boone.    8 Dec 1829
CULLOM, Tilman - Lewiston Twp, Montgomery Co.; took up a dark bay mare
    ae 3y appraised at $20 by Robert H. Patton Sr. &    14 Jun 1831
    Robert H. Patton Jr. Larking Carter JP.
CULPEPPER, Reid - appraised a stray taken up by Green B. Bush.    15 Jun 1830
CUNDIFF, James - appraised a stray taken up by James Boyers.    22 Dec 1829
CUNNINGHAM, Alexander - defendant in a suit for $600 by David V. Topper.    24 Apr 1832
    Thomas W. - offers 320 acres for sale on the main road from    2 Oct 1832
    St. Louis to St. Charles.
CURRY, James C. - Bonhomme Twp, St. Louis Co.; took up a roan horse ae 5y
    appraised at $55 by A. C. Blain & William Springgate.    2 Jun 1829
    Harris, JP.
CURTNER, James - Montgomery Co.; JP, stray taken up by Anthony Horton.    15 Feb 1831
    -    " by Hugh Logan.    5 Apr 1831
DAINSWOOD, Henry - bankrupt, St. Louis.    4 Oct 1831
DALEY, John J. - defendant in a suit for $1621.23 by Romulus Riggs
    and Robert B. Aertsen.    10 May 1831
DANIEL, Bracket & William - appraised a stray taken up by Robert Stuart.    24 Jan 1832
DANIELS, William - appraised a stray taken up by Philemon Plummer.    26 Aug 1828
    -    " by Andrew Tilford.    1 Jun 1830

MOR

72

DARBY, William M. - Spyers Palmer warns the public not to trade for a $55
    note which Darby gave him.                             9 Aug 1827
DARST, D. H. & Isaac - appraised a stray taken up by William Coshow.    10 Jan 1832
DAVIDSON, Abraham - appraised a stray taken up by Cornelius Howard.    7 Feb 1828
    Josiah H. - appraised a stray taken up by Walter Kinkead.    28 Dec 1826
DAVIS, Henry E. - appraised a stray taken up by Andrew Miller.    30 Nov 1826
    James - "waters of Loutre," Montgomery Co.; took up three mares
    appraised at $90 by Henry Logan & Adam Coble.    25 Jan 1831
                        John A. Morrison JP.
    John - Liberty Twp, Marion Co.; JP, stray taken up by William Ralls.    1 Feb 1831
    - appraised a stray taken up by Enoch Spry.    3 Nov 1829
    - " by Wm. Skinner (11 Jan 1831) & by John Smeltzer.    16 Oct 1832
    John B. - part of his property sold by trustee Smith Collins at
    the house of Thomas N. Graves, Montgomery Co.    6 Sep 1831
    Littleton - Clark Twp, Lincoln Co.; took up a gray mare ae 5y
    appraised at $20 by John S. Duncan & Christ Carter.    15 Feb 1831
                        Silas M. Davis JP.
    Robert - appraised a stray taken up by Michael J. Noyes.    21 Jun 1827
    Silas M. - Clark Twp, Lincoln Co.; stray taken up by Littleton
    Davis (see above) and by Thomas Slavens.    13 Mar 1832
    Semor - appraised a stray taken up by Thomas Cranch.    25 Dec 1832
DAVISS, John - appraised a stray taken up by Osias Heatherly.    26 May 1829
DAY, Francis - appraised a stray taken up by Moors B. Banks.    2 Mar 1830
DEAKER, George - bankrupt, St. Louis.    20 Nov 1832
DEAKERS, Richard - bankrupt, St. Louis.    13 Nov 1832
DEAN, John - "on Indian Creek," Washington Co.; took up a bay horse ae 10y
    appraised at $10 by Richard Summers & Archibald Roland.    18 Aug 1829
                     Charles Springer JP.
    William - will auction a mulatto boy age 18, property of
    Pierre Duchouquet.    27 Aug 1823
DEERING, William - advertises an improved lead-smelting furnace.    10 Jun 1828
DEFOE, John - appraised a stray taken up by Benjamin Ellenwood.    19 Jul 1831
DELAUNY,   David & Eleanor - defendants in a mortgage-foreclosure suit
(DELANAY)            by George P. Todson, Pike Co.    24 Jun 1828
    David - land sold for his debt to Abraham Like.    7 Mar 1832
DELAURIERE, Charles Fremon - bankrupt, St. Louis.    21 Oct 1828
DELISLE, Eugene - bankrupt, St. Louis.    25 Oct 1824
DEMERCE, Cornelius - appraised a stray taken up by Walter Kinkead.    28 Dec 1826
DENNIS, Jacob - appraised a stray taken up by James Keeney.    15 Feb 1831
DERING, William S. - advertises a "new hat manufactory."    10 Jun 1828
DES COMBES, Louis - "living on the plantation of P. Chouteau Jr." offers
    $5 reward for two horses strayed or stolen.    4 Jan 1827
DESLISLE, Baptiste - appraised a stray taken up by John Richardson.    18 Nov 1823
DETAILLIE, Genevieve versus Pierre, divorce.    7 Jun 1831
DEVORE, Uriah J. - defendant in a mortgage-foreclosure suit by the State
    of Mo. in the Pike Co. Circuit Court.    2 Nov 1826
    - JP, stray taken up by William W. Smith.    24 Jan 1832
DEWITT, A. B. - wants two apprentices for plastering and masonry.    26 Aug 1828
DICKERSON, Obadiah - sues Franklin Hallocks for $72.75 debt, Ralls Co.    15 Oct 1823
    - commissioner, Marion Co., announces lots for sale
    in Palmyra.    15 Jul 1828
DIGGS, Cole - Montgomery Co.; took up a mare and horse appraised at $25
    by Daniel Robinson & David M. Rice. W.G. Shackford JP.    17 Jan 1832
    David - took up a sorrel horse ae 5y appraised at $30 by J. L.
    Sitton & Elijah Myers. Wm. Hammock JP.    15 Feb 1827
    - appraised a stray taken up by John A. Woolfolk.    11 May 1830
DIO, Louis & Francois - took up a raft "floating adrift, which being
    perishable was offered for sale." St. Louis.    13 Apr 1826
DIVERS, Salathiel - sues Robert Wash, Spencer Pettis, Leo Mark & Wm.
    Rector to enjoin a judgment obtained for levy on a
    brick building claimed by Divers.    21 Sep 1826
DOBBINS, John B. - sues Henry Emert for $200.    13 Sep 1831
DOBYNS, DOBBINS, Edward B. - appraised a stray taken up by Wm. Triplett.    6 Jan 1829
    - his house, used as a carpenter shop, burned.    19 May 1829
DODSON, John W. - appraised a stray taken up by James Silvey.    25 Sep 1832
DONOHOE, John - defendant in a mortgage-foreclosure suit by the U. S.
    government, Perry Co. Circuit Court.    6 Sep 1827

MOR

73

DORSETT, Walter H. - Bonhomme Twp, St. Louis Co.; took up a dapple gray
          horse ae 10-11 y appraised at $40 by John P. Boice        19 Jul 1831
          & Wm. Miles.  H. Sappington JP.
          - appraised a stray taken up by Zachariah Tyler.     13 Nov 1832
DOUGHERTY, P. - offers $10 reward for a horse strayed or stolen from
          Mine Shibboleth; he lives near Mine-a-Breton.       13 Sep 1827
      Samuel F. - appraised a stray taken up by Alfonso Price.    7 Jul 1829
          - "   John Kent.                                17 Aug 1830
DOUGLASS, James S. - appraised a stray taken up by Absalom Holloway.  15 May 1832
DOWLING, Richard - his wife Martha has left his bed and board.     7 Apr 1829
DOWNING, Ezekiel - appraised a stray taken up by William Sitton.    20 Aug 1823
      Harrison - Bonhomme Twp, St. Louis Co.; took up a bright bay
          horse appraised at $20 by Samuel & Wm. Downing.     24 Aug 1830
          H. Sappington JP.
      Samuel - Bonhomme Twp, St. Louis Co.; took up a horse ae 11y
          appraised at $40 by George W. Elliott & Cain J. Brown.  14 Jul 1829
          A. P. Harris JP.
      William - St. Louis Co.; took up a bay mare ae 2y appraised at
          $8 by John Chapman & Samuel Downing. A.P. Harris JP.   3 Feb 1829
DOYEL, John - appraised a stray taken up by Eli Valentine.        1 Sep 1829
DRAKE, Elizabeth W. - treasurer of the Female Charitable Society.    8 Feb 1831
      Silas - dissolves partnership with Curtis Skinner.      27 Oct 1829
DRAPER, Daniel - Union Twp, Lincoln Co.; JP, stray taken up by Wm. Sitton. 20 Aug 1823
      - Appraised a stray taken up by Samuel Emily.       30 Jan 1828
      Edwin - dissolves partnership with Hampton Weed.       24 May 1831
      Zachariah G. - plaintiff, suit for $180 vs Robert K. Hamilton,
          Marion Co.                             15 Nov 1831
DuBOIS, Oliver - appraised a stray taken up by Caleb Brown.      9 Sep 1828
      - defendant, suit for $3000 by Charles Collins.       6 Sep 1831
DUDLEY, Aaron - appraised a stray taken up by Benjamin Horine.    27 Jun 1825
DUGAN, E. - Platin Twp, Jefferson Co.; JP, stray taken up by
          Henry Hendricks.                   10 Feb 1829
DULEY, Thomas - Hibernia, Callaway Co.; offers $10 reward for a runaway
          Negro age 50.                    14 Sep 1826
DULIN, Thaddeus G. - appraised a stray taken up by John Naylor.    19 Jan 1830
DUNCAN, C. K. - Monroe Twp, Lincoln Co.; JP, stray taken up by Edward Cottle. 8 Apr 1828
      - Clark Twp, Lincoln Co.; JP, stray taken up by James Forrest. 11 May 1830
      David - defendant, suit for $5000 by Thomas Ingram.      6 Sep 1831
      John S. - appraised a stray taken up by Littleton Davis.   15 Feb 1831
      Letitia - bought a plot of land from James & Elizabeth Lowe.  9 Oct 1832
      Marshall - appraised a stray taken up by Jack Johns Jr.   22 Dec 1829
      Richard - appraised a stray taken up by David Pursley.    1 Mar 1831
      William - appraised a stray taken up by Giles Sullivan.    3 Aug 1830
DUTTON, John H. - Prairie Twp, Montgomery Co.; JP, strays taken up by
          James Smith (17 Jun 1828), William Eades (9 Jun 1829),
          Reuben Pew (29 Dec 1829), Thornton Winscott & George Gray. 27 Dec 1831
DUVAL, Richard M. - St. Louis Twp, St. Louis Co.; took up a bay horse
          ae 12y appraised at $18 by James & Zephaniah      29 Mar 1831
          Sappington. T. Sappington JP.
DYER, Isaac - dissolves partnership with Jesse H. Rogers.       23 Mar 1830
EADES, William - Prairie Twp, Montgomery Co.; took up a gray horse ae 11y
          appraised at $25 by William Suggs & Thomas T. Elton.   9 Jun 1829
          John H. Dutton JP.
EADS, Granville - appraised a stray taken up by Owen Collins.     29 Dec 1829
EARLS, see HURLS
EASTIN, C. C. - Calumet Twp, Pike Co.; JP, strays taken up by Harris
          Spears (17 June 1828), Daniel McCugh (27 Apr 1830) and
          Joshua Wells.                     27 Dec 1831
      Christopher C. - next friend of Harriet Phelan in her divorce
          suit, Pike Co.                   3 Aug 1826
EATON, Abraham - took up a bay horse ae 9y appraised at $60 by Hezekiah
          Williams & Wm. Hagood.  Thomas Garvin JP.       19 Mar 1826
ECKERT, William - appraised a stray taken up by Antoine Thebo.    22 Apr 1828
EDGAR, L. - took over the Whitehall Tavern in Potosi.         24 May 1831
      Louis - appraised a stray taken up by John Hawkins.     13 Nov 1832
      Washington - Concord Twp, Washington Co.; took up a gray mare ae 9y
          appraised at $35 by George J. Hodges & Wm. Sutton.   31 Jul 1832
          I. A. Belknap JP

EDWARDS, John C. - attorney-at-law. 13 May 1828
      Lewis & Moses - appraised a stray taken up by Norman Pringle. 1 Nov 1831
ELDER, Sarah Ann - sues Augustine W. for divorce. 7 Jun 1831
ELLENWOOD, Benjamin - Bonhomme Twp, St. Louis Co.; took up a sorrel colt
      ae 2y appraised at $30 by William Page & 27 Apr 1830
      T. C. Trustee. Hartly Sappington JP.
      - took up a bay mare ae 8-9y appraised at $25 by John 19 Jul 1831
      Defoe & Samuel Whitley. H. Smith JP.
ELLINGTON, John - St. Ferdinand Twp, St. Louis Co.; took up a gray mare
      ae 4y appraised at $25 by Eddy Fortune & John Blue. 13 Nov 1832
      A. J. Whiteside JP.
      Peter - appraised a stray taken up by Jeremiah Ball. 23 Dec 1828
ELLIOTT, Benjamin - bankrupt, St. Louis. 30 May 1825
      George W. - appraised a stray taken up by Samuel Downing. 14 Jul 1829
      John - Howard Co.; offers a $50 reward for a runaway Negro, 9 Aug 1827
      ae 30; he was caught at Jefferson Barracks but got away.
      Mary L. - will soon open a school under the Baptist Church, her 7 Nov 1824
      engagement as instructress by Rev. Giddings has expired.
      Thomas J. - Buffalo Twp, Pike Co.; took up a sorrel horse ae 5y 4 Jan 1831
      appraised at $30 by James Benning & Wm. Penix.
      William - defendant, suit by Moses Thomas for $1000. 2 Oct 1832
ELLIS, Elisha - appraised a stray taken up by Anthony Thomas. 24 Aug 1830
      Isaac - appraised a stray taken up by Anthony Horton. 15 Feb 1831
      Samuel - a surgeon dentist, will be away for two months. 5 Jul 1824
ELTON, Thomas T. (Y?) - appraised a stray taken up by James Smith. 17 Jun 1828
      - " one by Wm. Eades, taken up by Reuben Pew. 29 Jun 1829
ELY, Joseph - advertises an auction and commission house, with 17 Aug 1830
      William H. Hopkins.
EMBRES, Elisha, M.D. - offers medicine and surgery; has a room in 13 Sep 1824
      . Mrs. Paddock's house on Main St., St. Louis.
EMERSON, Alexander H. - took up a brown horse ae 10 appraised at $25
      by Jacob Howdeshell, Stephen Burts, & William 15 Aug 1825
      McDowns. Thomas Whitesides JP.
      E. D. - appraised a stray taken up by Robert Allison. 15 Feb 1831
      Enoch - Buffalo Twp, Pike Co.; took up a dark sorrel mare ae 3y
      appraised at $8 by Abiel Roberson & William Knolton. 8 Mar 1827
      John Jordan JP.
      - announces the sale of town lots in Louisville, Lincoln Co. 5 Jun 1832
EMERT, Henry - defendant in a suit for $200 by John B. Dobbins. 13 Sep 1831
EMILY, Samuel - Union Twp, Lincoln Co.; took up a bay horse ae 4y 30 Jan 1828
      appraised at $20 by Samuel Gibson & Daniel Draper.
ENGLISH, Elkanah - candidate for Coroner, St. Louis. 26 Jun 1832
      Thomas & wife - their house on Myrtle St., St. Louis, sold to 8 Mar 1831
      satisfy a debt to Edward Tracy.
EOFF, Isaac - appraised a stray taken up by Ebner Terril. 2 Mar 1830
ERSKINE, Greene - dissolves partnership with Christopher Rhodes. 13 Nov 1832
ERWIN, Jared - Charrette Twp, Montgomery Co.; JP, strays taken up by
      James Hughes (14 Feb 1832) and by Scudder Smith. 9 Oct 1832
ESSEX, James C. - bought T. Houghan's stock, book store and bindery. 22 May 1832
ESTES, Easter - with others, defendants in a suit to regain possession 4 May 1826
      of a house. Plaintiff, David McNair. St. Charles Circ. Ct.
      Hiram - appraised a stray taken up by James Johnston. 9 Sep 1828
      H. - " by Ira Valentine. 8 Jun 1830
      James - appraised a stray taken up by Thomas Triplett. 29 May 1832
      Thomas - partnership of Gay & Estes dissolved, due to his death. 16 Nov 1830
      William - appraised a stray taken up by Benjamin Crump. 11 Apr 1825
EUELOE, Jesse - appraised a stray taken up by Uriah Burns. 13 Jul 1830
EVANS, Abraham - sues John Gray for $181.20 debt. 16 Jul 1823
FAHSNACHT, Jacob - offers "1¢ and a chew of tobacco" for runaway 1 Feb 1831
      apprentice John P. Brown, ca 18, 5'7 or 8".
FAIR, Elizabeth - her house on Chestnut St., St. Louis, sold to satisfy 8 Mar 1831
      a debt to J. Millington.
FARIS, Wilson - his land sold to satisfy the claim of George Collier. 3 Jul 1832
FARNSWORTH, Alden - appraised a stray taken up by Richard Puttmann. 2 Jul 1823
      - " by Allen Turnbow. 27 Aug 1823
      Biel - Dardenne Twp, St. Charles Co.; JP, stray taken up by 2 Jul 1823
      Richard Puttmann.
FARRANDO, Charles F. & Co. - advertises a real estate brokerage. 25 Sep 1832

MOR
75

FARRAR, Richard - appraised a stray taken up by Hannah Morris.      11 Jan 1831
FARREL, Michael - obtained a grocer's license, St. Louis.      29 May 1832
FARRIS, George - Bonhomme Twp, St. Louis Co.; took up a sorrel horse ae 4y
     appraised at $25 by A. W. Miller & Miner Farris.      29 May 1832
                  W. McCullough JP.
     Granville - appraised a stray taken up by Hiram Smith.      29 Dec 1829
FAUCET, William - appraised a stray taken up by Francis Lorine.      7 Oct 1828
FELLOWS, Hart - bankrupt, St. Louis.      16 Feb 1823
FELTS, Kindred S. - appraised a stray taken up by William Ralls.      1 Feb 1831
         - " by Thomas Forrest.      5 Apr 1831
FERGUSON, D. Jr. - partner of George Maguire, dry goods and groceries,
                "nearly opposite the St. Louis bookstore."      2 Dec 1828
     Fergus - St. Louis Co., stray taken up by Samuel Bay. (JP)      30 Mar 1830
         - St. Ferdinand Twp, St. Louis Co., " by David Martin.      10 Jan 1832
     John - appraised a stray taken up by Alfonso Price.      7 Jul 1829
         - Montgomery Co.; took up a sorrel horse ae 12y appraised
         at $25 by Christopher & Wm. J. Talbot. A. G. Irvine JP.      19 Jul 1827
     Moses - Richwoods Twp, Washington Co.; JP, stray taken up by
                      Benjamin Horine.      27 Jun 1825
         - appraised a stray taken up by John Hearst.      14 Apr 1829
     Peter - St. Louis Twp, St. Louis Co.; JP, stray taken up by
                      James Phillips.      19 Jun 1832
     William - Abraham Fox's property sold to satisfy a claim
         by Ferguson.      6 Nov 1832
FERRIS, Charles McLee - appraised a stray taken up by Adam Cluck.      2 Jun 1829
     Jabez - Bonhomme Twp, St. Louis Co.; took up a sorrel horse
         ae 5y appraised at $20 by Henry Raynor & George Sip.      23 Nov 1826
                      Caleb Bowles JP.
         - took up a bay mare ae 3y appraised at $15 by Mathias Sip
         & John Patterson. Bowles JP.      18 Jan 1831
FICKEAR, Paul - appraised a stray taken up by Joseph Racine.      30 Aug 1824
FICKLIN, Thomas H. - Belleview Twp, Washington Co.; JP, strays taken up by
         Luman Ruggie (11 Jul 1825) and by Gabriel Prewett.      23 Feb 1826
     Thompson -dissolves partnership with Hiram Alexander, Caledonia,
         Washington Co.; advertises a woolen factory.      10 Feb 1829
         - offers $50 reward for runaway "Buck," Potosi.      18 Aug 18??
FINDLEY, T. - appraised a stray taken up by Anthony Thomas.      24 Aug 1830
FINE, David - St. Louis Twp, St. Louis Co.; took up a brown horse colt
     ae 1y appraised at $10 by John Fine & James Hibbard.      23 Dec 1828
     Levi - appraised a stray taken up by Joseph Brown.      19 Jan 1830
     Peter - appraised a stray taken up by J. M. Baily.      24 Jun 1828
     Philip - appraised a stray taken up by Jordon McCormick.      2 Nov 1826
     Wilson - "south of the Meramec" took up a sorrel horse ae 7-8y,
         appraisers not shown; $40. T. Sappington JP.      19 Feb 1823
FINEGAN, John - appraised a stray taken up by J. M. Baily.      24 Jun 1828
FINNEY, J. & W. - with Joseph Tabor, offer miscellaneous merchandise in
         the stone warehouse at the steamboat landing, St. Louis.      30 Mar 1830
FISHER, George - Merrimack Twp, St. Louis Co.; took up a chestnut sorrel
         horse ae 8y appraised at $30 by Jeremiah Hamilton
         & Eli Short. Samuel Short JP.      9 Apr 1823
     Nicholas - appraised a stray taken up by Solomon Alkire.      27 Dec 1831
FITCH, T. E. - notice that anyone finding the body of 12-year-old Henry
         Fitch, who drowned 15 May when a yawl sank opposite the
         city, will receive parents' thanks and liberal reward.      28 May 1823
FITZGERALD, Carvel - appraised a stray taken up by Andrew Rice.      23 May 1826
     Thomas - took up a bright bay horse ae 5y appraised at $60 by
         Washington Fitzgerald & Jonathan Wiseman. H. Smith JP.      31 Jan 1832
FLAUGHERTY, Felix W. - defendant, with others, in a suit by David McNair
         to regain possession of a house, St. Charles.      4 May 1826
FLEMING,A. - appraised a stray taken up by Magness Tullock.      13 Apr 1826
     Arthur - a saddler on Main St., St. Louis, advertises an
         "improved patent horse checker."      10 May 1824
         - will be absent 3 months, Thornton Grimsley is his agent.      15 Jul 1828
     Luke - appraised a stray taken up by George Barnsback.      24 Jan 1828
FLETCHER, Clement B. - with others, authorized to build bridge over
         Joachim Creek at Herculaneum.      3 Feb 1829
         - assigns his property to his creditors.      27 Nov 1832

FLETCHER, D. - warns public not to trust or protect his wife Hannah, who
    has left him.                                                          4 May 1830
    William - Bonhomme Twp, St. Louis Co.; took up a sorrel mare
        ae 3y appraised at $28 by Enos McDonald & George         17 May 1827
        Sip. Caleb Bowles JP.
FLORE, Joseph - bankrupt, St. Louis.                      24 May 1824
FOLEY, Thomas - appraised a stray taken up by Daniel Clare.    22 Jun 1830
FOLGER, Jared W. - dissolves partnership with Martin Robinson.   21 Aug 1832
FOLY, Larkin - appraised a stray taken up by Richard Murrel.    30 Nov 1830
FORDE, John B. - "new goods of the most fashionable kind" in R. Paul's
    stone house, St. Louis.                         27 May 1828
FOREMAN, S. W. - advertises for a bright sorrel gelding stolen from the
    home of William Strode, 3m nw of St. Louis. Will give    29 Apr 1828
    $10 if found in St. Louis County, otherwise $25.
FORREST, James - Clark Twp, Lincoln Co.; took up a bright bay filly ae 3y
    appraised at $17 by William Hepmight & John Foster.   11 May 1830
                   C. K. Duncan JP.
    Thomas - Liberty Twp, Marion Co. - took up two horses appraised
        at $60 by Peter Pinkston & Kindred S. Felts.       5 Apr 1831
                John Davis JP.
FORTUNE, Eddy - appraised a stray taken up by John Ellington.   13 Nov 1832
    William - defendant in a suit to foreclose a mortgage by
        Francis Howell Sr., St. Charles.              11 Jan 1827
FOSTER, John - appraised a stray taken up by James Forrest.    11 May 1830
    Robert - JP, St. Charles Co., strays taken up by Moses Butcher  28 Jul 1829
        and by Thomas Spalding.                   2 Nov 1830
    Sarah -Washington Co.; sues Dabney Foster for divorce.    20 Sep 1824
    William Miles - with John Wetherill, auction & commission business.  3 Mar 1829
        - partnership dissolved.                     4 Aug 1829
        - whiskey, dry goods, etc. from the business sold by
        the sheriff upon the action of John O'Rourke        11 May 1830
        and John G. Stevenson.
FOUNT, Elmsly - Charrette Twp, Montgomery Co.; took up two horses
    appraised at $55 by John Hyatt & Edward Baber.      28 Jun 1831
               Beston Callahan JP.
FOX, Abraham - his property sold to satisfy a claim of Wm. Ferguson.  6 Nov 1832
FRANKLIN, Napoleon B. - obtained a grocer's license, St. Louis.   29 May 1832
FRASIER, Ann - Merrimac Twp, Franklin Co.; took up a bay mare with a colt,
    appraised at $37, and a stud horse ae 2y, $15, by S. B.   19 Jul 1827
    Wheeler, Daniel Wheeler, & Perry Moore. Samuel Conn JP.
FRAZIER, Keziah & Harriet - divorce petition in the Mo. Legislature.  25 Jan 1831
    Thomas S. - bankrupt, Marion Co.                  26 May 1829
FRAZER, Robert - St. John's Twp, Franklin Co.; took up a black horse
    ae 7y appraised at $15 by Valentine Hunter & Thomas   22 Jun 1826
    Wall. John Caldwell JP.
FREEMAN, Daniel - appraised a stray taken up by Coonrod Cashman.  12 Feb 1823
    John - Loutre Twp, Montgomery Co.; took up a bright bay mare with
    a colt appraised at $35 by Thomas Freeman & James Alfrey.   5 Jan 1830
               Joseph Howard JP.
    John & Thomas - appraised a stray taken up by William Lugs.   31 May 1831
FRISSELL, Willard - appraised a stray taken up by Prudence Beavis.   1 Mar 1831
FROST, Simon - appraised a stray taken up by John Stuart.      22 Dec 1825
FRUIT, Enoch - 9-Mile-Prairie Twp, Callaway Co.; JP, strays taken up
    by Samuel Boone (8 Dec 1829) and by Levi McMurtry.    31 Jul 1832
FRY, Thomas - runaway apprentice of carpenter Phineas Bartlett. He was
    "stout, clumsy," about 17 or 18, light hair, blue eyes.   24 Aug 1830
FRYER, Alexander - his property in St. Louis sold to satisfy a note
    for $300 to Sullivan Blood.                  24 Jan 1832
FULBRIGHT, David - appraised a stray taken up by George Smithers.  23 Feb 1826
    Morton - "on Ozan Fork of Forche a Toway," Harmony Twp,
        Washington Co.; took up a yellow sorrel horse       1 Aug 1825
        appraised at $30 by Daniel Fulbright & Allen
        Hinesly. Charles Springer JP.
GAINES, John - sues John W. Merritt & Wm. Bagley for $500.     28 Aug 1832
GAITHER, Dr. H. - physician and surgeon, office on Main St., St. Louis.  20 Jan 1829
GALLAWAY, James - appraised a stray taken up by David Markle.    20 Jan 1829

GAMALE, John - appraised a stray taken up by Joshua Herrington.                24 Jun 1828
GANITCHIE, Joseph - appraised a stray taken up by James McDonald.             16 Aug 1831
GANNON, Timothy - bankrupt, St. Louis.                                        31 May 1824
GARA, Michael - Perry Twp, St. Francois Co.; JP, stray taken up by
                 George Barnsback.                                            24 Jan 1828
GARDNER, Isaac C. - defendant, suit by Curtis Skinner for $500 and by
                 William Tighe for $300, St. Louis.                            6 Sep 1831
             - defendant, suit by George Hood and John C. Abbott
                 for $300, St. Louis.                                         13 Sep 1831
        Johnston - defendant, suit by Clayton Tiffin for $150, St. Louis.     30 Aug 1831
GARNER, Sarah - sues Thruston Garner for divorce, Montgomery Co., by
                 next friend Hugh McDermed.                                   27 Aug 1823
GARNET, Lewis - appraised a stray taken up by William Mills.                   2 Dec 1828
GARRATY, J. W. - Platin Twp, Jefferson Co.; JP, stray taken up by
                 Antony Wilkson.                                              30 Jun 1829
         W. H. - opens a House of Entertainment on Main St., St. Louis.       24 May 1831
GARVIN, Joseph - appraised a stray taken up by William Haines.                19 Mar 1823
        Thomas - JP, stray taken up by William Haines.                               "
GASH, John - appraised a stray taken up by William Anderson.                  12 Oct 1830
      William - Fabius Twp, Marion Co.; JP, strays taken up by Jacob
                 Weaver (7 Jul 1829) and by William Anderson.                 12 Oct 1830
GAY, David - dissolved partnership with Elisha S. Beebee.                     19 Mar 1823
     Elizabeth - sues David for divorce, St. Louis Circuit Court.             10 Apr 1832
     George W. - runaway apprentice of R. Millegan, St. Louis. Age 19.        19 Jul 1824
     John H. - asks debtors of late firm Gay & Estes to pay.                   4 Jan 1831
GEIGER, Charles L. - took up a pale blue skiff, opposite Herculaneum.
                 Appraised at $15 by Rees Cadwallader, William                25 May 1830
                 McDonald, and Benjamin Johnston Sr. Notice by
                 John Geiger.
        John - appraised a stray taken up by Edward Cottle.                    8 Apr 1828
GENTRY, Joshua - Liberty Twp, Marion Co.; took up a sorrel mare ae 4-5y
                 appraised at $25 by Rodes Gentry & Robert Van Schoiacke.      1 Mar 1831
                 James F. Mahan JP.
GEORGE, Edward - appraised a stray taken up by Asa Griffith.                   1 Jun 1830
        Sidney - "at his plantation in Fabius Twp," Marion Co.; took up a
                 black mare ae 3y appraised at $25 by John Johnson &          29 Nov 1831
                 Alexander Shannon. James Spears JP.
GERNSEY, L. - Principal of the Missouri Literary & Classical Academy,
                 St. Louis.                                                   15 Sep 1829
GIBSON, Archibald - Elkhorn Twp, Montgomery Co.; took up a bay filly
                 ae 2y appraised by John Zumwalt & Thomas K---?               20 Jan 1829
                 John Cross JP.
        John - appraised a stray taken up by Francis Withinton.               29 Jun 1830
        Samuel - appraised a stray taken up by John Shrum.                    31 Aug 1826
             -    " by Samuel Emily.                                          30 Jan 1828
GIEGER, John - appraised a stray taken up by Samuel Moore.                     9 Sep 1828
GILBERT, William - appraised a stray taken up by Welch Allison.               14 Dec 1826
GILL, John - Dardenne Twp, St. Charles Co.; took up a brown mare ae 6-7y
                 appraised at $30 by T. D. Stephenson & John Howell.           6 Aug 1823
                 John B. Stone JP.
GILLEY, John B. - defendant, suit for $10,000 damages by James D.
                 Breckenridge, St. Louis Circuit Court.                       25 Jan 1827
GILMAN, Solomon - appraised a stray taken up by Peter Vinyard.                27 Dec 1831
GILMORE, John - appraised a stray taken up by Daniel Clare.                   22 Jun 1830
GIMBLIN, Henry - appraised a stray taken up by Abner Ball.                    14 Jun 1831
GLADNEY, Samuel - appraised a stray taken up by Martin McCoy.                  2 Sep 1828
GLASGOW, William - dissolves partnership with John Niven, Herculaneum.         2 Mar 1826
GLOVER, Philip - Prairie Twp, Montgomery Co.; JP, stray taken up by
                 Joseph Brown.                                                19 Jan 1830
GODAIRE, Baptiste - bankrupt, St. Louis.                                      25 Oct 1824
GOE, Talton - appraised a stray taken up by James McDonald.                   16 Aug 1831
GOFORTH, Andrew - Black River Twp, Washington Co.; JP, stray taken up by
                 Laban Miner.                                                  5 Jul 1827
              - Bellevue Twp, Washington Co.; JP, strays taken up by
                 Wm. Hewitt (28 Jul 1829), Uriah Hull (8 Jun 1830)
                 and William Campbell.                                        15 Mar 1831

GOFORTH, John L. - appraised a stray taken up by William Hewitt.                          28 Jul 1829
          - " by William Campbell.                                                        15 Mar 1831
GOLDSCHMIDT, W. L. & Co. - owners of a clothing store in St. Louis,
                    " opposite Mr. Paul's."                                               13 Apr 1830
GOODALL, J. - offers a reward for a runaway mulatto, Eliza.                                4 Aug 1829
GOODFELLOW, John - dissolves partnership with James W. Park.                              22 Mar 1831
GOODRICH, James - appraised a stray taken up by Evin Lemasters.                           10 Jul 1832
GOODYEAR, W. - a "boot and shoe manufacturer" on the east side of
              Main St., St. Louis.                                                        28 Jun 1831
GORDON, Alfred - appraised a stray taken up by Thomas Jackson.                            13 Sep 1827
        George - warns the public not to accept notes he gave Nathan
                 Ramey for land to which Ramey had no good title.                          3 Nov 1829
               - appraised a stray taken up by George Lewis.                              31 Aug 1830
GORE, Reuben - appraised a stray taken up by Joshua Herrington.                           24 Jun 1828
GRAHAM, George W. - appraised a stray taken up by David Hilderbrand.                       2 Feb 1830
        Robert - Loutre Twp, Montgomery Co.; JP, stray taken up by
                 Daniel Peveler.                                                          26 Jul 1827
        Samuel - took up a chestnut sorrel horse ae 8y appraised at $25
                 by Leonard Couch & Jacob Wilson. B. Hansell JP.                          11 Apr 1825
               - Jefferson Co.; JP, stray taken up by James Owens.                        22 Dec 1829
        Thomas Jr. - dissolves partnership with John S. Boyd, but will
                     continue the business.                                                6 Nov 1832
GRANJEAN, Julian Ann - sues Abraham F. Granjean for divorce.                               7 Jun 1831
GRANVILLE, Asa - appraised a stray taken up by Nicholas Long.                             30 Nov 1830
GRATE, William - appraised a stray taken up by Leaden Posey.                              27 Nov 1832
GRAVES, Thomas N. - Montgomery Co.; his home was the site of the sale of
                    part of John B. Davis' property by trustee Smith Collins.              6 Sep 1831
GRAY, George - took up a sorrel mare ae 3y appraised at $30 by Isaac Gray
               & Thornton Winscott; Dutton JP. Same day appraised a stray                 27 Dec 1831
               taken up by Winscott.
     Isaac - appraised a stray taken up by James Smith.                                   17 Jun 1828
           -        "        Thornton Winscott.                                           27 Dec 1831
     John - defendant in a suit for $181.20 debt by Abraham Evans.                        16 Jul 1823
     Samuel - plaintiff, suit for $1000 against John Clark.                                1 May 1832
     William - appraised a stray taken up by Pleasant Stewart.                            14 Jul 1829
GREEN, Benjamin - with George W. Martin sues Charles Collins for $1200.                   13 Sep 1831
      Bernard - Mine-a-Breton; offers $30 reward for Thomas Hamilton,
                "a swindler," who had lived at Green's place for 11                        23 Feb 1824
                months before running away.
              - dissolves partnership with Andrew Burt at Mine-a-Breton
                and Mine-a-Valle, Jefferson Co.                                           14 Sep 1826
      J. G. - appraised a stray taken up by Samuel Hutton.                                11 May 1830
      James - St. Charles Twp, St. Charles Co.; JP, stray taken up by
              Evin Lemasters.                                                             10 Jul 1832
GREENE, George S. - advertises public sale of furniture, bedding, etc.
                    of the City Hotel, St. Louis.                                         14 Oct 1828
                  - sells the City Hotel to E. Towne.                                     10 Mar 1829
                  - "resumes his former practice as a surgeon-dentist."                   16 Mar 1830
       Dr. George - his household goods, brick house, farm on the
                    River des Peres, and a mulatto boy for sale.                          30 Nov 1830
       George W. - opens the Missouri Hotel, $5 per week boarding and
                   lodging, or $1 per day.                                                29 Nov 1831
GREENSTREET, Allen & Enoch - appraised a stray taken up by John Sullens.                  31 May 1827
            James - appraised a stray taken up by Thomas Maupin.                          25 Jan 1831
GREGORY, Uriah B. - appraised a stray taken up by Eli Merill.                             20 Sep 1831
GRIFFITH, Asa - appraised a stray taken up by Michael Keeny.                               3 Oct 1825
         Daniel - JP, stray taken up by Michael Keeny.                                     3 Oct 1825
         Asa - Portage des Sioux Twp, St. Charles Co.; took up a sorrel
               horse ae 7y appraised at $50 by Edward George & Robert                      1 Jun 1830
               Cresswell. Joseph Sumner JP.
         Ezra - lost a pocketbook with several hundred dollars in cash,
                either in St. Louis or between St. Louis & Vandalia.                      20 Dec 1831
GRIFFIN, James H. - Perry Twp, St. Francois Co.; took up a bay horse
                    ae 8y appraised at $10 by William Y. Craig & P. D.                     9 Sep 1828
                    Blunt. George McGahan JP.
GRIMES, John J. - appraised a stray taken up by Harris Spears.                            17 Jun 1828
GRIMSLEY, Thornton - advertises for saddlers & harness-and-trunk makers.                  22 Apr 1828

          MOR                    79

GRIMSLEY, William R. - advertises for runaway apprentice Edward Lessieur.          25 Mar 1828
              - dissolves partnership with Samuel Willett.                         10 Jun 1828
              - advertises for runaway apprentice Sydenham Wilson.                  5 Oct 1830
              - dissolves partnership with Wm. A. Lynch.                           19 Apr 1831
GROOM, Aaron - Loutre Twp, Montgomery Co.; took up a small bay horse               14 Jul 1829
              appraised at $15 by Jacob Groom & Joseph Counts.
            - took up a sorrel mare ae 20y appraised at $10 by Elias                6 Jul 1830
              Widdle & Esau Baker.  S. Baker JP.
GUELBERTH, Auguste - advertises watches and jewelry.                               26 Jul 1831
GUFFEE, Young - Jefferson Co., JP, stray taken up by Joshua Herrington.             5 Oct 1829
GUILLORY, Philip - bankrupt, St. Louis.                                            24 May 1824
GUION, Joseph - appraised a stray taken up by Louis Barada.                        21 Oct 1828
GUITARD, Louis - offers a 130-acre farm for sale, 9 miles from St. Louis.           7 Oct 1828
GURNO, Lewis - appraised a stray taken up by Lewellen Turnbo.                      10 Apr 1832
GUNSOLIS, James - his property sold to satisfy claims of David Kyle                 5 Jul 1831
              and John McCausland.
GUTHRIE, Robert - appraised a stray taken up by Benjamin Crump.                    11 Apr 1825
GUY, Ervin - appraised a stray taken up by William Watt.                           31 May 1831
GUYER, Ervin - appraised a stray taken up by Isaac Blanton.                        14 Jul 1829
HAAB, Victor - manufacturer of wooden pumps at Rock Branch.                         9 Jan 1830
HAGOOD, William G. - appraised a stray taken up by Abraham Eaton.                  19 Mar 1823
HAIGH, Joseph - Breton Twp, Washington Co.; took up a piebald roan filly            8 Feb 1827
              ae 3y appraised at $15 by John McIlvain & Amos J. Bruce.
                                                   Henry Shurlds JP.
HAINES, William - took up a chestnut sorrel, shod, appraised at $60 by             19 Mar 1823
              Joseph Neel & Joseph Garvin.  Thomas Garvin JP.
HALDEMAN, Peter - defendant in a damage suit by Ralph Clayton.                     30 May 1825
HALL, Charles R. - appraised a stray taken up by Robert Quarles Jr.                22 Jan 1823
     Isaac - St. Ferdinand Twp, St. Louis Co.; took up a brown horse ae 3y          1 Sep 1829
              appraised at $30 by John Mulhall & John J. Brown.
                                                   Joel Musick JP.
     John - defendant in a suit for $350 damages by Richard Mason.                 16 Jul 1823
          - Buffalo Twp, Pike Co.; took up a bay mare ae 6y appraised at           25 Jan 1831
              $16 by Robert Jordan & Joseph Burnett.  John Price JP.
     R. - carver and gilder, Market between Main-Church, St. Louis.                26 Jul 1831
     Thomas C. - wants to hire journeyman shoemakers at his shop below              1 Nov 1827
              the Market House, St. Louis.
HALLIDAY, James L. - appraised a stray taken up by John Bray.                      10 Jun 1828
HALLOCK, Franklin - defendant in a suit for $72.75 debt by Obadiah                 15 Oct 1823
              Dickerson, Ralls Co. Court.
HAMILTON, Andrew Jr. - appraised a stray taken up by James Boyer.                  17 May 1831
     Ninian -                    "                                                      "
     Jeremiah - appraised a stray taken up by George Fisher.                        9 Apr 1823
     John - appraised a stray taken up by Reuben Sollar.                           29 Nov 1831
     Richard W. - bankrupt, St. Louis.                                             21 Sep 1826
     Robert K. - defendant, suit for $180 by Zachariah Draper,                     15 Nov 1831
                                                   Marion Co.
     Thomas - accused of theft by Bernard Green, Mine-a-Breton.                    23 Feb 1824
HAMMACK, Brice - Hurricane Twp, Lincoln Co.; JP, stray taken up by                 29 Jun 1830
                                                   Francis Withinton.
     William - Hurricane Twp, Lincoln Co.; JP, stray taken up by                    2 Sep 1828
                                                   Martin McCoy.
HAMMOCK, William - JP, stray taken up by David Diggs.                              15 Feb 1827
HAMMOND, Alden - Joachim Twp, Jefferson Co.; took up a bay horse ae 6y             30 Aug 1831
              appraised at $30 by C. S. Rankin & G. W. Johnston.
                                                   Chauncey Smith JP.
     G. - Joachim Twp, Jefferson Co.; JP, strays taken up by James                  1 Mar 1831
              Smith (16 May 1825), Moses B. Austin (9 Nov 1826), Silas
              Huskey (6 Apr 1830) and Prudence Beavis.
HAMMONS, Thomas - Union Twp, Lincoln Co.; JP, stray taken up by                    21 Feb 1832
                                                   Elijah Marden.
HAMTRAMCK, John F. - sues John Calvert for $200.                                   17 May 1831
HANCOCK, Benjamin - appraised a stray taken up by John Jump.                        4 Jan 1827
              -       "       by Elijah Bryan.                                      11 Sep 1832
     Stephen - Bonhomme Tp, St. Louis Co., took up a bay mare ae 11-12y
              and a bay mare with a colt ae 2y, each appraised at $19
                                                   (cont)
     MOR
                                   80

HANCOCK, Stephen - James Long & Thomas Caulk. Hartly Lanham JP.                          15 Apr 1828
    cont.      - took up a bay mare ae 5y appraised at $20 by Hugh Miller              27 Dec 1831
                 and James Long. Henry Smith JP.
    William - Charrette Twp, Montgomery Co.; took up a bay horse                       21 Jul 1829
                 appraised at $20. James Hughes JP.
HANEY, Joseph - Jefferson Co.; took up a flatboat appraised at $50 by                  28 Apr 1829
                 Henry Hendrick and William Slater.
    Thomas - JP, stray taken up by George Reed.                                        31 Mar 1829
HANKINSON, A. C. - "new and cheap" goods, wholesale, retail, in the                     8 Nov 1831
                 building formerly occupied by John Lee, St. Louis.
HANLY, Barnabas - offers the farm of John Kinkade, near Florissant, for sale.           3 Mar 1829
* HANNA, William - appraised a stray taken up by William Triplett.                      6 Jan 1829
HANSFORD, Hiram - appraised a stray taken up by Joshua Wells.                           27 Dec 1831
* HANNA, William - appraised a stray taken up by Jonathan St. Clear.                    9 Mar 1826
HANSELL, B. - JP, stray taken up by Samuel Graham.                                     11 Apr 1825
HANSON, A. - appraised a stray taken up by James Robinson.                              9 Sep 1828
HARBISON, Abner - appraised a stray taken up by Thomas Keathley.                       12 Jan 1830
HARDWICK, Margaret - defendant, with others, in a suit by David McNair to               4 May 1826
                 regain possession of a house, St. Charles.
HARBISON, Harvy - Bonhomme Twp, St. Louis Co.; took up a roan filly ae ly             12 Jan 1830
                 appraised at $15 by Abner Harbison & William Hooper.
                                                           Henry McCullough JP.
               - took up a bay filly ae 2y appraised at $15 by Abner                   15 Nov 1831
                 Harbison & A. W. Miller. McCullough JP.
    Thomas - Bonhomme Twp, St. Louis Co.; took up a roan horse                         15 Nov 1831
                 ae 3y appraised at $20 by Jonathan St. Clair &
                 Abner Harbison. McCullough JP.
HARDESTY, John - Bonhomme Twp, St. Louis Co.; took up a sorrel horse ae                 5 Jan 1830
                 6 y appraised at $15 by Jeremiah Smith & John B. Wheeler.
HARRIS, Audley P. - Bonhomme Twp, St. Louis Co.; JP, strays taken up by
                 Joshua Burckhartt (25 May 1826), John Jump (4 Jan 1827)
                 Spyrus Palmer (15 Apr 1828) and William Downing.                       3 Feb 1829
    Benjamin - appraised a stray taken up by Andrew Rice.                              23 Nov 1826
HARRISON, Ferry - Merrimack Twp, Franklin Co.; took up an iron gray mare                8 Feb 1831
                 ae 2y appraised at $16 by Wm. Harrison & Macom Wheeler.
                                                           Samuel Conn JP.
    G. H. - opens an. Academy in the house of Mr. Coles at 4th &                        1 Nov 1831
                                                           Locust, St. Louis.
    Jesse - his house in St. Charles has been taken by H. B. Talbot                    11 Dec 1832
                 who will open a House of Entertainment there.
    Joshua - appraised a stray taken up by Justus Post.                                29 May 1832
    Reuben - St. John's Twp, Franklin Co.; took up a bay horse                         24 Feb 1829
                 ae 6-7y appraised at $30 by Phineas Adams & Oliver McEwn.
    Thomas - St. Louis Twp, St. Louis Co.; took up a sorrel mare                       14 Dec 1826
                 ae 4y appraised at $15 by Mark Sappington & Isaac
                 Kirkland. Thomas Sappington JP.
               - took up a bright bay horse ae 9-10y appraised at $20                   4 May 1830
                 by Andrew King & Learden Posey.
    William - Washington Co., 25 miles west of Potosi,offers $20                       30 Nov 1830
                 reward for runaway Negro Peter Inks.
               - appraised a stray taken up by John Twetty.                            31 Jul 1832
HART, Armstrong - St. John's Twp, Franklin Co.; JP, stray taken up by                  19 Feb 1828
                                                           Isaiah Todd.
    John S. & William S. - form Hart, Black & Co., druggists, with                     19 Apr 1831
                                                           J. R. Black.
    John J. - appraised a stray taken up by David Martin.                              10 Jan 1832
HARTLEY, James - a wagon-maker, took over Edward Harrington's shop.                    18 Aug 1829
               - moved carriage and blacksmith shop to 2nd & Pine.                      3 May 1831
HARVY, David - runaway apprentice of George Morton, carpenter.                          2 Aug 1824
HASCALL, E. N. - offers a liberal reward for information about three large
                 steers strayed from the farm of Capt. R. H. Price at                   9 Nov 1826
                 Mine-a-Breton.
               - offers $5 reward for a strayed bay mare, supposed to have             11 Feb 1827
                 a colt with her, near St. Louis.
HASKILL, Charles - defendant, suit for $500 by William H. Savage, in                   10 Jan 1825
                                                           Franklin Co.

                MOR

HAWKINS, John "on his plantation" in Washington Co., took up a pale
    sorrel mare ae 6-7y appraised at $37.50 by Lewis Edgar  13 Nov 1832
    and Robert W. Boggs.  John Brickey JP.
HAYDEN, James H. - appraised a stray taken up by Samuel McMillan.   6 Sep 1831
HAYES, Boone - appraised a stray taken up by Samuel Boone.     8 Dec 1829
HAYS, Delilah - petition for divorce in the Legislature, but her
    husband's name is not shown.           25 Jan 1831
  Elizabeth - "late Glanton," petition for divorce from Greenup
    Hays in the Legislature.            3 Feb 1829
  James - Loutre Twp, Montgomery Co.; took up a bay mare ae 3y and a
    red bay mare ae 2y appraised at $50 total by John & Samuel  29 Jul 1828
    Hays.  Joseph Howard JP.
  William - sues Henry McLaughlin, a dispute over land ownership,   4 Jan 1827
    in the St. Charles Circuit Court.
HEARST, John - Richwoods Twp, Washington Co.; took up a bay mare ae 3y
    appraised at $25 by Charles Yets & Ovesey Baker.    14 Apr 1829
    Moses Ferguson JP.
HEATHERLY, Osias - Franklin Co.; took up a sorrel horse ae 12-13y
    appraised at $35 by William Brown & John Daviss.    26 May 1829
    Jesse McDonald JP.
HEBERT, Bazile - bankrupt, St. Louis.           16 Feb 1824
HEIFNER, Thomas - appraised a stray taken up by Daniel Sullivan.  20 Oct 1829
HELM, Benjamin F. - appraised a stray taken up by John Massey.   7 Aug 1832
HEMPSTEAD, John - appraised a stray taken up by Spyrus Palmer.   15 Apr 1828
  - Bonhomme Twp, St. Louis Co.; took up a dark bay horse
    ae 13y appraised at $19 by Jedediah Kingsley & William   17 Feb 1829
    Page.  Audley P. Harris JP.
  - appraised a stray taken up by Andrew Kinkead.      16 Nov 1830
  - " by Zachariah Tyler.             13 Nov 1832
  Thomas & Cornelia - divorce petition in the Legislature.   25 Jan 1831
HENDERSHOT, John D. - defendant, suit for $300 by Wm. H. Savage.  2 Oct 1832
HENDRICK, Harrison - Cuivre Twp, Pike Co.; JP, strays taken up by Vincent
    Moor (17 Jun 1828), John Crow (29 Jun 1830) and
    Henry Branstutter.              10 Jan 1832
HENDRICKS, D. - Liberty Twp, Marion Co.; JP, stray taken up by   23 Sep 1828
    Zephaniah Robnett.
HENDRICKS, Henry - Platin Twp, Jefferson Co.; took up a brown horse ae 12y
    appraised at $10 by William Bartlett & Robert     10 Feb 1829
    Jamieson.  E. Dugan JP.
  - appraised a flatboat taken up by Joseph Haney.     28 Apr 1829
HENRY, Malcolm - his wife Elizabeth has left his bed and board.   6 Oct 1829
  Mrs. R. - "milliner and mantua-maker," opens a business in the  7 Feb 1825
    house of Mme. Primm, St. Louis.
  Thomas - Bowles Twp, Franklin Co.; JP, strays taken up by Robert
    Chunning (19 Jul 1827), Jacob Cole (29 Nov 1827), Uriah
    Burns (13 Jul 1830) and Hannah Morris.      11 Jan 1831
HENSLEY, Fleming - appraised a stray taken up by Barksdale Sledd.  15 Feb 1831
HEPMITH, William - appraised a stray taken up by James Forrest.   11 May 1830
HERRINGTON, Edward - advertises for runaway apprentice Nicholas Tiernan. 27 May 1828
  - wagonmaker James Hartley takes over his shop.     18 Aug 1829
  - offers $5 reward for runaway apprentice Joseph Bartole. 15 Mar 1831
  Joshua - Joachim Twp, Jefferson Co.; took up a chestnut sorrel
    ae 9y appraised at $25 by Charles Stuart & George   5 Oct 1826
    Wash.  Young Guffee JP.
  - took up a bright bay filly ae 4y appraised at $10 by   29 Mar 1827
    Michael Brindley & Hezekiah Wright. Chauncey Smith JP.
  - took up a brown mare ae 11y appraised at $10.50 and
    a bright bay mare ae 4y at $13 by John Gamale &   24 Jun 1828
    Reuben Gore.  Smith JP.
HERVIN, Ferdinand - Perry Twp, St. Francois Co.; took up a bay mare ae 7y 18 Dec 1832
    appraised at $30 by Robert Chapman & Constantine Perkins.
HEWITT, James - Belleview Twp, Washington Co.; took up a sorrel horse ae
    11y appraised at $4 and a bay filly at $4 by John   5 Jul 1827
    Johnston & Thomas Brock.  A. Goforth JP.
  Lemuel - suit in chancery in Washington Co. vs Wm. Boydston et al. 27 Sep 1824
  William - Belleview Twp, Washington Co.; took up a dark sorrel
    mare ae 3y appraised at $17.50 by John Johnson &   28 Jul 1829
    John L. Goforth.  Andrew Goforth JP.

    MOR

HIBBARD, James - appraised a stray taken up by David Fine.                                    23 Dec 1828
HIBLER, Daniel - his wife Lydia has left his bed and board.                                    4 May 1826
    Thomas - took up a bay mare ae 4y appraised at $25 by Wm. Page &                          14 Dec 1830
        W. C. Kinkead. H. Sappington JP.
HICKEY, Nathaniel - appraised a stray taken up by Palmer Breckenridge.                        13 Sep 1827
HICKMAN, Jesse - appraised a stray taken up by Richard Lowe.                                  24 Jul 1832
    Noah & William - appraised a stray taken up by John Wilson.                               27 Nov 1832
    Thomas - near Franklin, Howard Co.; offers a liberal reward                               16 Aug 1827
        for a runaway Negro.
    William - Bonhomme Twp, St. Louis Co.; took up a chestnut sorrel
        horse ae 4y appraised at $30 by John Wilson and                                       27 Nov 1832
        Noah Hickman. H. Smith JP.
HICKS, Henry - appraised a stray taken up by Joseph Neill Sr.                                 31 May 1831
    Lewis - offers a $5 reward for a strayed horse; he lives near                             29 Jul 1828
        Mr. Foulk's grocery.
HIGGINS, Dennis - obtained a grocer's license in St. Louis.                                   29 May 1832
HIGHSMITH, David - appraised a stray taken up by Francis Witherton.                           24 Mar 1829
HIGH, John - William Bonnet warns the public not to accept a note                             26 Jul 1827
        he gave Hight.
HILDERBRAND, David - Jefferson Co.; took up a sorrel horse ae 17y
        appraised at $11 by Thomas Medley & George W.                                          2 Feb 1830
        Graham. Samuel Graham JP.
HILL, Ames - offers $20 reward for two horses strayed or stolen, at the                        1 Nov 1827
        North St. Louis Steam Mill.
    William - dissolves partnership with William McGunnegle in a                              14 Oct 1828
        commission house in St. Louis.
    - sues Oliver Hudson for $2000 damages, St. Louis.                                        26 Apr 1831
HIMES, George W. - has bought an interest in Wm. Truesdell's mills on                         15 Nov 1827
        the Gasconade River where a saw mill is being built;
        lumber will be sent to him.
    - not responsible for transaction made by Truesdell;                                      28 Oct 1828
        Truesdell says the same thing in the same issue.
HINESLEY, Allen - appraised a stray taken up by Morton Fulbright.                              1 Aug 1825
HINKSON, Benjamin Harrison - Liberty Twp, Washington Co.; took up a horse
        ae 3y appraised at $27.50 by John Morrison                                            30 Jan 1828
        & James Renfrow. W. Hinkson JP.
    - appraised a stray taken up by John Twetty.                                              31 Jul 1832
    William - JP, stray taken up by John Twetty.                                              31 Jul 1832
HINSON, John - appraised a stray taken up by Hugh Logan.                                       5 Apr 1831
HODGES, Benjamin - appraised a stray taken up by George Barnes.                               25 May 1826
    David - dissolved partnership with James Keyte.                                            3 May 1831
    George J. - appraised a stray taken up by Washington Edgar.                               31 Jul 1832
HOFFA, John - bankrupt, St. Louis.                                                            9 Nov 1826
HOFFMAN, H. L. - St. Louis; offers "a fresh supply of kine pock matter,
        parents and others wishing to avail themselves of this                               16 Feb 1826
        sure protection against smallpox can be vaccinated . . "
        (at their own home or at his store).
    - asks for information about a stolen saddle.                                              3 Jan 1832
HOGELAND, William - "near Columbia in St. Louis County," took up a brown
        mare ae 7y appraised at $50 by John Pulman, William                                  28 Jun 1824
        Paul, & James James. W. Hunt JP.
HOLBERT, E. G. - appraised a stray taken up by Samuel Welborn.                                 3 Aug 1830
    James - Pendleton Twp, St. Francois Co.; took up a brown bay
        horse ae 10-12y appraised at $20 by E. G. Holbert &                                    3 Aug 1830
        Lewis Kennon. John Sherrill JP.
HOLDEN, Edward - living on Salt River, advised that his runaway Negro                         30 Oct 1832
        is in jail in St. Louis.
HOLLMAN, Frederick - sued for trespass by Robert Pogue, surviving                             17 Dec 1823
        partner of Robert & George Pogue.
HOLLYMAN, John - sues Charles N. Calbert for $150 damages in the                               7 Dec 1830
        Marion Co. Circuit Court.
HOLLOWAY, Absalom - St. Louis Co.; took up a bay horse ae 6y appraised                        15 May 1832
        at $35 by James S. Douglass & Thomas Baber.
        Fergus Ferguson JP.
HOLTON, George - advertises a new book store, Main St., St. Louis.                            24 Aug 1830
    Miss H. S. - opens a Seminary for Young Ladies, St. Louis.                                 8 Feb 1831
HONEY, John W. - dissolves partnership with Elias Bates, Herculaneum.                         22 Mar 1831

        MOR

HOOD, George - with John C. Abbott, sues Isaac G, Gardner for $300.                    13 Sep 1831
HOOK, C. - has taken over the livery stable of John Kerr.                              11 Nov 1828
HOOPER, William - appraised a stray taken up by Harvy Harbison.                        12 Jan 1830
HOOPS, David - Grey Twp, Gasconade Co.; JP, stray taken up by Joseph Racine.  30 Aug 1824
HOPKINS, Thomas - appraised a stray taken up by James Stark.                           17 Mar 1829
         - Femme Osage Twp, St. Charles Co.; JP, strays taken up by
           Solomon Alkire (27 Dec 1831) and by James Silvey.                           25 Sep 1832
    Walker - appraised a stray taken up by Joseph Brown.                               19 Jan 1830
    William H. - partner of Joseph Ely, auction & commission house.                    17 Aug 1830
HORINE, Benjamin - Washington Co.; took up a bay mare ae 4-5y appraised
           at $22 by Aaron Dudley & Philip Menedy; Moses Ferguson JP.  27 Jun 1825
HORNER, E. B. & Co., druggists -their former building taken over by
                                 by J. S. Pease's hardware store.                      23 Nov 1830
HORRELL, Thomas - offers the dwelling house where he lives for rent.                    8 Jul 1828
HORTON, Anthony - Montgomery Co.; took up a horse and mare appraised at
           $40 by James G. Smith & Isaac Ellis. John Curtner JP.       15 Feb 1831
    Hezekiah - appraised a stray taken up by John Carter.                              13 Nov 1832
HOSE, P. W. - appraised a stray taken up by Dr. Frederick Clarke.                      10 Nov 1829
HOSTELLER, John - Peno Twp, Pike Co.; took up a dark iron gray filly ae 2y
           appraised at $22.50 by Alfred Mefford & John                               29 Mar 1831
           McAlister. Alexander Wagoner JP.
HOUGH, Daniel & Asa E. - closing their retail business.                                15 Feb 1831
         - sue George Casner for $300.                                                 10 Jan 1832
HOUGHAN, Thomas - advertises "new books," stationery etc., St. Louis.                   1 Apr 1828
         - asks debtors of later firm Essex & Houghan to pay.                           8 Apr 1828
         - his stock, book store & bindery bought by James C. Essex.  22 May 1832
HOUSE, Joseph - appraised a stray taken up by James L. Kilby.                          11 Aug 1829
HOWARD, Andrew - appraised a stray taken up by Scudder Smith.                           9 Oct 1832
    Benjamin - appraised a stray taken up by Philemon Plummer.                         26 Aug 1828
    Cornelius - Lewiston Twp, Montgomery Co.; took up a brown horse
           ae 9y appraised at $27.50 by Abraham Davidson &                              7 Feb 1828
           Joseph Taylor. James W. Taylor JP.
         - appraised a stray taken up by Shelton Ray.                                  22 Jun 1830
    David - appraised a stray taken up by Benjamin Sharp.                              24 May 1827
    Joseph - Loutre Twp, Montgomery Co.; JP, stray taken up by
           James Hays (29 Jul 1828), by John Freeman (5 Jan 1830)
           and by William Lugs.                                                        31 May 1831
HOWDESHELL, Jacob - appraised a stray taken up by Alexander Emerson.                   15 Aug 1825
HOWELL, John - appraised a stray taken up by John Gill.                                 6 Aug 1823
    Newton - appraised a stray taken up by Mordecai Morgan.                            30 Aug 1831
HOYLE, Lawrence - obtained a merchant's license. St. Louis.                            29 May 1832
HUBBARD, David - appraised a stray taken up by Francis Witherton.                      24 Mar 1829
** HUDSPETH, A. W. - Harmony Twp, Washington Co.; JP, strays taken up by
           John P. Webb (20 Jul 1830) and by Thomas Sterman.                           31 Jul 1832
HUDSON, Isaac - Waverly Twp, Lincoln Co.; took up a chestnut sorrel horse
           ae 9y appraised at $30 by William Hudson & William                          2 Jun 1829
           Owens. Caleb McFarland JP.
    Oliver - opens a new store "opposite Scott & Rule" in St. Louis.                   10 Nov 1829
         - defendant, suit for $2000 damages by Wm. Hill, St. Louis.                   26 Apr 1831
    Thomas - appraised a stray taken up by Joseph W. Sitton.                           13 Jul 1826
** HUDSPETH, Ayres - Harmony Twp, Washington Co.; JP, strays taken up by
           George Smithers (23 Feb 1826) & John Stuart.                                22 Dec 182
         - appraised a stray taken up by Luman Ruggie.                                 11 Jul 1825
         -     " Palmer Breckenridge.                                                  27 Sep 1827
    William - appraised a stray taken up by George Smithers.                           23 Feb 1826
HUETT, L. - appraised a stray taken up by John P. Webb.                                20 Jul 1830
HUFF, John - Washington Co.; took up a sorrel mare ae 7y appraised at $20
           by Wm. C. Smith & John Perry. H. Shurlds JP.               5 Nov 1823
HUGH, John M. - appraised a stray taken up by Jonathan Cottle.                          9 Aug 1827
HUGHES, James - Charrette Twp, Montgomery Co.; JP, strays taken up by
           Micajah Ousley (1 Feb 1827), Dugal Wyatt (7 Feb 1828),
           Wm. Hancock (21 Jul 1829), John Tice (22 Jun 1830), and
           James Noland.                                                               15 Feb 1831
         - took up a dark gray colt appraised at $15, no appraisers                    14 Feb 1832
           shown. Jared Erwin JP.
    Mark - appraised a stray taken up by John Buford.                                   1 Jun 1830
HULL, Uriah - Belleview Twp, Washington Co.; took up an iron gray horse
           ae 2y appraised at $5 by Wm. Montgomery & Wm. Sullied.                       8 Jun 1830
           A. Goforth JP.

                    MOR
                                              84

HUME, John - St. Ferdinand Twp, St. Louis Co.; took up a bay horse ae
   about 10 appraised at $25 by James L. Musick, Vincent                2 Sep 1828
   Browner, & John G. James.  Hugh O'Neil JP.
HUNT, Wesley - Prairie Twp, Montgomery Co.;took up a bay horse ae10-11y
   appraised at $30 by James & Wm. Smith. Horatio Cox JP.               27 Nov 1832
   Warren - bankrupt, St. Louis.                                        13 Sep 1824
HUNTER, Valentine - appraised a stray taken up by Robert Frazer.        22 Jun 1826
HURLS (EARLS), Samuel - believed a principal in the shooting death of
   Charles Rouse at New London.                                         29 Dec 1829
HURRED, Thomas L. - appraised a stray taken up by James Sapp.           29 Jun 1830
HUSKEY, Silas - Joachim Twp, Jefferson Co.; took up a dark bay horse ae 8y
   appraised at $40 by Moses B. Austin & Joseph M. Speed.               6 Apr 1830
   G. Hammond JP.
HUTCHINGS, Green - Dardenne Twp, St. Charles Co.; JP, strays taken up by
   Thomas H. Kelly (16 Dec 1828) & Benjamin Teters.                     29 Dec 1829
   Thomas - appraised a stray taken up by Laban Miner.                  28 Jun 1827
HUTTON, Samuel - Boeuf Twp, Franklin Co.; took up a black mare ae 5-6y,
   appraised by Oliver McEune & J. G. Green, amount not                 11 May 1830
   shown.  Owens JP.
HYATT, John - appraised a stray taken up by Elmsly Fount.               28 Jun 1831
IMBODEN(S), Benjamin - appraised a stray taken up by Wm. Bounds.        19 Mar 1823
   - " by Henry H. Snider.                                              29 Aug 1825
   David - appraised a stray taken up by Gabriel Prewett.               23 Feb 1826
INGOLDSBY, Felix - with Jacob S. Platt & Aquilla G. Stout, sues
   William M. Read for $2000.                                           2 Oct 1832
INGRAM, Arthur - dissolves partnership with Henry Reily.                14 Jun 1824
   Thomas - dissolves partnership with Richard H. McGill.               4 Jan 1831
   - sues David Duncan for $5000.                                       6 Sep 1831
INKS, Elisha G. - appraised a stray taken up by Robert Kelso.           18 Oct 1831
   Peter - a runaway Negro; William Harrison, Potosi, offers a $25
   reward. (Actually, shown as 25m west of Potosi.)                     30 Nov 1830
INSKEEP, James - has lost a hair trunk shipped from Fever River on a
   keel boat.                                                           18 Oct 1827
IRVINE, Albert G. - Loutre Twp, Montgomery Co.; JP, strays taken up by
   John Ferguson (19 Jul 1827), Lewis Jones (13 Dec 1827)
   and John Best.                                                       2 Jun 1829
   John A. - dissolves partnership with B. F. Payne, Potosi.            4 Aug 1829
   Robert - appraised a stray taken up by Jeremiah Moore.               2 Jul 1823
   - JP, stray taken up by James L. Kilby.                              11 Aug 1829
ISLER, Stephen - appraised a stray taken up by William Burns.           15 Dec 1829
IVERS, J. T. - dissolves partnership with Thomas Barnett.               8 Nov 1831
JACKSON, Elisha - appraised a stray taken up by James Martin.           29 Mar 1831
   Joseph vs Mary, divorce, Pike Co. Circuit Court.                     11 Jun 1823
   Thomas - Hurricane Twp, Lincoln Co.; took up two horses appraised
   at $50.50 by Alfred Gordon & Robinson Copeland.                      13 Sep 1827
   Benjamin Allen JP.
JAMES, James - appraised a stray taken up by William Hogeland.          28 Jun 1824
   John G. - appraised a stray taken up by John Hume.                   2 Sep 1828
   Robert - Howard Co., "near Foster's Prairie," offers a reward
   for runaway Negro Ned.                                               15 Mar 1831
   William - appraised a stray taken up by Dugal Wyatt.                 12 Aug 1828
JAMESON, Allen - took up a bay mare ae 10y appraised at $12 by Sherman
   Cottle & Robert E. Mott. William W. Woodbridge JP.                   30 Nov 1826
JAMIESON, Robert - appraised a stray taken up by Henry Hendricks.       10 Feb 1829
JAMISON, Allen - appraised a stray taken up by Thomas Slavens.          13 Mar 1832
   George - Union Twp, Washington Co.; JP, stray taken up by
   Hardy Merrill.                                                       27 May 1828
   Hugh M. - took up a bay horse ae 7y appraised at $35 and a bay
   horse ae 10-11y appraised at $20 by Bennett and                      4 Mar 1828
   Richard Lowe, Thomas Mason JP; also appraised a
   stray taken up by Benjamin Bennett.
   Hubbard and Joseph - St. John's Twp, Franklin Co.; took up a black
   horse ae 9-10y appraised at $15 by Isaac                             15 Jun 1830
   McCormick & John Prather.  W. G. Owens JP.
   John vs Nancy, divorce, Pike Co.                                     16 Mar 1830
JANNERET, Harriet - asks customers who left watches with her late husband
   to retrieve them.                                                    12 Oct 1830
JAQUES, Lewis - sues Thomas Byrn for $3000.                             6 Sep 1831

   MOR

85

JEFFRIES, Charles R. - Bowles Twp, Franklin Co.; took up a black mare ae
   8-9y appraised at $50 by James W. Lewis & Matthew  21 Jul 1829
   Cole. Jonathan Potts JP.
JOHNS, Henry - appraised a stray taken up by Henry Robust.  26 Jun 1832
  Jack Jr. - Calvy Twp, Franklin Co.; took up a black filly ae 3y
   appraised at $25 by Marshall Duncan & William King.  22 Dec 1829
   Jonathan Potts JP.
JOHNSON, Evens - picked up two sorrel mares 16 miles below St. Charles. 17 Nov 1829
  Henry - dissolved partnership with Philip Cassilly.  31 Mar 1829
  A. L. & Co. - open a new store at Main & Olive in St. Louis in  20 Jul 1830
   building formerly occupied by Graham & Kerr.
   - moved to Boonville.  30 Aug 1831
   - own a sawmill at Hannibal, want to buy oak, ash,  5 Jun 1832
   walnut, cherry, and maple.
  John - appraised a stray taken up by Green B. Baxter.  21 Sep 1826
   - " by William Hewitt.  28 Jul 1829
   - " by James Boyers.  22 Dec 1829
   - " by Sidney George.  29 Nov 1831
   - " by Joshua Wells.  27 Dec 1831
  John A. - appraised a stray taken up by Thomas Shores.  14 Apr 1829
  Josiah - Liberty Twp, Washington Co.; JP, stray taken up by  14 Apr 1829
   Thomas Shores.
   - took up a sorrel horse ae 9-10y appraised at $25 by  2 Oct 1832
   Richard Summers & Wm. McKinzie. Charles Springer JP.
JOHNSTON, Benjamin Sr. - appraised a skiff taken up by Charles Geiger. 25 May 1830
  G. W. - appraised a stray taken up by Alden Hammond.  30 Aug 1831
  James - Boeuf Twp, Franklin Co.; took up a yellow bay mare ae 6y, 9 Sep 1828
   with a colt, appraised at $20 by Hiram Estes & John Jump.
   - took up a bay mare ae 7y appraised at $25 by Nathan  2 Mar 1830
   Richardson & Hiram Estes. Wm. G. Owens JP.
  John - appraised a stray taken up by James Hewitt.  5 Jul 1827
JONES, David - Pendleton Twp, St. Francois Co.; took up a dark bay mare
   ae 8y appraised at $50 by Joshua Kinworthy & Benjamin  16 Feb 1830
   Burnhard. Richard Murphy JP.
  J. H. - advertises moss and cotton mattresses.  5 Aug 1828
  James - appraised a stray taken up by Michael J. Noyes.  21 Jun 1827
   - found "adrift in the Mississippi, about 4 miles north of  2 Oct 1832
   Herculaneum," a one-horse cart painted blue, with a dead
   horse harnessed to it. Value $30; will owner please claim.
  John - took up a brown bay mare ae 4y appraised at $20 by William 8 Jun 1826
   Twitty & Alexander Lasley. Jonathan Potts JP.
   - appraised a stray taken up by Richard Lowe.  24 Jul 1832
  John L. - defendant in a suit for $500 by John Carman and one for 13 Sep 1831
   $300 by William A. Coons.
  Lewis - Loutre Twp, Montgomery Co.; took up a mare ae 4y appraised 13 Dec 1827
   at $30 by Mathias McGirk & L. H. Neill. Albert Irvine JP.
  Stephen - his property sold to satisfy a claim of James Tanner. 6 Nov 1832
   - appraised a stray taken up by Thomas Cranch.  25 Dec 1832
  Theodore - Clerk of the Marion Circuit Court.  7 Dec 1830
JORDAN, John - Buffalo Twp, Pike Co.; JP, stray taken up by Enoch Emerson. 8 Mar 1827
  Robert - appraised a stray taken up by John Hall.  25 Jan 1831
JUMP, John - Bonhomme Twp, St. Louis Co.; took up a bright bay mare ae 5y 4 Jan 1827
   appraised at $20 by Benjamin Hancock & Peter Jump.
   A. P. Harris JP.
   - appraised a stray taken up by James Johnston.  9 Sep 1828
KASSON, Archy - with William Leavenworth, defendant in a suit for $300 21 Aug 1832
   damages by Thomas Barnett.
   - defendant in a suit for $500 by Peter & Robert McQueen. 28 Aug 1832
KEADY, Samuel - sues Alanson Mead for $800, St. Charles.  30 Aug 1831
KEATHLEY, Thomas - Bonhomme Twp, St. Louis Co.; took up a bay filly ae 2y 
   appraised at $18 by Henry Scroggins & Abner  12 Jan 1830
   Harbison. McCullough JP.
KEATLEY, William - Bonhomme Twp, St. Louis Co.; took up a dark bay horse 
   ae 2y appraised at $10 by Diedrick Schultze & John  2 Mar 1826
   Calvert. Thomas Mason JP.
KEEN, R. L. - partner of J. H. Page in a commission business.  18 May 1830
KEENEY, James - Peno Twp, Pike Co.; took up a claybank horse appraised at 15 Feb 1831
   $18 by E. B. Sinclair & Jacob Dennis. Alex'r Waggener JP.

KEENY, Michael - took up a bay horse ae 2-3y appraised at $28 by Asa
    Griffith & Archibald Caldwell. Daniel Griffith JP. ........ 3 Oct 1825
KEER, Thomas G. - appraised a stray taken up by John Crow. ........ 29 Jun 1830
KEESACKER, John - offers for sale a two-story log house in St. Louis,
    on a 20' x 80' lot. ........ 1 Aug 1825
KELLY, Christopher - appraised a stray taken up by Thomas Triplett. ........ 29 May 1832
    Thomas H. - Dardenne Twp, St. Charles Co.; took up a bright
        sorrel mare ae 4y appraised at $35 by Lazarus ........ 16 Dec 1828
        McFall & Louis Strong. Green Hutchings JP.
KELSO, Robert - Bonhomme Twp, St. Louis Co.; took up a yellow bay mare
    ae 7y appraised at $40 by Henry Votaw & Elisha Inks. ........ 18 Oct 1831
        Henry McCullough JP.
KEMPER, John F. - sues Joseph Swager for $1848.25. ........ 17 May 1831
KENNEDA, Abraham - appraised a stray taken up by Thomas Chambers. ........ 15 Jul 1828
KENNEDY, Azeriah - lost a pocketbook containing $100 cash. ........ 19 Jul 1831
    James - appraised a stray taken up by Alexander Smith. ........ 27 May 1828
    John - appraised a stray taken up by Laken Walker. ........ 18 Dec 1832
    Sarah - Elkhorn Twp, Montgomery Co.; took up a yellow bay mare
        ae 5y appraised at $30 and a bay horse ae 3y, $30, and a ........ 17 Aug 1826
        colt, $5, by Guyan (Gekkendy?) and Thomas Chambers.
        George Clay JP. (Probably should be Guyan Kennedy?)
KENNEL, Etienne - appraised a stray taken up by Sylvester Baradan. ........ 2 Apr 1823
KENNETT, James - partner of James M. White, Selma. ........ 10 Aug 1830
KENNON, Lewis - appraised a stray taken up by James Holbert. ........ 3 Aug 1830
KENT, John - Elkhorn Twp, Montgomery Co.; took up a mare and foal
    appraised at $52 by Neil McCan and Samuel F. Dougherty. ........ 17 Aug 1830
        Benoni McClure JP.
KERR, John - his livery stable taken over by C. Hook. ........ 11 Nov 1828
    Matthew & John - dissolve partnership, business will be taken over ........ 14 Jan 1824
        by John & Augustus Kerr.
    Richard - next friend of Elizabeth Steele in her divorce suit. ........ 28 Oct 1828
    William - next friend of Margaret Brown in her divorce suit, ........ 18 Oct 1831
        Pike Co.
KEYTE, James - dissolves partnership with David Hodges. ........ 3 May 1831
KIAN, Anthony - appraised a stray taken up by John Wright. ........ 5 Jan 1830
KIBBY, Amos - of St. Charles; warns the public not to accept a mortgage
    given him by Solomon Whitley for "certain Negroes." ........ 1 Oct 1823
KILBY, James L. - took up two horses appraised at $90 by Jeremiah Moore &
    Joseph House. Robert Irvine JP. ........ 11 Aug 1829
KINEMONT, Garrison B. - appraised a stray taken up by Gabriel Prewett. ........ 23 Feb 1826
KING, Andrew - appraised a stray taken up by Thomas Harrison. ........ 4 May 1830
    - " by Leaden Posey, one (22 Nov 1831) and another. ........ 27 Nov 1832
    George - appraised a stray taken up by Alexander McCourtney Jr. ........ 8 Jun 1826
    - Bonhomme Twp, St. Louis Co.; took up a bay horse ae 5y
        appraised at $25 by Jeremiah Smith and Jonathan Carder. ........ 7 Dec 1830
        Henry Smith JP.
    Samuel - Boon Twp?; took up a dark bay mare ae 6y appraised at
        $17.50 by Thomas Apling & George W. Perry. ........ 13 Jul 1830
        William Truesdell JP.
    Solomon - St. Louis Co.; took up a black horse ae 7y appraised at
        $25 by Henry Watson & James McDonald. Fergus Ferguson JP. ........ 8 Jun 1830
    William - appraised a stray taken up by Samuel Whitworth. ........ 23 Feb 1826
    - " by Plato Cole (2 Dec 1828) and by Jack Johns Jr. ........ 22 Dec 1829
KINGSLEY, Jedediah - appraised a stray taken up by John Hempstead. ........ 17 Feb 1829
KINKEAD, Alexander - Bonhomme Twp, St. Louis Co.; took up a bright sorrel
    horse ae 14y appraised at $20 by Thomas Mason ........ 20 Oct 1829
        & Lawrence Carder. Henry Smith JP.
    Andrew - appraised a stray taken up by William Orr. ........ 2 Sep 1828
    - Bonhomme Twp, St. Louis Co.; took up a black horse
        ae 3y appraised at $45 by John Hempstead and ........ 16 Nov 1830
        U. C. Kinkead. H. Sappington JP.
    W. C. - appraised a stray taken up by Thomas Hibler. ........ 14 Dec 1830
    Walter - Bonhomme Twp, St. Louis Co.; took up a white horse
        ae 4y appraised at $17 by Cornelius Demerce and ........ 28 Dec 1826
        Josiah H. Davidson. Hartley Lanham JP.
KINNE, O. A. - St. Louis; advertises cornmeal, beans, corn, butter, rice,
    green coffee, sugar, etc. ........ 31 Jul 1832
    - advertises produce, a brokerage, a commission house, ........ 7 Aug 1832
        at Water & Chestnut Sts.
    MOR

KINWORTHY, Joshua - appraised a stray taken up by David Jones.                                16 Feb 1830
KIRKER, James - his land sold to satisfy a debt to George W. Scott,
                                                      St. Charles.                            7 Mar 1832
           - suit for $1000 damages in the St. Louis Circuit Court.                           26 Apr 1831
KIRKLAND, Isaac - appraised a stray taken up by Thomas Harrison.                              14 Dec 1826
KIRKPATRICK, Wallace - appraised a stray taken up by Thomas Spalding.                          2 Nov 1830
KISSINGER, Henry -Pike Co., four miles south of Clarksville, took up a
                 sorrel mare ae 3y appraised at $25 by John Stark &                            3 Jan 1832
                 William Mountjoy. C. C. Eastin JP.
KIZER, James - defendant, suit for $125 debt by James Pool, St. Louis.                         8 Jun 1826
KLUNK, Joseph - St. Louis; offers two houses at the corner of 3rd-Chestnut
                 for sale or rent.                                                            28 Dec 1826
KNOLTON, William - appraised a stray taken up by Enoch Emerson.                                8 Mar 1827
KNOTT, Osborn - appraised a stray taken up by William Watson.                                  8 Jun 1826
           - " by Joseph Spalding.                                                             8 Feb 1827
KNOX, George Jr. - of Franklin; taken into the firm of White & Lane,
                 which will be renamed Lane, Knox & Co.                                       18 Oct 1827
KOPMAN, Joseph - new drygoods store on Main St., St. Louis.                                    5 Jan 1830
KYLE, David - Property of James Gunsolis sold to satisfy a claim of
                 Kyle & John McCausland.                                                       5 Jul 1831
           - advertises a "new establishment" on Main St., St. Louis -
                 hardware, groceries, liquor, etc.                                             3 Jan 1832
           - moving from St. Louis, selling out.  (29 May 1832) but
                                                     still in business.                       27 Nov 1832
LaBEAUME, P. A. - bankrupt, St. Louis.                                                         9 Nov 1830
LADUKE, Morris vs Eulalie, divorce, St. Charles Circuit Court.                                20 Oct 1829
LAMBETH, Aaron - appraised a stray taken up by Reuben League.                                 21 Oct 1828
LANE, James S. - partner of H. C. Simmons, auction & commission house.                         7 Dec 1830
LANHAM, Hartly - Bonhomme Twp, St. Louis Co.; JP, strays taken up by
                 Green B. Baxter (21 Sep 1826) & Stephen Hancock.                             15 Apr 1828
        James B. - John Shannons warns the public not to accept a note
                 he gave Lanham.                                                              30 Nov 1830
LANIUS, Jacob - bankrupt, Washington Co.                                                       6 Oct 1829
LARRABEE, Russell - bankrupt, St. Louis.                                                      28 Mar 1825
LARSH, Abraham - obtained a merchant's license, St. Louis.                                    29 May 1832
LASIEUR, Francis - Portage des Sioux Twp, St. Charles Co.; JP, stray
                 taken up by John Smeltzer.                                                   16 Oct 1832
LASLEY, Alexander - appraised a stray taken up by John Jones.                                  8 June 1826
           - " by Plato Cole.                                                                  2 Dec 1828
           - Franklin Co.; his wife Agnes has left his bed & board.                           23 Sep 1828
LAVENDER, Anderson - defendant in a mortgage-foreclosure suit by
                 Francis Howell Sr., St. Charles.                                             11 Jan 1827
LAWLESS, Armstead - defendant in a suit by S. T. & James G. McKenney
                 for $500.                                                                    21 Aug 1832
LAWRENCE, Daniel - principal of the Lawrence Seminary for Young Ladies.                       29 Mar 1831
LEACH, F. B. - offers $10 reward for the delivery of two strayed horses
                 to him at Farmers' Hotel, Main St., St. Louis.                                6 Dec 1827
LEAGUE, Reuben - Perry Twp, St. Francois Co.; took up a dun horse ae 3y
                 appraised at $8 and a sorrel horse ae 15y, $9, by                            21 Oct 1828
                 Aaron Lambeth & Jacob Mostillers. H. Poston JP.
           - appraised a stray taken up by Stokely Parker.                                    24 Mar 1829
LEAMING, Thomas F. - sold his interest in a store in St. Louis to
                 James Clemens Jr.                                                            28 Jun 1824
LeDUC, Lewis - advertises dyeing and scouring.                                                24 May 1831
LEE, James - defendant, suit for trespass, $200, by Edward Tracy &
                 Charles Wahrendorf.                                                          30 Aug 1827
        John - dissolves partnership with W. A. Beard.                                        19 May 1829
           - Elkhorn Twp, Montgomery Co.; took up a black horse ae 6y
                 appraised at $40 by James Long & Talton Martin. C. Williams JP.              12 Apr 1831
        Joseph - barber and hairdresser, moved to Main & Prune, St. Louis.                    17 Mar 1829
LEMASTERS, Evin - St. Charles Twp, St. Charles Co.; took up a dapple gray
                 mare ae 5-6y appraised at $30 by James Goodrich &                            10 Jul 1832
                 John Oliver. James Green JP.
LEPS, Samuel - appraised a stray taken up by James Longwith.                                  26 Apr 1827
LESSIEUR, Edward - runaway apprentice of W. R. Grimsley. Ae 19, 5'6",
                 dark, freckled. $5 reward if taken in the state,                             25 Mar 1828
                 $20 if taken outside.

                 MOR

LESTER, Daniel - Black River Twp, Washington Co.; JP, stray taken up by       1 Jun 1830
                                                        John Buford.
        Jesse - appraised a stray taken up by John Buford.                    "
LETCHER, Isaac A. - sued Daniel McConnel for $500.                            31 May 1831
LEWALLEN, Samuel - Peno Twp, Pike Co.; JP, stray taken up by John Tally.      17 Jun 1828
LEWIS, George - River des Peres, St. Louis Co.; took up a chestnut sorrel
        mare ae 6y appraised at $30 by Thornton Grimsley &                    31 Aug 1830
        George Gordon. Garnier JP.
        James W. - appraised a stray taken up by Charles R. Jeffries.         21 Jul 1829
        Samuel - appraised a stray taken up by William Sitton.                20 Aug 1823
        Samuel H. - appraised a stray taken up by David Markle.               20 Jan 1829
        William W. - next friend of Parthenia Boyce in her divorce suit.      10 Mar 1829
LIGGETT, Joseph - his copper-and-tin manufactory bought by Thomas &           14 Sep 1826
                                                        William Andrews.
        - dissolves partnership with Thomas Andrews.                          17 Mar 1829
LIKE, Abraham - David Delanay's land sold to justify a debt to Like.          7 Mar 1832
LILES, Joseph - appraised a stray taken up by Thomas Chambers.                15 Jul 1828
LILLY, John Jr. - appraised a stray taken up by William Watson.               8 Jun 1826
LINDSEY, John - Hurricane Twp, Lincoln Co.; JP, stray taken up by             1 Jun 1830
                                                        Andrew Tilford.
        - Monroe Twp, Lincoln Co.; JP, " by Robert Stuart.                    24 Jan 1832
LINE, William - Wayne Co.; defendant, suit for debt by Richard Cowan.         5 Sep 1825
LINK, Allen - Bonhomme Twp, St. Louis Co.; took up a bay mare & colt
        appraised at $25 by James Votaw & Nathaniel W. Morris.                26 Jul 1831
                                                        H. McCullough JP.
        Alton - appraised a stray taken up by John Brackenridge.              11 May 1830
        Campbell - appraised a stray taken up by William Hawkins.             2 Nov 1830
        Henry - Bonhomme Twp, St. Louis Co.; took up a bay horse ae 5-6y      9 Jun 1829
        appraised at $25 by C. G. & Andrew Link. A.P. Harris JP.
        John M. - appraised a stray taken up by Ennis Vaughn.                 26 Jun 1832
LIVERMORE, Samuel - defendant in an attachment suit in the St. Louis Co.
                        Court, by William F. Peterson & Israel Monroe.        10 Dec 1823
LOCKLAND, George - Bonhomme Twp, St. Louis Co.; took up a bay mare ae 10
                appraised at $15 by W.M. Bills & John P. Boice.               27 Nov 1832
                                                        H. Sappington JP.
LOGAN, David - Logan Twp, Wayne Co.; took up a chestnut sorrel mare ae 7y
                appraised at $30 by James & Clark Biggers & Phinehas          15 Nov 1854
                Williams. John Logan JP.
        George M. - lost a flat gold seal, offers $5 reward.                  13 Mar 1832
        Henry - appraised a stray taken up by James Davis.                    25 Jan 1831
        Hugh - Montgomery Co.; took up a deep red sorrel mare ae 2y           5 Apr 1831
                appraised at $20 by John Hinson & James G. Smith. Curtner JP.
LOISE, Paul - bankrupt, St. Louis.                                            25 Oct 1824
LONG, Andrew J. - appraised a stray taken up by Mordecai Morgan.              30 Aug 1831
        James - appraised strays taken up by Stephen Hancock (15 Apr 1828),
                John Lee (12 Apr 1831), and another by Stephen Hancock.       27 Dec 1831
        Nicholas - Bonhomme Twp, St. Louis Co.; took up a bay horse ae 5y     30 Nov 1830
                appraised at $45 by James Bacon & Asa Granville. H. Smith JP.
        Reuben - Bonhomme Twp, offers $10 reward for a brown horse,           2 Aug 1831
                                                        strayed or stolen.
        William - Bonhomme Twp; took up a dark bay horse ae 6y appraised at   17 Jan 1828
                $40 by G. Baxter & John P. Bacon. H. Lanham JP.
LONGWITH, James - Bonhomme Twp, St. Louis Co.; took up a sorrel mare ae 4y    26 Apr 1827
                appraised at $30 by Enos McDonald, Samuel Leps, &
                Samuel Ridge. C. Bowles JP.
        Joseph - Bonhomme; took up a sorrel mare ae 15y appraised at          23 Feb 1826
                $25 by Henry Reynor & George Sip. Caleb Bowles JP.
LORINE, Francis - St. Ferdinand Twp, St. Louis Co.; took up a dark bay
                horse ae 6-7y appraised at $45 by Joel Musick &               7 Oct 1828
                William Faucet. Hugh O'Neal JP.
LOVE, Andrew - Pike Co.; took up a gray horse ae 5y appraised at $30 by       15 Mar 1831
                James Love & M. Mann. M. J. Noyes JP.
LOWE, Richard - appraised a stray taken up by Benjamin Bennett, also one      4 Mar 1828
                by Hugh Jamison.
        - Bonhomme Twp, St. Louis Co.; took up a gray mare ae 12y             24 Jul 1832
                appraised at $40 by John Jones & Jesse Hickman.
                                                        H. Smith JP.

        MOR                     89

LUGS, William - Upper Loutre Twp, Montgomery Co.; took up a chestnut sorrel
          stud ae 11y appraised at $25 by John & Thomas Freeman.        31 May 1831
                              Joseph Howard JP.
LYLE, James S. & Elizabeth - their property sold to satisfy a debt to
          Sullivan Blood.                                                9 Oct 1832
LYNCH, James C. - opens a bottling cellar under Jenneret's store on
          Main St., St. Louis.                                           6 May 1828
          - announces a special meeting of the Hibernian Relief
          Society at the home of John Pigott on Church St.              14 Oct 1828
          - opens the new St. Louis Brewery, offers 75¢ per
          bushel for barley.                                             1 Nov 1827
     William A. - dissolves partnership with W. A. Grimsley.            19 Apr 1831
LYNN, Joseph - appraised a stray taken up by George Allen.             29 Jun 1830
McALLISTER, Alexander - Bonhomme Twp, St. Louis Co., offers a $30 reward
          for a runaway Negro.                                         28 Feb 1825
          - took up a yellow bay mare ae 4y appraised at $20
          by William Grimsley & Adam Charters.                          2 Jun 1829
McAYEAL, John - opens a porter cellar on Main St., St. Louis, offers
          "Pittsburgh Point Porter and Ale."                            9 Mar 1826
McCABE, John G. - appraised a stray taken up by Andrew Casey.          27 Jul 1830
McCAN, Neil - Elkhorn Twp, Montgomery Co.; took up a sorrel horse ae 3y
          appraised by William S. Penn & Jesse McCan, amount not       14 Dec 1830
          shown.  Benoni McClure JP.
          - appraised a stray taken up by John Kent.                   17 Aug 1830
          - took up a bay mare & a sorrel horse appraised at $50 by
          Nathaniel Pendleton & Benoni McClure. William Skinner JP.    11 Dec 1832
McCARTAN, Thomas - opens "The Sign of the Golden Boot" next to
          McKenney's Saddlery, St. Louis.                               2 Sep 1828
McCAUSLAND, John - with David Kyle, won a claim against James Gunsolis.  5 Jul 1831
McCLELLAND, James J. - obtained a grocer's license, St. Louis.         29 May 1832
          Robert - Bourbon Twp, Callaway Co.; took up an iron gray
          filly ae 2y appraised at $25 by Robert Baker &               12 Jan 1830
          Thomas McClelland.  Isaac Black JP.
McCLENNY, James - appraised a stray taken up by Elijah Bryan.          11 Sep 1832
McCLURE, Benoni - Elkhorn Twp, Montgomery Co.; JP, strays taken up by
          Alfonso Price (7 Jul 1829) and by John Kent.                 17 Aug 1830
          - appraised a stray taken up by Neal McCan.                  11 Dec 1832
McCONNEL, Daniel M. - defendant, suit for $500 by Isaac A. Letcher.    31 May 1831
McCLURG, Mary - late Brotherton, petitioned for divorce from Joseph
          in the Mo. Legislature.                                       3 Feb 1829
McCORD, James - appraised a stray taken up by Vincent Moor.            17 Jun 1828
McCORMIC, William - appraised a stray taken up by Andrew Cobb.         29 Jul 1828
McCORMICK, Isaac - appraised a stray taken up by Joseph & Hubbard Jamison. 15 Jun 1830
          Isaac N. - offers two farms for sale, one near Sappington's
          Ox Mill.                                                     21 Aug 1832
          James - Plattin Twp, Jefferson Co.; offers $100 reward for
          runaway Negro Watt.                                          23 Jun 1829
          Jardon M. - took up a brown mare ae 7y appraised at $13.50
          by James Sappington & Philip Fine; T. Sappington JP.          2 Nov 1826
          Samuel - took up a bright bay mare ae 14-15 y appraised at $40
          by Mark Sappington & James McCormack. T. Sappington JP.      19 Jul 1827
McCORTNEY, John - defendant in a suit for $837.06 damages by
          Jonathan Walton.                                             16 Jul 1823
          William R. - Bonhomme Twp, St. Louis Co.; took up a bay horse
          ae 8y appraised at $75 by John Carrel &                      16 Jun 1829
          Alexander McCortney.
McCOURTNEY, Alexander Jr. - Bonhomme Twp, St. Louis Co.; took up a dark
          bay horse ae 12y appraised at $32.50 by John                  8 Jun 1826
          Bell & George King.  Thomas Mason JP.
McCOY, Martin - Hurricane Twp, Lincoln Co.; took up a bay horse appraised
          at $40 by Samuel Gladney & Joseph Sitton. W. Hammack JP.      2 Sep 1828
McCREERY, Allen - appraised a stray taken up by James Sapp.            29 Jun 1830
McCUGH, Daniel - Calumet Twp, Pike Co.; took up a yellow bay yearling
          appraised at $12 by Joshua Wells & William Mountjoy.         27 Apr 1830
          C. C. Eastin JP.
McCULLOUGH, Henry - Bonhomme Twp, St. Louis Co.; JP, strays taken up by
          Hiram Smith (29 Dec 1829), Allen Link (26 Jul 1831)
          (cont.)

          MOR

McCULLOUGH, Henry, cont. -and Henry Votaw.               3 Jul 1832
- took up a sorrel horse ae 6y appraised at $30 by
    Michael Smith & Thomas Robinson. Henry Smith JP.   15 Mar 1831

   W. - Bonhomme Tp, St. Louis Co.; appraised a stray taken up
     by George Farris.                              29 May 1832
McDERMED, Hugh - next friend of Sarah Garner in her divorce suit vs
    Thruston Garner, Montgomery Co.              27 Aug 1823
McDONALD, Archibald - took up a bay horse ae 11y appraised at $50 by
    William Walton & Joseph McDonald. James Walton JP.  22 Jan 1823
   Benjamin - appraised a stray taken up by Peter Massie.     19 Jul 1831
   Enos - appraised a stray taken up by James Longwith.      26 Apr 1827
          -    " by William Fletcher.                 17 May 1827
   James - appraised a stray taken up by James Brown Jr.    6 May 1828
   James A. - appraised a stray taken up by Solomon King.   8 Jun 1830
   Jesse - Boeuff Twp, Franklin Co.; JP, strays taken up by John
    Sullens (31 May 1827), Lawson Collins (20 Jul 1830)
    and Peter Massie (19 Jul 1831). In Rock Twp, by
    James Brown Jr. (6 May 1828), Osias Heatherly
    (26 May 1829) and James Criswell.               23 Mar 1830
   John - appraised a stray taken up by Jacob Wickerham.   10 Mar 1829
   Patrick - obtained a grocer's license in St. Louis.     29 May 1832
   William - Franklin Co.; took up a bay horse ae 3y appraised at
    $22.50 by Talton Goe & Joseph Ganitchie.
                             Jesse McDonald JP.   16 Aug 1831
    - appraised a skiff taken up by Charles Geiger.       25 May 1830
McDONOUGH, P. - selling a house and lot formerly owned by James O'Tool.  12 Sep 1825
   Patrick - bankrupt, St. Louis.                   14 Mar 1825
McDOWNS, William - appraised a stray taken up by Alexander Emerson.  15 Aug 1825
McEUNE, McEWN, Oliver - appraised a stray taken up by Reuben Harrison.  24 Feb 1829
          -    " by Samuel Hutton.                    11 May 1830
McFALL, Lazarus - appraised a stray taken up by Fleming Miller.    3 May 1827
    - appraised a stray taken up by Thomas H. Kelly.     16 Dec 1828
McFARLAND, Caleb - Waverly Twp, Lincoln Co.; JP, stray taken up by
    Isaac Hudson.                            2 Jun 1829
McGAHAN, George - Perry Twp, St. Francois Co.; JP, strays taken up by
    James H. Griffin (9 Sep 1828) and Benjamin Crump.   11 Apr 1825
McGILL, Richard H. - dissolves partnership with Thomas Ingram.    4 Jan 1831
    - moves his business to Market St.              9 Oct 1832
McGINNISS, Neal - appraised a stray taken up by Austin Shelton.   27 Jul 1830
McGIRK, I. C. - offers for sale a house, kitchen, smokehouse, stable, and
    large garden plot on the Hill near the public square.  23 Mar 1826
    (St. Louis; probably "Hill" refers to the big Mound.)
   Mathias - appraised a stray taken up by Lewis Jones.      13 Dec 1827
McGOLDRICK, Robert - bankrupt, St. Louis.                28 Mar 1825
McGRORY, Samuel - appraised a stray taken up by Joseph Neill Sr.   31 May 1831
McGUIRE, Richard - runaway apprentice of Thomas Andrews who offers $10
    reward. May have gone to New Orleans. Height 5'6",    16 Oct 1832
    ae 17 or 18, "sullen."
   Thomas - defendant in a mortgage foreclosure suit by the State.  17 Dec 1823
   William - bankrupt, St. Louis.                   29 Jun 1830
McGUNNEGLE, Wilson - dissolves partnership with Wm. Hill, commission house.  14 Oct 1828
McILROYE, Sam - appraised a stray taken up by George Barnsback.   24 Jan 1828
McILVAIN, John - appraised a stray taken up by Joseph Haigh.     8 Feb 1827
McINTIRE, John - St. John's Twp, Franklin Co.; took up a fleabitten gray
    mare ae 7-8 appraised at $27 by A. Chambers &       19 Feb 1828
    A. Ranson. Wm. H. Owens JP.
McKEE, S. - selling a house and lot formerly owned by James O'Tool.  12 Sep 1825
   Stewart - dissolves partnership with Joseph Bates & Robert
    Cathcart in the Union Steam Mill.              4 Sep 1832
McKENNEY, R. T. - dissolves partnership with William Starr.     13 Apr 1830
   Samuel T. - appraised a stray taken up by Caleb Brown.    9 Sep 1828
    - dissolves partnership with J. G. A. McKenney,
    Samuel will continue the business.             21 Feb 1832
   Samuel T. & James G. - sue Armstead Lawless for $500.    21 Aug 1832
McKINZIE, William W. - appraised a stray taken up by Josiah Johnson.  2 Oct 1832
McKNIGHT, Alfred - assigns his goods to his creditors.

McKNIGHT, James - ordered to appear for trial in St. Louis Circuit Court.    9 Aug 1824
    - an order in favor of James Walker vs McKnight & Hartly
      Sappington, all of McKnight's interest in 300 arpents    28 Nov 1825
      on Little Creve Coeur Creek seized and levied upon.
    - appraised a stray taken up by Joshua Burckhartt.    25 May 1826
    - " by Spyrus Palmer (15 Apr 1828) & William Hawkins.    2 Nov 1830
McLAUGHLIN, Henry - defendant, St. Charles Circuit Court, suit by    4 Jan 1827
    William Hays Jr. over land ownership.
McMEANS, David - appraised a stray taken up by Edmund Burgess.    30 Jun 1829
McMILLAN, William - Joachim Twp, Jefferson Co.; JP, strays taken up by
    Edmund Burgess (30 Jun 1829) & Avington K. Wilson.    31 Jul 1831
    Samuel - Cuivre Twp, Pike Co.; took up two horses appraised at    6 Sep 1831
    $60 by James H. Hayden & Jacob Pritchett. L. Rogers JP.
McMILLIN, Joseph - appraised a stray taken up by Mathew McPeck.    19 Oct 1826
    Samuel - Plattin Twp, Jefferson Co.; JP, stray taken up by    19 Oct 1826
    Mathew McPeck.
McMINAMY, Bernard - appraised a stray taken up by Elijah Weaver.    17 Jul 1832
McMORRIS, Edmund - bankrupt, St. Louis.    2 Mar 1826
McMULLEN, Joseph - defendant, suit for $600 damages by John Taylor.    16 Jul 1823
    Samuel - JP, Jefferson Co., stray taken up by Peter Vinyard.    27 Dec 1831
McMURPHY, Miss - will teach "the art of English grammar," starting    3 Apr 1832
    24 April, $5 per session. (St. Louis)
McMURTRY, Levi - 9-Mile-Prairie Twp, Callaway Co.; took up a light brown
    mare ae 4y appraised at $30 by Caleb E. Berry &    31 Jul 1832
    George W. Burt. Enoch Fruit JP.
McNAIR, David - plaintiff in a suit to regain possession of a house, St.
    Charles Circuit Court, vs Margaret Hardwick, Easter    4 May 1826
    Eades, Felix W. Flaugherty et al.
McNULTY, M. & B., bakers, offer a reward for a runaway Negro Bob, ae ca 14.    10 Jan 1832
McPEAKE, Matthew - offers a $50 reward for a lost or stolen pocketbook    16 Oct 1832
    containing $210 in bank notes and other valuables.
McPECK, Mathew - Plattin Twp, Jefferson Co.; took up a sorrel mare ae 4y
    appraised at $22 by James Pollard & Joseph McMillin.    19 Oct 1826
    Samuel McMillin JP.
McQUEEN, John A. L. - appraised a stray taken up by Ephraim Cannon.    16 Nov 1830
    - " by John A. Woolfolk.    11 May 1830
    Peter W. & Robert - sue John W. Merritt & William Bagley for
    $500 and Arch Kasson & William Leavenworth    28 Aug 1832
    for $500, St. Louis Circuit Court.
    Thomas - Calumet Twp, Pike Co.; JP, strays taken up by Isaac
    Blanton (14 Jul 1829) and William Watt.    31 May 1831
McQUIE, Walter - obtained a merchant's license, St. Louis.    29 May 1832
MACE, Nathaniel W. - appraised a stray taken up by Antoine Thebo.    22 Apr 1828
MACK, George - appraised a stray taken up by John Tally.    17 Jun 1828
    N. W. - took up a roan horse swimming in the Missouri River, which
    is now at his stable in St. Charles.    5 May 1829
MACKAY, Zeno - appraised a stray taken up by Paul Robert.    8 Mar 1827
MADDOX, William P. - dissolves partnership with Augustus Bowles.    10 Aug 1830
    - defendant in a suit for $300 by Martin Simpson.    24 Apr 1832
MAGEE, Alexander - opens a writing school on Main St., St. Louis; will    1 Jun 1826
    also teach the art of stenography (shorthand).
MAGIN, Charles - his wife Emily Beyon has left his bed and board.    2 Jul 1823
MAGUIRE, George - partner of D. Ferguson Jr. in a dry goods and grocery    2 Dec 1828
    store, "nearly opposite the St. Louis Bookstore."
MAHAN, James F. - Liberty Twp, Marion Co.; JP, stray taken up by Joshua Gentry.1 Mar 1831
MALLOW, Jacob - appraised a stray taken up by Andrew Miller.    30 Nov 1832
MANN, M. - appraised a stray taken up by Andrew Love.    15 Mar 1831
MARCH, E. C. - offers a "patent threshing machine" at Main & Market Sts.,    21 Feb 1832
    St. Louis.
    - his stock bought by Cross & Shaw.    29 May 1832
MARDEN, Elijah - Union Twp, Lincoln Co.; took up a bay mare ae 6-8y    21 Feb 1832
    appraised at $20 by John Cox & Statia Webb.
    Thomas Hammons JP.
MARINIER, Jacques - bankrupt, St. Louis.    3 May 1824
MARKLE, David - Union Twp, Lincoln Co.; took up a sorrel filly ae 2y
    appraised at $18 and a dark brown colt 1y, $15, by    20 Jan 1829
    Samuel H. Lewis & James Gallaway. Lawrence H. Sitton JP.
MARLE, Michael - bankrupt, St. Louis.    24 May 1824

MOR

92

MARLOW, John S. - "near the mouth of the Wyaconda, Marion Co."; took up a mare and colt appraised at $60. Robert Sinclair JP.   19 Jul 1831

MARQUIS, James - of Franklin Co.; has taken up a runaway Negro woman said to belong to Mme La Brosse; she has been in the custody of the sheriff for some time and will be sold unless someone proves ownership and pays the fees.   5 Feb 1823

MARTEL, Joseph - warns the public not to accept a note that Simon Bertrand "fraudulently obtained" from him.   15 Jan 1823

MARTEN, Talton - appraised a stray taken up by John Lee.   12 Apr 1831

MARTIN, David - St. Ferdinand Twp, St. Louis Co.; took up a sorrel horse ae 12y appraised at $25 by John J. Hart & Thomas Baber. Fergus Ferguson JP.   10 Jan 1832

George W. - with Benjamin Green, sues Charles Collins for $1200.   13 Sep 1831

J. - opens a tailoring business with J. W. Riggs, Main St., St. Louis.   4 May 1826

James - Peno Twp, Pike Co.; took up a dark bay filly ae 2y appraised at $15 by Thomas Spencer & Elisha Jackson. A. Wagoner JP.   29 Mar 1831

James W. - Calumet Twp, Pike Co.; JP, stray taken up by Thomas Triplett.   29 May 1832

M. - a doctor, graduate of the University of Pennsylvania, with office over Charless' drug store, St. Louis.   25 Dec 1832

Robert N. - appraised a stray taken up by Benjamin B. Ray.   25 Sep 1832

MASON, John - appraised a stray taken up by Adam Cluck.   2 Jun 1829

John L. - appraised a stray taken up by Jonathan St. Clear.   9 Mar 1826

Mrs. M. - offers private boarding for "six or eight gentlemen" at 25 Chouteau Tow, St. Louis.   17 May 1824

Richard - sues John Hall for $350 damages.   16 Jul 1823

** Thomas - Bonhomme Twp, St. Louis Co.; JP, strays taken up by William Keatley (9 Mar 1826) and Benjamin Bennett.   4 Mar 1828

MASSEY, John - St. Ferdinand Twp, St. Louis Co.; took up a sorrel mare
* * ae 12-13y appraised at $40 by Benjamin F. Readman & Benjamin F. Helm. A. J. Whiteside JP.   7 Aug 1832

MASSIE, D. - offers for sale a 4-year-old horse left with him by the owner who has disappeared and whose address is not known.   6 Dec 1824

H. A. - sells "flour, cheese, and fruit," Ferry Landing, St. Louis.   8 Apr 1828

Peter - Boeuff Twp, Franklin Co.; took up a black horse ae 8y appraised at $15 by Benjamin McDonald & George Mitchell. Jesse McDonald JP.   19 Jul 1831

* * MASON, Thomas also was JP for strays taken up by William Orr -   2 Sep 1828
and Alexander Kinkead.   20 Oct 1829

* * MASSEY, John - also appraised a stray taken up by Abner Ball.   14 Jun 1831

MATSON, Enoch - gives a detailed description of a stray mare at his home on Salt River "near the mouth of Peno," Pike Co.   2 Aug 1827

Richard - named accessory in the shooting of Charles Rouse at New London.   29 Dec 1829

MAUPIN, Daniel - appraised a stray taken up by Andrew Rice.   6 Dec 1831

Thomas - "head of Boeff," Franklin Co.; took up a black mare ae 3y appraised at $18 by Zimri Smith & John Greenstreet. Jesse McDonald JP.   25 Jan 1831

MAXWELL, Robert - Belleview Twp, Washington Co.; took up a bay horse ae 6y appraised at $40 by Andrew Perry & Hezekiah Williams. G. Ashbrook JP.   30 Aug 1824

MAYFIELD, James H. - attorney and counselor-at-law, St. Louis.   27 Nov 1832

MEAD, Alanson - defendant, suit for $800 by Samuel Keady, St. Charles.   30 Aug 1831

MEARA, John - defendant, mortgage-foreclosure suit by Morton & Rocheblave.   30 May 1825

MEDLEY, Thomas - appraised a stray taken up by David Hilderbrand.   2 Feb 1830

MEECH, S. W. - opens the Franklin Book Store and paper agency on Main St., St. Louis.   31 July 1832

MEFFORD, Alfred - appraised a stray taken up by John Hosteller.   29 Mar 1831

MEGARY, John - offers a reward for a stolen bay horse.   7 Jun 1831

MELTON, William - appraised a stray taken up by Gabriel Rush.   16 Feb 1830

William N. - offers $100 reward for the apprehension of a thief who stole $224 from him.   2 Nov 1830

MENEDY, Philip - appraised a stray taken up by Benjamin Horine.   27 Jun 1825

MERILL, Eli - "at the crossing of the North Fabius," Marion Co.; took up a sorrel mare ae 6y appraised at $25 by Wm. Pritchard & Uriah B. Gregory. Robert Sinclair JP.   20 Sep 1831

MERRILL, Hardy - Union Twp, Washington Co.; took up a brown mare appraised at $20 by Stephen Bryan & Nathan Pinson. Geo. Jamison JP.   27 May 1828

MOR

93

MERRITT, John W. - defendant (with William Bagley) in a suit for $500 damages 21 Aug 1832
 by Thomas Barnett & Peter & Robert McQueen, St. Louis.
 - defendant in a suit by John Gaines for $500. 28 Aug 1832
METCALF, Nancy - by next friend H. Hendrick sues Washington Metcalf for 21 Feb 1825
 divorce, Jefferson Co. Circuit Court.
MILES, William - appraised a stray taken up by Walter Dorsett. 19 Jul 1831
MILLEGAN, Richard - warns public not to trust or harbor his runaway 19 Jul 1824
 apprentice George W. Gay, ae 19, who absconded 10 July.
 - " his apprentice James Sutton who left about 16 months ago.5 Jan 1826
 - " his apprentice Richard Morton, who was indentured. 2 Feb 1826
 - will be absent from the state for some time, Joseph 29 Jun 1826
 Woods will conduct his business.
MILLER, A. W. - appraised a stray taken up by Harvy Harbison. 15 Nov 1831
 - " George Farris. 29 May 1832
 Andrew - Washington Co.; took up a bay horse ae 6-7y appraised at 30 Nov 1826
 $20 by Jacob Mallow & Henry E. Davis. H. Shurlds JP.
 David - sues Thomas C. Bell for $300, Pike Co. Circuit Court. 21 Feb 1832
 Fleming - Dardenne Twp, St. Charles Co.; took up a mare ae 13y &
 two colts, appraised at $23 by James Silvey & 3 May 1827
 Lazarus McFall. Thos. D. Stephenson JP.
 Hugh - Bonhomme Twp, St. Louis Co.; took up a bay horse ae 12y
 appraised at $30 by Stephen Hancock & Lawrence Carden. 31 Aug 1830
 H. Smith JP.
 - appraised a stray taken up by Stephen Hancock. 27 Dec 1831
 - " by Sarah Caulk. 26 Jun 1832
 John - Bonhomme Twp, St. Louis Co.; took up a sorrel horse ae 15y
 appraised at $10 by Joseph Snell & John Brackenridge. 1 Mar 1831
 H. McCullough JP.
 Thomas J. - with Jacob R. Stine, proposes to publish the 17 Feb 1829
 St. Louis _Times_.
MILLINGTON, Seth - offers white mulberry trees for sale. 24 Mar 1829
 - writes a long, interesting letter about silk-raising. 7 Apr 1829
MILLS, Henry L. - Sheriff, St. Louis Co., offers $10 reward for a Negro 20 Jun 1825
 man escaped from jail.
 William - Spencer Twp, Ralls Co.; took up a dark bay horse appraised 2 Dec 1828
 at $40 by Lewis Garnett & Wm. Sims. Richard Boyce JP.
MINER, Laban - Black River Twp, Washington Co.; took up a bay mare ae 5y
 appraised at $20 by Thomas Hutchings & Henry Miner. 28 Jun 1827
 Andrew Goforth JP.
MINTONGE, Eli - sues Selleck B. Andrews for $150. 13 Sep 1831
MITCHELL, George - appraised a stray taken up by Peter Massie. 19 Jul 1831
 William - appraised a stray taken up by William Arthur. 26 Aug 1828
 Willis - Buffalo Twp, Pike Co.; JP, strays taken up by M. J.
 Noyes (21 Jun 1827) and Robert H. Allison. 15 Jan 1831
MOHER, B. - a resident of Potosi; Stephen Molony, now missing, had 20 Jan 1829
 boarded with him.
MOLONY, Stephen - a citizen of Potosi, disappeared from the house of
 B. Moher, where he boarded; foul play suspected. 20 Jan 1829
 A Native of Ireland, ae 60-65, height 5'6 or 7".
MONROE, Israel - with Wm. F. Peterson, sues Samuel Glover, St. Louis. 10 Dec 1823
MONTGOMERY, John - appraised a stray taken up by Michael J. Noyes. 21 Jun 1827
 William - appraised a stray taken up by Uriah Hull. 8 Jun 1830
 - " by William Ralls. 1 Feb 1831
MOOR, Vincent - Cuivre Twp, Pike Co.; took up a chestnut sorrel horse
 ae 12y appraised at $25 by James McCord & Mathew B. Moore. 17 Jun 1828
 Harrison Hendrick JP.
MOORE, Alfred L. - offers for sale at auction, St. Louis, tea in
 quantities of 5-catty (6 lb.), 10-catty (13 lb.), 22 Jun 1826
 bales, half-chests, and whole chests.
 Daniel - appraised a stray taken up by William Adams. 23 Dec 1828
 Elizabeth - has taken a room on Myrtle St., St. Louis, and offers 25 Jan 1827
 her services as a midwife.
 James D. - appraised a stray taken up by William Coshow. 10 Jan 1832
 Jeremiah - took up a gray mare appraised at $35 by Vincent Moore 2 Jul 1823
 & Jonathan Oylear. Robert Irvine JP.
 - appraised a stray taken up by James L. Kilby. 11 Aug 1829
 Mathew B. - appraised a stray taken up by Vincent Moor. 17 Jun 1828

  MOR

MOORE, Perry - appraised a stray taken up by Ann Frasier. 19 Jul 1827
Quintin - appraised a stray taken up by William Wiley. 24 Jun 1828
Samuel - Joachim Twp, Jefferson Co.; took up a dark bay horse ae 8y
appraised at $35 by John Gieger & Isaac Roberts; C. Smith JP. 9 Sep 1828
MOORES, Arthur - bankrupt, St. Louis. 3 Oct 1825
MORGAN, Mordecai - Elkhorn Twp, Montgomery Co.; took up a dark bay horse
ae 6y appraised at $40 by Newton Howell & Andrew J. Long. 30 Aug 1831
William Skinner JP.
MORIN, Henry - bankrupt, St. Louis. 25 Oct 1824
MORRIS, Hannah - Boles Twp, Franklin Co.; took up a bay horse ae 14y
appraised at $17 by Richard Farrar & John B. Brown. 11 Jan 1831
Thomas Henry JP.
John - appraised a stray taken up by Robert Chunning. 19 Jul 1827
- " by Jacob Cole. 29 Nov 1827
Nathaniel W. - appraised a stray taken up by Allen Link. 26 Jul 1831
Philip - appraised a stray taken up by Charles Philips. 21 Feb 1832
MORRISON, James - offers the Boons Lick Saltworks for sale, including five
salt springs, a coal bank, furnaces, etc., 12 miles 9 Aug 1831
from Franklin, Fayette, and Chariton.
John A. - appraised a stray taken up by Daniel Peveler. 26 Jul 1827
- JP, Montgomery Co., stray taken up by James Davis. 25 Jan 1831
William - dissolves partnership with Samuel Veacock. 11 Dec 1832
MORRISS, Richard & Hepselia - divorce petition in the Mo. Legislature. 25 Jan 1831
MORRISSON, John - appraised a stray taken up by Benj. H. Hinkson. 30 Jan 1828
MORSE, Lewis & Henry - the Sheriff is selling 24 pigs of iron seized from
them upon the action of John S. Rundlett. 11 May 1830
MORTON, George - a carpenter, warns the public against his runaway
apprentice David Harvy. 2 Aug 1824
Richard - runaway apprentice of Richard Millegan. 2 Feb 1826
Samuel - Palmyra; offers a reward for a strayed dun horse. 24 Nov 1829
MOSELY, John - sues Moses Singleton & Thomas Phillips for $342.11. 2 Oct 1832
MOSTILLERS, Jacob - appraised a stray taken up by Reuben League. 21 Oct 1828
MOTT, Robert E. - appraised a stray taken up by Allen Jameson. 30 Nov 1826
MOUNTJOY, William - appraised a stray taken up by Daniel McCugh. 27 Apr 1830
- " by Henry Kissinger. 3 Jan 1832
MOUTRY, James H. - appraised a stray taken up by Anthony Wilkson. 30 Jun 1829
MULDOON, Andrew - appraised a stray taken up by Waddy Cobbs. 16 Dec 1828
MULHALL, John - appraised a stray taken up by Isaac Hall. 1 Sep 1829
MUNDY, E. & R. - advertise a blacksmith shop, St. Louis, Locust St. 22 Jun 1830
Edward & Roland - dissolve partnership. 12 Oct 1830
MUNROE, Lockwood - appraised a stray taken up by James Brotherton. 30 Nov 1826
Dockweed - appraised a stray taken up by John Bray. 3 Jun 1828
MURPHY, Dennis - obtained a grocer's license, St. Louis. 29 May 1832
James - a wagonmaker, advertises for apprentices, at L. Newell's
establishment, St. Louis. 30 Mar 1830
Richard - Pendleton Twp, St. Francois Co.; JP, stray taken up by
David Jones. 16 Feb 1830
- St. Francois Twp, St. Francois Co.; JP, stray taken up
by Laken Walker. 18 Dec 1832
William - appraised a stray taken up by James Criswell. 23 Mar 1830
MURREL, Richard - took up a gray horse ae 12-13y appraised at $25 by Mark
Sappington & Granville Eads. Thomas Sappington JP. 27 Jul 1830
- took up a roan horse ae 12-13 appraised at $35 by Larkin
Foley & Granville Eads. Sappington JP. 30 Nov 1830
MURRY, Thomas - appraised a stray taken up by Green B. Baxter. 21 Sep 1826
MUSICK, James L. - appraised a stray taken up by John Hume. 2 Sep 1828
Joel - appraised a stray taken up by Francois Lorine. 7 Oct 1828
- JP, stray taken up by Isaac Hall. 1 Sep 1829
- ", stray taken up by Benjamin B. Ray. 25 Sep 1832
Robert - appraised a stray taken up by John Withinton. 22 Mar 1831
MUSSETT, John - appraised a stray taken up by Jeremiah Brickey. 5 Apr 1827
MYERS, Elijah - appraised a stray taken up by David Diggs. 15 Feb 1827
NASON, Mary - by next friend, sues Cuthbert Nason for divorce, St. Louis.
They were married in Mo. in 1821, he left her in Nov. 1823. 20 Dec 1827
NAYLOR, John - Dardenne Prairie; took up a bay filly ae 2y appraised at
$8 by Thaddeus Dulin & Benj. Baugh. John Smith JP. 19 Jan 1830
John C. - St. Louis; offers a reward for a bay horse strayed from
his property. 12 Jul 1827

MOR

NEEL, Joseph - appraised a stray taken up by William Haines.                          19 Mar 1823
NEILL, Joseph - appraised a stray taken up by Chukesberry Redmound.                   17 Mar 1829
       Joseph Sr. - Concord Twp, Washington Co.; took up an iron gray mare
                     ae 5y appraised at $25 by Samuel McGrory & Henry Hicks.          31 May 1831
                                             O. A. Belknap JP.
       L. H. - appraised a stray taken up by Lewis Jones.                             13 Dec 1827
NELSON, D. - announces the start of teaching at Marion College, tuition
             $5-$10 for five-month session; boarding $1 per week.                     20 Mar 1832
NEWELL, Louis - testifies as to the quality of Van Leer iron.                         19 May 1829
             - bankrupt, St. Louis.                                                   15 May 1832
NEWMAN, John - attorney and counselor-at-law, Main St., St. Louis.                    25 Nov 1828
NEWMAN, Jonas & Thomas - dissolve partnership.                                        23 Mar 1824
NICHOLSON, William - appraised a stray taken up by John Carter.                       13 Nov 1832
NICKELL, A. - a portrait painter, "recently from Virginia."                            5 Jul 1831
NIVIN, John - dissolves partnership with William Glasgow, Herculaneum.                 2 Mar 1826
NIX, Caleb - appraised a stray taken up by Eli Valentine.                             17 Jan 1832
NOEL, Joel - appraised a stray taken up by Elliott Burton.                            12 Aug 1828
NOLAND, James - Charrette Twp, Montgomery Co.; took up an iron gray mare
                ae 3y appraised at $25.  James Hughes JP.                             15 Feb 1831
NORMAN, Nathan - offers a reward for a horse strayed from his residence
                 near the Methodist Meeting House, St. Louis.                         21 Jun 1824
NORTHERAFT, James F. - appraised a stray taken up by Sampson Anderson.                17 Nov 1829
NORTON, Joshua - appraised a stray taken up by John Bray.                             10 Jun 1828
NOYES, Michael J. - Buffalo Twp, Pike Co.; JP, strays taken up by Welch
                Allison (14 Dec 1826), Andrew Love (15 Mar 1831)
                and Betsy Parry.                                                      22 Mar 1831
              - took up a sorrel mare ae 7y appraised at $35 and a
                roan colt $10 by James Jones, John Montgomery, and                    21 Jun 1827
                Robert Davis.  Willis Mitchell JP.
NYE, Seth W. - sues John Bostwick for $404.00½ debt, St. Louis.                       16 Jul 1823
O'BANNON, John - Boeuf Twp, Franklin Co.; JP, strays taken up by William
                 Roark, first -18 Nov 1828; second -                                 17 Nov 1829
         Thomas - runaway mulatto of James Russell; ca 30, 6' tall.                    9 Sep 1828
OBER, Samuel - sues Robert Pogue for $3000 damages; St. Louis Circuit Ct.             9 Aug 1824
O'BUCHON, Francois - bankrupt, St. Louis.                                             24 May 1824
OGLE, Thomas - appraised a stray taken up by James Smith.                             16 May 1825
       William - appraised a stray taken up by Moses B. Austin.                        9 Nov 1826
OLDENBURG, Justus - bankrupt, St. Louis.                                              25 Mar 1828
OLIVER, John - appraised a stray taken up by Evin Lemasters.                          10 Jul 1832
OLMSTED, W. S. - agent for the Sunday School Bible and Tract Depository,
                 St. Louis, announces a move to Main & Locust.                        20 Nov 1832
O'NEIL, Hugh - St. Francois Co.; JP, strays taken up by James Brotherton -            30 Nov 1826
               John Bray (3 Jun 1828) and Francis Lorine.                              7 Oct 1828
ONSTATT, William - appraised a stray taken up by John Tally.                          17 Jun 1828
ORME, Archibald - dissolves partnership with Joseph Walton.                           16 Feb 1830
O'ROURKE, John - joins John G. Stevenson in a court action against
                  Wetherill & Foster, St. Louis.                                     11 May 1830
ORR, William - Bonhomme Twp, St. Louis Co.; took up a dark bay horse ae 15y
               appraised at $20 by James C. Curry & Andrew Kinkead.                    2 Sep 1828
                                             Thomas Mason JP.
OSBERN, John - appraised a stray taken up by Barksdale Sledd.                         15 Feb 1831
O'TOOL, James - the brick house and lot at the Ox Mill, which he formerly
                owned, now for sale by P.C. McDonough & S. McKee.                     12 Sep 1825
OUSLEY, Micajah - Charrette Twp, Montgomery Co.; took up a bay mare ae 12y
                  appraised at $10.  James Hughes JP.                                  1 Feb 1827
OWEN, Talbot - offers a family carriage and horse for sale, St. Louis.                19 Nov 1823
OWENS, James - Jefferson Co.; took up a chestnut sorrel horse ae 7y
               appraised at $40 by James Royen & King White. S. Graham JP.            22 Dec 1829
       William G. - St. John's Twp, Franklin Co.; JP, stray taken up by
                                                              John McIntire.          19 Feb 1828
               - same township, JP, stray taken up by                                15 Jun 1830
                 Joseph & Hubbard Jamison.
               - Boeuf Twp, Franklin Co.; JP, stray taken up by Andrew
                 Rice (23 Nov 1826) and by James Johnston.                             2 Mar 1830
               - appraised a stray taken up by Isaac Hudson.                           2 Jun 1829
OYLEAR, Jonathan - appraised a stray taken up by Jeremiah Moore.                       2 Jul 1823
PAGE, J. H. - partner of R. L. Keen, commission business.                            18 May 1830
       William - appraised strays taken up by John Hempstead (17 Feb 1829,
                 Benj. Ellenwood (27 Apr 1830) and Thomas Hibler.                     14 Dec 1830

       MOR

PAINE, Noah - his wife Polly has left his bed and board.                                              31 Jan 1825
PALMER, Joel - appraised a stray taken up by Felix Brown.                                             15 Sep 1829
    Spyers - warns the public not to accept two $55 notes given to
      him by Wm. M. Darby.                                              9 Aug 1827
    Spyrus - Bonhomme Twp, St. Louis Co.; took up a white mare ae 14y
      appraised at $27.50 by John Hempstead & James McKnight.         15 Apr 1828
                        A. P. Harris JP.
PARISIEN, Victor - bankrupt, St. Louis.                                                               24 May 1824
PARK, James W. - dissolves partnership with John Goodfellow.                                          22 Mar 1831
PARKE, Jonah - appraised a stray taken up by Paul Robert.                                              8 Mar 1827
PARKER, Stokely M. - Perry Twp, St. Francois Co.; took up a brown horse
    ae 6-7y appraised at $15 by Reubin League &                                    24 Mar 1829
    Leonard Parker. H. Poston JP.
    William G. - wants a job in a grocery or dry goods store.                       30 Oct 1832
PARKS, Marshall - appraised a stray taken up by Jeremiah Blackwell.                                    6 Jul 1826
PARMELEE, S. - intends to leave St. Louis, asks debtors to settle.                                    15 Feb 1827
PARMER, John - appraised a stray taken up by William Anderson.                                        12 Oct 1830
    - " by John Smeltzer.
PARRY, Betsey - Buffalo Twp, Pike Co.; took up a dark sorrel filly ae 2y
    appraised at $13 by Joseph Stevens & William N. Allen.                         22 Mar 1831
                      M. J. Noyes JP.
PARSONS, N. G. - advertises a "Looking Glass Manufactory" in the old
      St. Louis Bank Building.                                           5 Jan 1830
    Samuel A. - broke jail; accused of larceny; is about 25, 5'8 or 9",
      with light sandy hair and grey eyes.                               2 Oct 1832
    William - bankrupt, St. Louis.                                                  28 Oct 1828
    - announces the opening of business as a turner in
      brass, iron, or wood.                                              20 Dec 1827
PARTEN, Daniel L. - obtained a pedlar's license, St. Louis.                                           29 May 1832
PATTER, Green - appraised a stray taken up by William Campbell.                                       15 Mar 1831
PATTERSON, John - appraised a stray taken up by Jabez Ferris.                                         18 Jan 1831
    N. - offers a "splendid assortment" of dry goods, groceries,
      hardware, shoes, hats, etc.; wants "a boy to assist."           24 May 1831
    Samuel - defendant, damage suit by John Perry, Washington Co.
      Circuit Court.                                                     19 Aug 1828
PATTON, Robert Sr. & Jr. - appraised a stray taken up by Tilman Cullom.                               14 Jun 1831
    Robert - appraised a stray taken up by Andrew Rice.                             6 Dec 1831
    William and wife Martha, nee Mark; divorce petition in the
      Mo. Legislature.                                                   3 Feb 1829
PAUL, William - appraised a stray taken up by Wm. Hogeland.                                           28 Jun 1824
PAULDING, John W. - advertises a "hat manufactory."                                                   15 Sep 1829
PAXTON, Joseph - appraised a stray taken up by Roger B. Pollard.                                      14 Dec 1830
PAYNE, B. F. - dissolves partnership with John A. Irvine, Potosi.                                      4 Aug 1829
    Thomas J. - offers lots for sale or lease, central St. Louis.                  12 Jun 1832
PEARCE, George - obtained a grocer's license, St. Louis.                                              29 May 1832
PEARSON, Alonzo & Eliza - divorce petition in the Mo. Legislature.                                    25 Jan 1831
    Eliza vs Daniel, divorce, St. Charles Circuit Court; he deserted
      her, she has one child living with her.                             4 Jan 1827
PEASE, J. S. - advertises a new hardware store at 68 Main St., St. Louis,
      building formerly occupied by E. B. Horner, druggist.            23 Nov 1830
    Joseph S. - wants a position as clerk or bookkeeper.                            9 Oct 1832
PECK, W. B. - offers a 14-16 year old Negro boy for sale at "the yellow
      house on 3rd St.," St. Louis.                                     28 Sep 1826
PEERS, John D. - sues Abram Wilcox for $196.62½ debt and damages, St. Louis.  28 Aug 1832
    V. J. - Troy, Lincoln Co.; offers a wool carding establishment                22 Dec 1829
      for sale.
PEERY, Andrew - appraised a stray taken up by Robert B. Maxwell.                                      30 Aug 1824
PEGION, Hyacinthe - bankrupt, St. Louis.                                                              16 Feb 1824
PENDLETON, Nathaniel - appraised a stray taken up by Neal McCan.                                      11 Dec 1832
PENN, William - appraised a stray taken up by Thomas J. Elliott.                                       4 Jan 1831
PENROSE, C. B. - JP, raft taken up by Louis & Francois Dio, St. Louis.                                13 Apr 1826
PENN, William S. - appraised a stray taken up by Neil Mc Can.                                         14 Dec 1830
PERKINS, Constantine - appraised a stray taken up by Ferdinand Hervin.                                18 Dec 1832
PERRY, George W. - appraised a stray taken up by Samuel King.                                         13 Jul 1830
    John - appraised a stray taken up by John Huff.                                 5 Nov 1823
    John & Co. - advertises iron furnace and forges, near Potosi.                  15 Jul 1828
    John vs Samuel Patterson, damages, Washington Co. Ct.                          19 Aug 1828
                (cont.)

MOR

97

PERRY, John, cont. - offers the Missouri Iron Works for sale, including
    Springfield Furnace, Cedar Creek forge, and
    other property.                                   8 Mar 1831
   Montgomery - St. Charles Twp, St. Charles Co.; JP, stray taken
    up by Lewellen Turnbo.                              10 Apr 1832
   Samuel - Washington Co.; offers $20 reward for runaway mulatto.    8 Sep 1829
PETERSON, Henry - bankrupt, St. Louis Co.                     10 Aug 1826
   William F. - with Israel Monroe, sues Samuel Livermore in the
    St. Louis Co. Circuit Court.                          10 Dec 1823
PEVELER, Daniel - Loutre Twp, Montgomery Co.; took up two horses, ae 6y
    appraised at $30 and ae 2y, $10 by John Craig &
    John A. Morrison. Robert Graham JP.                  26 July 1827
PEW, Reuben P. - Prairie Twp, Montgomery Co.; took up a sorrel mare ae 2y
    appraised at $20 by Thomas Y. Elton & Pressly Anderson.    29 Dec 1829
    John H. Dutton JP.
   - took up a pale chestnut sorrel mare ae 4y appraised at
    $37.50 by Jacob Sharp & Benj. Bryan. John Curtner JP.    28 Jun 1831
PHELPS, Fealdon - runaway apprentice of tanner R. Clayton who offers $5
    reward at River. des Peres. Phelps was about 19,
    5' 8 or 9", fair haired, "tolerably heavy set."    10 Mar 1829
PHELAN, Harriet - by next friend Christopher C. Eastin sues for divorce
    in Pike Co.                                       3 Aug 1826
PHILLES, Dr. A. - office at 36 N. Main, St. Louis.           17 May 1824
PHILIPS, Bernard - information wanted by his sister Bridget, traveling in
    search of him. He was 26 or 27, 6' tall, from Co.
    Monaghan Ire.; last heard from in St. Louis, thought to
    be still in Mo.                              5 Sep 1825
   Charles - Boeff Twp, Franklin Co.; took up a roan mare ae 8-9y
    appraised at $15 by Samuel Rule & Philip Morris.    21 Feb 1832
    Jesse McDonald JP.
PHILLIPS, James - St. Louis Twp, St. Louis Co.; took up a chestnut sorrel
    horse ae 8y appraised at $20 by John W. Wasson,  Noah    19 Jun 1832
    Revis, & Jacob Albert. Peter Ferguson JP.
   Samuel - appraised a stray taken up by Joseph Sullivan.    13 May 1828
   Thomas - with Moses Singleton, defendant in a suit for $342.11
    by John Mosely.                                2 Oct 1832
PIERCE, David - defendant in a mortgage-foreclosure suit by Robert Sloan
    in the Washington Co. Circuit Court.                  5 Aug 1828
PIGOTT, John - a special meeting of the Hibernian Relief Society, St. Louis,
    to be held at his home on Church St.               14 Oct 1828
PILES, James - offers $5 reward for an iron gray horse strayed or stolen
    from Rock Spring.                           7 Aug 1832
PINKSTON, Peter - appraised a stray taken up by Thomas Forrest.    5 Apr 1831
PINSON, Nathan - appraised a stray taken up by Hardy Merrill.    27 May 1828
PITMAN, D. K. - advertises his horse Prince Hal at stud 12 miles west of
    St. Charles on the Boons Lick Road.                21 Feb 1832
PITTMANN, John - appraised a stray taken up by Richard Puttmann.    2 Jul 1823
      -    " by Allen Turnbow.                      27 Aug 1823
PLATT, A. S. - bankrupt, St. Louis.                         24 May 1824
   Jacob S. - with Aquilla Stout & Felix Ingoldsby sues William M.
    Read for $2000.                              2 Oct 1832
PLUMMER, Joseph - bankrupt, Lincoln Co.                    9 Nov 1830
    Philemon - took up an iron gray mare ae 4y appraised at $30 by
    Wm. Daniels & Benj. Howard. Benjamin Allen JP.    26 Aug 1828
POGUE, Robert - surviving partner of George & Robert Pogue sues Frederick
    Hollmann for trespass, St. Louis.                17 Dec 1823
   - defendant, suit for $3000 damages by Samuel Ober.    9 Aug 1824
POLAND, James - bankrupt, St. Louis, first: 28 Mar 1825.   Second -    6 Dec 1827
POLLARD, James - appraised a stray taken up by Mathew McPeck.    19 Oct 1826
   Roger B. - Union Twp, Lincoln Co.; took up two horses appraised
    at $65 by Joseph Paxton & Wm. Whitesides. Smiley JP.    14 Dec 1830
POOL, James - sues James Kizer for $125 debt, St. Louis.    8 Jun 1826
POSEY, Leaden - St. Louis Twp, St. Louis Co.; took up a sorrel horse ae 4y
    appraised at $30 by Richard Sappington & Andrew King.    22 Nov 1831
   - took up a black horse ae 6y appraised at $20 by Andrew
    King & Wm. Grate. Thomas Sappington, JP, both times.    27 Nov 1832
   - appraised strays taken up by Owen Collins    29 Dec 1829
        and by Thomas Harrison.    4 May 1830

POST, Justus - Bonhomme Twp, St. Louis Co.; took up a dark bay horse ae 5y
    appraised at $37 by Jonathan Carder & Joshua Harrison.     29 May 1832
                 Henry Smith JP.
POSTON, H. - Perry Twp, St. Francois Co.; JP, stray taken up by Reuben League. 21 Oct 1828
POTTER, Nathaniel - dissolves partnership with John Cleveland.     10 May 1824
POTTS, J. B. - offers 151 acres for sale at Cerre's Saline, with two
    springs, a good square log house, smoke house, shingled barn.     21 Aug 1832
    Jonathan - Bowles Twp, Franklin Co.; JP, stray taken up by Charles R.
    Jeffries (21 Jul 1829) and one by John Withinton in
    Calvy Twp, Franklin Co.     22 Mar 1831
    Joseph - River des Peres, St. Louis Co.; took up a gray mare ae 6-7y
    appraised at $40, appraisers not shown. Sappington JP.     26 Jan 1824
POWELL, Peter and Joseph - dissolve partnership with George Collier,
    Powells will continue business.     12 Oct 1830
    Richard & Barbara - divorce petition, Mo. Legislature.     25 Jan 1831
POWERS, E. H. - Hurrican Twp, Lincoln Co.; JP, stray taken up by
            Ephraim Cannon.     16 Nov 1830
PRATHER, John - Merrimac Twp, Franklin Co.; took up a dark bay horse ae 8y
    appraised at $80 by William Stuart & John Thurman.     23 Dec 1828
    - appraised a stray taken up by Joseph & Hubbard Jamison.     15 Jun 1830
PRESLEY, Jacob - Bedford Twp, Lincoln Co.; took up an iron gray filly ae 2y
    appraised at $20 by John Bell & Shedriot Woodson.     15 Nov 1831
            Charles Wheeler JP.
PREWETT, Gabriel - Belleview Twp, Washington Co.; took up a red sorrel
    colt ae 1y appraised at $15 by Garrison B. Kinemont &     23 Feb 1826
    David Imboden. Th. H. Ficklin JP.
PRICE, Alfonso - Elkhorn Twp, Montgomery Co.; took up a bay mare ae 3y
    appraised at $20 by John Ferguson & Samuel F. Daugherty.     7 Jul 1829
            Benoni McClure JP.
    James - appraised a stray taken up by Hiram Smith.     29 Dec 1829
     -  " by Reuben Sollar.     29 Nov 1831
    John - Buffalo Twp, Pike Co.; JP, stray taken up by John Hall.     25 Jan 1831
PRICHARD, William - appraised a stray taken up by Eli Merill.     20 Sep 1831
PRINGLE, Norman - Charrette Twp, Montgomery Co.; took up a yellow sorrel
    mare appraised at $45 by Lewis & Moses Edwards &     1 Nov 1831
    Greenberry Spires. H. E. Welch JP.
PRITCHETT, Jacob - appraised a stray taken up by Samuel McMillan.     6 Sep 1831
PULMAN, John - appraised a stray taken up by William Hogeland.     28 Jun 1824
PURDOM, Elijah & John - appraised a stray taken up by Henry Branstütter.     10 Jan 1832
    Thomas - named accessory in the shooting of Charles Rouse
         at New London.     29 Dec 1829
PURSLEY, David - Bowles Twp, Franklin Co.; took up a bay horse ae 5y
    appraised at $17 by Andrew Caldwell & Richard Duncan.     1 Mar 1831
            Thomas Henry JP.
PUTNAM, John - warns the public not to harbor or trade with Michael Russell,
    age about 16, his indentured apprentice.     30 Aug 1827
    - as guardian of Russell, offers 6¼¢ reward for his capture.     28 Nov 1828
PUTTMANN, Richard B. - Dardenne Twp, St. Charles Co.; took up a dark sorrel
    horse ae 9-10y appraised at $45 by John Pittmann     2 Jul 1823
    & Alden Farnsworth. Biel Farnsworth JP.
QUARLES, Robert Jr. - St. Ferdinand Twp, St. Louis Co.; took up a sorrel
    horse ae 6y appraised at $30 by Charles R. Hall &     22 Jan 1823
    Joseph D. Beauchamp. W. G. Robinson JP.
QUIGLEY, Patrick - secretary of the Mo. Hibernian Relief Soc., St. Louis.     14 Oct 1828
RACINE, Joseph - Gray Twp, Gasconade Co.; took up a bay horse ae 6-7y
    appraised at $50 by Fontaine Seif & Paul Fickear.     30 Aug 1824
            David Hoops JP.
RAGSDALE, Richard - opens a new livery stable on Chestnut St., St. Louis.     17 Jul 1832
RAGSDALL, James - appraised a stray taken up by Ephraim Cannon.     16 Nov 1830
RAISNER, John - takes over the St. Louis Comb Factory.     12 Jun 1832
RALLS, William - Liberty Twp, Marion Co.; took up two strays appraised at
    $53 by Enoch Barnett & Wm. Montgomery & a filly appraised     1 Feb 1831
    by Kindred S. Felts (?) John Davis JP. (Probably all
    three animals were appraised by the three appraisers and
    the $53 covered them all.)
RALSTON, Gavin - sued Pierre Seguin for damages, St. Louis.     3 Feb 1829
RAMEY, Nathan - George Gordon warns the public not to accept notes he gave
    Raney for land, to which he says Raney has no good title.     3 Nov 1829

       MOR

RAMIREZ, Luis - will teach the Spanish language; apply at the bar of the Union Hotel, St. Louis.                                                18 Sep 1832
RANDOLPH, J. C. F. - advertises a bakery at Pine & 2nd, St. Louis - bread, biscuits, cakes, etc. "From New York."                                25 Sep 1832
RANKIN, C. S. - appraised a stray taken up by Alden Hammond.                    30 Aug 1831
RANSON, A. - appraised a stray taken up by John McIntire.                       19 Feb 1828
RAVENSCRAFT, James - his property sold to satisfy a claim of James Tanner.       6 Nov 1832
RAY, Benjamin B. - took up a brown horse ae 13y appraised at $20 by Joseph Walton & Robert N. Martin.  Joel Musick JP.                           25 Sep 1832
    Shelton - Lewiston Twp, Montgomery Co.; took up a sorrel mare ae 3y appraised at $35 by Cornelius Howard & Jesse Ritter.
                                                James W. Taylor JP.             22 Jun 1830
RAYBURN, J. N. - Belleview Twp, Washington Co.; JP, stray taken up by William Rownds.                                                            19 Mar 1823
    Joseph - appraised a stray taken up by Henry H. Snider.                     29 Aug 1825
    Samuel W. - appraised a stray taken up by William Rownds.                   19 Mar 1823
RAYNOLD, John - appraised a stray taken up by William Adams.                    23 Dec 1828
RAYNOR, Henry - appraised a stray taken up by Jabez Ferris.                     23 Nov 1826
READ, William M. - defendant, suit for $2000 by Jacob S. Platt, Felix Ingoldsby, and Aquilla G. Stout.                                           2 Oct 1832
READMAN, Benjamin F. - appraised a stray taken up by John Massey.                7 Aug 1832
REDMOUND, Chukesberry - St. Louis Co.; took up a bay horse ae 6y appraised by Joseph Neill & Hiram Shattuck. J. C. Brown JP.                    17 Mar 1829
REED, Gabriel - appraised a stray taken up by William Wiley.                    24 Jun 1828
    George - Bowles Twp, Franklin Co.; took up a bay filly ae 2y ($15) & a brown filly ae 3y ($10) appraised by John Colvin & Henry Reed.  Thomas Haney JP.                                               31 Mar 1829
    Henry - Gray Twp, Gasconade Co.; took up a brown mare ae 7y appraised at $10 by Thomas Bettick & Bartlet Renfro.
                                                William Bumpass JP.             23 Feb 1826
    James & Samuel - dissolve partnership.                                      16 Nov 1826
    J. H. - St. Louis; offers a reward for a strayed sorrel horse.              19 Aug 1828
    William - shop he formerly occupied taken over by Coleman & Sutton.          3 Aug 1830
    William B. - property sold at auction.                                      16 Aug 1831
REEVES, Widow - Merrimack Twp, Franklin Co.; her little daughter found a bundle of clothes.                                                       9 Aug 1831
REID, George - Bonhomme Twp, St. Louis Co.; took up a bright bay horse ae 11-12y appraised at $25 by Zachariah Blackwell & A. C. Blain.  A. P. Harris JP.                                                5 May 1829
REILLY, Michael - resigns as alderman, North Ward, St. Louis.                   23 Sep 1828
REILY, Henry - dissolves partnership with Arthur Ingram.                        14 Jun 1824
         - "surviving partner" of Ingram & Reily, announces auction.            23 Sep 1828
RENFRO, Bartlett - appraised a stray taken up by Henry Reed.                    23 Feb 1826
RENFROW, James - appraised a stray taken up by Benj. H. Hinkson.                30 Jan 1828
RENICK, Willing - appraised a stray taken up by Thomas Shores.                  14 Apr 1829
    William - appraised a stray taken up by Ira Valentine.                       8 Jun 1830
REVIS, John - appraised a stray taken up by John Wright.                         5 Jan 1830
    Noah - appraised a stray taken up by James Phillips.                        19 Jun 1832
REYNOLDS, John - appraised a stray taken up by Joshua Burckhartt.               25 May 1826
    Otis - appointed deputy by constable Sullivan Blood, who is leaving St. Louis for 3 or 4 months.                                             21 May 1823
REYNOR, Henry - appraised a stray taken up by Joseph Longwith.                  23 Feb 1826
RHODES, Christopher - dissolved partnership with Greene Erskine.                13 Nov 1832
RICE, Andrew - Boeff Twp, Franklin Co.; took up a bay horse ae 8y appraised at $30 by Benjamin Harris & Carvel Fitzgerald. W.G. Owens JP.       23 Nov 1826
         - took up two horses appraised at $70 by Daniel Maupin & Robert Patton.  Jesse McDonald JP.                                             6 Dec 1831
    David M. - appraised a stray taken up by Cole Diggs.                        17 Jan 1832
    John - appraised a stray taken up by Andrew Casey.                          27 Jul 1830
RICHARDS, Hugh - offers cash for "merchantable leaf tobacco."                   17 Sep 1823
         - dissolves partnership with Tracy & Wahrendorff.                       7 Nov 1824
         - Edward Smith, barber, moves next door to him.                        27 Jul 1826
RICHARDSON, John - found a bay gelding on the road from Herculaneum to St. L.    6 May 1828
         - St. Louis Twp.; took up a bright sorrel horse appraised at $25 by Baptiste Deslisle & Isidore Barada.
                                                J. R. Stine JP.                 18 Nov 1821
    Daniel & Richard - appraised a stray taken up by Lawson Collins.            20 Jul 1830

MOR

100

RICHARDSON, Nathan - appraised a stray taken up by James Johnston.                    2 Mar 1830
RICKARD, T. J. - took over the plane manufactory of M. Stout.                        24 Jan 1832
RIDGE, Samuel - appraised a stray taken up by James Longwith.                        26 Apr 1827
RIGG, J. W. - opens a tailoring business with J. Martin on Main St.,
                                                                 St. Louis.           4 May 1826
RIGGIN, John - the partnership of Riggin & Marshall is dissolved, due to
                 Marshall's death.                                                   13 Nov 1832
RIGGS, Romulus - with Robert B. Aertsen, sues John J. Daley for $1621.23.            10 May 1831
RINGO, Samuel - dissolves partnership with Robert Aull, Liberty.                      8 Feb 1831
RIPLEY, Richard - appraised a stray taken up by Jonathan Cottle.                      9 Aug 1827
RITTER, Jesse - appraised a stray taken up by Shelton Ray.                           22 Jun 1830
ROACH, Benjamin - wants to buy 25 or 30 "likely young Negroes."                      24 Jul 1832
ROARK, William - Boeuf Twp, Franklin Co.; took up a bay horse ae 3y
                 appraised at $25 by Abraham Shobe & Thomas Roark.                   18 Nov 1828
                 John O'Bannon JP.
             - took up a deep sorrel mare ae 2y appraised at $20 by
                 Abraham Shobe & John Breeding.  O'Bannon JP.                         17 Nov 1829
ROBBINS, Elizabeth & Mary - teachers at Lawrence's Seminary for young ladies.        29 Mar 1831
         S. H. - offers $30 reward for a stolen dapple-gray horse.                   19 Apr 1831
ROBERSON, Abiel - appraised a stray taken up by Enoch Emerson.                        8 Mar 1827
ROBERT, Paul - took up a bright bay horse ae 5y appraised at $20 by Zeno
                 Mackay & Jonah Parke.  Thos. Sappington JP.                          8 Mar 1827
ROBERTS, Isaac - appraised a stray taken up by Samuel Moore.                          9 Sep 1828
             - offers $10 reward for a gray mare strayed or stolen, St. L.            2 Mar 1830
         Michael - appraised a stray taken up by James Boyer.                        17 May 1831
ROBERTSON, George - offers "choice groceries" in G. Paul's former coffee house.       9 Jun 1829
ROBIDOUX, Francis - bankrupt, St. Louis.                                              7 Jul 1829
ROBINSON, Alonzo - appraised a stray taken up by Lewellen Turnbo.                    10 Apr 1832
         Daniel - appraised a stray taken up by Cole Diggs.                          17 Jan 1832
             - postmaster at Loutre Lick, Montgomery Co., announces
                 that the name has been changed to Middletown.                        4 Sep 1832
         James - Franklin Co.; took up a brown horse ae 3y appraised at
                 $25 by A. Chambers & A. Hanson.                                      9 Sep 1828
             - "of Manchester;" advertises a tanning establishment for
                 rent, including "never failing springs."                            14 Aug 1832
         John - appraised a stray taken up by Felix Brown.                           15 Sep 1829
         Martin - dissolves partnership with Jared W. Folger.                        21 Aug 1832
         Thomas H. - appraised a stray taken up by Henry McCullough.                 15 Mar 1831
         W. G. - St. Ferdinand Twp, St. Louis Co.; JP, stray taken up by
                                                           Robert Quarles Jr.        22 Jan 1823
         Westly - appraised a stray taken up by Thomas Slavens.                      13 Mar 1832
ROBIRDS, Hardin - sues John Clark for $550, St. Louis.                               30 Aug 1831
ROBNETT, Zephaniah - Liberty Twp, Marion Co.; took up a brown horse ae 15y
                 appraised at $15 by Squire Burton & Gabriel Rush.                   23 Sep 1828
                 D. Hendricks JP.
ROBUST, Henry - Bowles Twp, Franklin Co.; took up a yellow sorrel horse
                 ae 13y appraised at $15 by Martin Alexander & Henry                 26 Jun 1832
                 Johns.  Russell Twetty JP.
ROGERS, C. H. & Co. - Main St., St. Louis, offers "a splendid new
                 assortment of clothing from New York."                               3 May 1831
         Jesse H. - dissolves partnership with Isaac Dyer.                           23 Mar 1830
         L. - Cuivre Twp, Pike Co.; JP, stray taken up by Sam'l McMillan.             6 Sep 1831
ROLAND, Archibald - appraised a stray taken up by John Dean.                         18 Aug 1829
ROLETTE, H. - offers "excellent claret wine," St. Louis.                             20 Jun 1825
ROSS, Daniel C. - with James Brown, defendant in a suit by Washington West,
                                                                 St. Louis.          10 Dec 1823
ROSSINS, J. N. - offers "patent invalid bedsteads," St. Louis.                        4 Oct 1831
ROSZEL, S. W. - a doctor, "formerly of Baltimore," #52 Main St., St. Louis.
ROUSE, Charles B. - an attorney at New London; shot fatally on the porch of
                 Green V. Caldwell, innkeeper. Samuel Hurls (Earls) was              29 Dec 1829
                 the principal suspect; Richard Matson, Alexander
                 Boarman, Thomas Purdom, believed accessories.
ROYEN, James - appraised a stray taken up by James Owens.                            22 Dec 1829
RUDDOR, Jacob - bankrupt, St. Louis.                                                 16 Feb 1830
RUGGIE, Luman - Belleview Twp, Washington Co.; took up a bay horse ae 8-9y
                 appraised at $27 by Ayres Hudspeth & David Black. Ficklin JP.       11 Jul 1825

                 MOR        101

RUGGLES, Martin - offers $25 reward for a runaway slave, Peter, at Potosi.    6 Jul 1826
RULE, Samuel - appraised a stray taken up by Charles Philips.                21 Feb 1832
RUNDLETT, John S. - advertises a new store, 2nd door south of Simmons
               Auction House, St. Louis.  Dry goods.                        14 Apr 1829
            - as a result of an action by Rundlett against Lewis &
               Henry Morse, the sheriff sold 24 pigs of iron                 11 May 1830
               seized from them.
RUSH, Gabriel - appraised a stray taken up by Zephaniah Robnett.            23 Sep 1828
             - Mason Twp, Marion Co.; took up a sorrel horse ae 3y
               appraised at $20 by Samuel Conway & William Melton.          16 Feb 1830
RUSHVILLE, Henry - bankrupt, St. Louis.                                     21 Feb 1832
RUSSELL, Henry A. H. - appraised a stray taken up by George Allen.          29 Jun 1830
         James - advertises for a runaway mulatto, Thomas O'Bannon.          9 Sep 1828
         Michael - a runaway; his guardian John Putnam offers 6¢ reward.    18 Nov 1828
               He was 15.
St. CLAIR, Jonathan - appraised a stray taken up by John Brackenridge.      11 May 1830
              -      "      by Thomas Harbison.                             15 Nov 1831
St. CLEAR, Jonathan - Bonhomme Twp, St. Louis Co.; took up a brown mare
               ae 10y appraised at $30 by Wm. Hanna & John L.                9 Mar 1826
               Mason.  Thomas Mason JP.
St. CYR, Hyacinthe - bankrupt, St. Louis.                                   25 Oct 1824
St. LEGER, Doctor - opens a French academy, will also practice medicine;
               "30 years experience."  St. Louis.                           26 Oct 1830
SALING, Richmond - appraised a stray taken up by Elliott Burton.            12 Aug 1828
SALMON, John - dissolves partnership with W. A. Beard.                      18 Nov 1828
SAMUEL, John - appraised a stray taken up by Laken Walker.                  18 Dec 1832
SAPP, James - Calumet Twp, Pike Co.; took up a bright bay horse ae 11y
               appraised at $20 by Thomas L. Hurred & Allen McCreery.       29 Jun 1830
                               C. C. Easton JP.
SAPPINGTON, Hartly - Bonhomme Twp, St. Louis Co.; JP, strays taken up by
               Benj. Ellenwood (27 Apr 1830), Andrew Kinkead -              16 Nov 1830
               Walter H. Dorsett (19 Jul 1831) & Ennis Vaughn.              26 Jun 1832
            - appraised a stray taken up by Isaiah Todd.                    19 Feb 1828
         James - appraised a stray taken up by Jordon McCormick.             2 Nov 1826
         James & Zephaniah - appraised a stray taken up by Rich'd Duval.    29 Mar 1831
         Mark - appraised strays taken up by Thomas Harrison (14 Dec 1826),
               Samuel McCormick (19 Jul 1827) and Richard Murrel.           27 Jul 1830
         Richard - appraised a stray taken up by Leaden Posey.              22 Nov 1831
         Thomas  - JP, strays taken up by Wilson Fine (19 Feb 1823),
               Joseph Wright, Bonhomme Twp, 8 Aug 1825; also in
               Bonhomme, Jordon McCormick, 2 Nov 1826; in St. Louis
               Twp, by Richard Murrel (27 Jul 1830) & Leaden Posey.         22 Nov 1831
SAUNDERS, Christopher - advertises a new store on Main St., St. Louis.      20 Jul 1830
               - lost a bag of coffee, at the landing, from
                                the Carrollton.                             26 Jul 1831
SCHLOTTER, William - sued for $1300, trespass, by Theodore Hunt.            16 Jul 1823
SCHULTZE, Diedrick - appraised a stray taken up by Wm. Keatley.              9 Mar 1826
SCHWIMMER, Nancy vs John, divorce, desertion, Pike Co. Circuit Ct.          9 Nov 1826
SCOTT, George W. - St. Charles; James Kirker's land sold to pay a debt
                                to Scott.                                    7 Mar 1832
               - see above; the suit for $1000 was in the St. Louis Court.  26 Apr 1831

         James - his wife Meeky has left his bed and board.                 15 Mar 1831
         Moses - St. Louis Co.; JP, stray taken up by Coonrod Cashman.      12 Feb 1823
SCROGINS, Henry - appraised a stray taken up by Thomas Keathley.            12 Jan 1830
SEGUIN, Pierre - defendant in a damage suit by Gavin Ralston, St. Louis.     3 Feb 1829
SEIF, Fontaine - appraised a stray taken up by Joseph Racine.               30 Aug 1823
SEIRS, John - obtained a grocer's license, St. Louis.                       29 May 1832
SERVARY, J. - with P. Walsh, opens an Academy on Main St., St. Louis.       18 May 1826
SEVERSON, Beloney - obtained a grocer's license, St. Louis.                 29 May 1832
SHACKFORD, Willis G. - Montgomery Co.; JP, stray taken up by Cole Diggs.    17 Jan 1832
SHANNON, Alexander - appraised a stray taken up by Sidney George.           29 Nov 1831
         John - warns the public not to accept a note he gave James B.
               Lanham, "paid and illegally withheld from me."               30 Nov 1830
SHARP, Benjamin - Charrette Twp, Montgomery Co.; took up a mare and horse
               appraised at $43.91 by Francis Bivens & David Howard.        24 May 1827
                               James Hughes JP.
            MOR
                                       102

SHARP, Jacob L. - appraised a stray taken up by Reuben Pew.                           28 Jun 1831
SHATTUCK, Hiram - appraised a stray taken up by Chukesberry Redmound.                 17 Mar 1829
SHELTON, Austin - Bonhomme Twp, St. Louis Co.; took up a dark bay mare
            ae 10y appraised at $30 by John Calvert & Neal                            27 Jul 1830
            McGinniss. Henry Smith JP.
SHEPHERD, David - advertises for a strayed or stolen large sorrel horse               17 Jan 1828
    SHEPPERD        and a roan mare; he lives near the courthouse, St. Louis.
                - agent for Michael Tranor while Tranor is absent.                    28 Apr 1829
SHERRILL, John - Pendleton Twp, St. Francois Co.; JP, stray taken up by                3 Aug 1830
                    James Holbert.
SHOBE, Abraham - appraised strays taken up by William Roark, first -                  18 Nov 1828
            later 17 Nov 1829; and one by Solomon Alkire.                             27 Dec 1831
    Archibald - Femme Osage Twp, St. Charles Co.; JP, stray taken up by               31 May 1827
                    James Brumfield.
SHORES, Thomas - Liberty Twp, Washington Co.; took up a claybank colt ae 2y
            appraised at $18 by John A. Johnson & Willing Renick.                     14 Apr 1829
                    Josiah Johnson JP.
SHORT, Eli - appraised a stray taken up by George Fisher.                              9 Apr 1823
          - " by James Caldwell.                                                       6 Aug 1823
    Samuel - Merrimac Twp, St. Louis Co.; JP, stray taken up by                        9 Apr 1823
                    George Fisher.
           - Calvy Twp, Franklin Co.; JP, strays taken up by James
            Caldwell ( 6 Aug 1823) and Samuel Whitworth.                              23 Feb 1826
SHRUM, John - Union Twp, Lincoln Co.; took up a bay horse ae 3y appraised
            at $22.50 and a sorrel colt ae 1y, $15, by Samuel Gibson &                31 Aug 1826
            W. B. Sitton. Philip Sitton JP.
SHUMATE, W. D. - advertises a boarding school at Manchester, tuition                   5 July 1831
            $60 per quarter.
SHURLDS, Henry - Washington Co.; JP, strays taken up by John Huff -                    5 Nov 1823
            and by Jeremiah Blackwell.                                                 6 Jul 1826
SIDDON, J. H. - appraised a stray taken up by James Walton.                           22 Feb 1827
SILVEY, James - appraised a stray taken up by Fleming Miller.                          3 May 1826
            - Femme Osage Twp, St. Charles Co.; took up a sorrel mare
            appraised at $60 by John W. Dodson & James B. Brumfield.                  25 Sep 1832
                    Thomas Hopkins JP.
SIMMONS, H. C. - partner of J. S. Lane, auction and commission house.                  7 Dec 1830
    Nancy S. - daughter of Samuel (late Hibler) sues Wm. M. Simmons                    8 Dec 1829
            for divorce, St. Louis.
SIMPSON, Martin - sues Wm. P. Maddox for $300.                                        24 Apr 1832
            - signs over his goods for the benefit of his creditors.                   4 Sep 1832
    R. - Sheriff of St. Louis Co., offers a reward for the capture                    26 Oct 1826
            of three who broke jail.
    Samuel - sues Perrine Barker for $100, Pike Co.                                   21 Feb 1832
SIMS, Bartlett - former owner of a runaway Negro now belonging to                      7 Jun 1827
            J. M. White of Mine Shibboleth.
    William S. - appraised a stray taken up by William Mills.                          2 Dec 1828
SINCLAIR, E. B. - appraised a stray taken up by James Keeney.                         15 Feb 1831
    Robert - Marion Co., "mouth of the Wyaconda;" JP, stray taken up                  19 Jul 1831
            by John S. Marlow.
SINGLETON, Moses - with Thomas Phillips, defendant in a suit for $324.11               2 Oct 1832
            by John Mosely.
SIP, George - appraised strays taken up by Joseph Longwith (23 Feb 1826),
    Jabez Ferris (23 Nov 1826), Wm. Fletcher (17 May 1827), Jacob
            Wickerham (10 Mar 1829) and another by Ferris.                            18 Jan 1831
SITTON, J. L. - appraised a stray taken up by David Diggs.                            15 Feb 1827
    Joseph - appraised a stray taken up by Martin McCoy.                               2 Sep 1828
    Joseph W. - Union Twp, Lincoln Co.; took up a bay horse ae 8-9y
            appraised at $20.50 by Thomas Hudson & Jesse Cox.                         13 Jul 1826
                    Philip Sitton JP.
    Lawrence - Union Twp, Lincoln Co.; JP, stray taken up by                          20 Jan 1829
                    David Markle.
    Philip - see Joseph W. Sitton.
    W. B. - appraised a stray taken up by John Shrum.                                 31 Aug 1826
    William - Union Twp, Lincoln Co.; took up a chestnut sorrel mare
            ae 10-11y with a yearling colt, appraised at $37.50 by                    20 Aug 1823
            Ezekiel Downing & Samuel Lewis. Daniel Draper JP.

```
SKINNER, Alfred - will pay cash for clean cotton and linen rags, also will      22 Jan 1823
                     wants to buy ox horns.
                   - closes the business of Alfred & William Skinner.            1 Nov 1827
        Curtis - dissolves partnership with Silas Drake.                        27 Oct 1829
               - opens a new store on Market St., St. Louis.                    17 Nov 1829
               - sues Isaac G. Gardner for $500.                                 6 Sep 1831
        Francis - Lewiston Twp, Montgomery Co.; took up a sorrel mare
                     ae 13-14y appraised at $10 by Daniel & John Skinner.        24 May 1827
                                                    Hugh Skinner JP.
        Hugh - see above.
        William - dissolves partnership with William Smith.                      31 May 1827
                - partnership with Alfred Skinner dissolved.                      1 Nov 1827
        William - Elkhorn Twp, Montgomery Co.; took up a roan filly ae 2y
                     appraised at $20 by John Davis & Heath Woodland.            11 Jan 1831
                                                    Caleb Williams JP.
                - appraised a stray taken up by Mordecai Morgan.                 30 Aug 1831
                - " by Neal McCan.                                               11 Dec 1832
SLATER, John - St. Charles Twp, St. Charles Co.; JP, stray taken up by            2 Apr 1823
                                                    Sylvester Baradan.
        William - appraised a flatboat taken up by Joseph Haney.                 28 Apr 1829
SLAVENS, Thomas - Clark Twp, Lincoln Co.; took up a light sorrel filly
                     ae 2y appraised at $15 by Westly Robinson & Allen           13 Mar 1832
                     Jamison.  Silas M. Davis JP.
SLEDD, Barksdale - St. Louis Co.; took up a sorrel horse ae 14y appraised        15 Feb 1831
                     at $20 by Fleming Hensley & John Osbern. Garnier JP.
SLOAN, Robert - sues David Pierce, mortgage foreclosure, Washington Co.           5 Aug 1828
SMELSER, Peter - Portage des Sioux Twp, St. Charles Co.; took up a brown
                     mule ae 12y appraised at $10 by Edward Cheneli, John        24 Jan 1828
                     Bienvenu, & Napoleon Lesier.  Wm. Christy Jr. JP.
SMELTZER, John - Portage des Sioux Twp, St. Charles Co.; took up a bay
                     mare ae 12y appraised at $17 by John Davis & John Parmer.   16 Oct 1832
                                                    Francis Lasieur JP.
SMILEY, Samuel - Union Twp, Lincoln Co.; JP, stray taken up by Roger Pollard.    14 Dec 1830
SMITH, Alexander - Bonhomme Twp, St. Louis Co.; took up a bay mare ae 10y
                     appraised at ($30?) and a bright bay horse, $14,            27 May 1828
                     by James Kennedy & Wm. Cole.  H. Lanham JP.
                - appraised a stray taken up by John M. Collins.                 15 Mar 1831
                - " by Abner Blize.                                              12 Jun 1832
        Chauncey - Joachim Twp, Jefferson Co.; JP, stray taken up by             29 Mar 1827
                                                    Joshua Herrington.
                - " by Samuel Moore (9 Sep 1828), Anthony Thomas -               24 Aug 1830
                     and Alden Hammond.                                          30 Aug 1831
        Darling - appraised a stray taken up by Eli Clay.                         2 Mar 1830
        Edward F. - will continue business as barber and hairdresser at the
                     shop adjoining Hugh Richards' tobacco manufactory,          27 Jul 1826
                     St. Louis; will also repair curls for ladies " in the
                     neatest style." Also sells wigs and curls.
        Elijah - bankrupt, Marion Co.                                             7 Dec 1830
        Henry - Bonhomme Twp, St. Louis Co.; JP, strays taken up by
                     Alexander Kinkead (20 Oct 1829), Austin Shelton (27 Jul 1830),
                     Joseph Snell (14 Jun 1831) and Justus Post.                 29 May 1832
        Henry - moved from Clarksville to Bowling Green, opens a House of        15 Feb 1831
                     Entertainment (building form/occupied by W. Crow).
        Hiram - Bonhomme Twp, St. Louis Co.; took up a sorrel mare ae 12y
                     appraised at $30 by James Price & Granville Farris.         29 Dec 1829
                                                    Henry McCullough JP.
        J. J. - believed to have stolen a mare, saddle and bridle from            2 Aug 1827
                     Jefferson Barracks; notice by N. Ranney.
        James - (Joachim Twp?); took up a bay horse ae 9-10y appraised at        16 May 1825
                     $50 by J. Boring & Thomas Ogle.  G. Hammond JP.
                - appraised a stray taken up by James Wheeling.                  30 Jan 1828
                - Prairie Twp, Montgomery Co.; took up a dark bay mare ae 7y
                     appraised at $25 by Thomas T. Elton & Isaac Gray.           17 Jun 1828
                                                    John H. Dutton JP.
                - appraised a stray taken up by John Bently.                      2 Mar 1830
        James G. - appraised a stray taken up by Hugh Logan.                      5 Apr 1831
                - " by Anthony Horton.                                           15 Feb 1831

        MCR                          104
```

SMITH, James & William - appraised a stray taken up by Wesley Hunt.                27 Nov 1832
        Jeremiah - appraised a stray taken up by John Hardesty.                     5 Jan 1830
              -  "  by George King.                                                27 Dec 1830
        John - Femme Osage Twp, St. Charles Co.; JP, stray taken up by
                    George Chapman.                                                15 Jun 1826
             - Dardenne Twp, St. Charles Co.; JP, stray taken up by
                    John Naylor.                                                   19 Jan 1830
        Michael - appraised a stray taken up by Henry McCullough.                  15 Mar 1831
        Samuel - appraised a stray taken up by William Watt.                       31 May 1831
        Scudder - St. John's Twp, Franklin Co.; took up a bay horse ae 6y
                    appraised at $18 by Joshua Brock & Thomas Burros.              23 Jun 1829
                    John Callwell JP.
               - Charrette Twp, Montgomery Co.; took up a fleabitten gray
                    horse ae 11-12y appraised at $18 by James Bland &              9 Oct 1832
                    Andrew Howard.  Jared Erwin JP.
        William - dissolved partnership with Wm. Skinner, St. Louis.               31 May 1827
        William C. - appraised a stray taken up by John Huff.                       5 Nov 1823
        Zimri - appraised a stray taken up by Thomas Maupin.                       25 Jan 1831
        William W. - "near Potosi;" took up a dark bay mare ae 3y appraised
                    at $22.50 by Robert W. Boggs & John A. Strickland.             24 Jan 1832
                    U. J. Devore JP.
SMITH G., John - reopens his store in St. Louis, opposite the Market.               5 Jan 1831
SMITHERS, George - Harmony Twp, Washington Co.; took up a bay horse ae 10y
                    appraised at $50 by William Hudspeth & David                   23 Feb 1826
                    Fulbright.  A. W. Hudspeth JP.
SNELL, Joseph - Bonhomme Twp, St. Louis Co.; took up a sorrel horse ae 5y
                    appraised at $20 by W. E. Alley & Lawrence Carder.             14 Jun 1831
                    Henry Smith JP
             - appraised a stray taken up by John Miller.                          1 Mar 1831
SNIDER, Henry H. - Belleview Twp, Washington Co.; took up a black horse
                    ae 6y appraised at $60 by Benjamin Imboden & Joseph            29 Aug 1825
                    Rayburn.  Thomas Ficklin JP.
SNOW, Henry H. - opens a School of Music at the Baptist Church, St. Louis.         15 Jan 1823
SOLLAR, Reuben - Bonhomme Twp, St. Louis Co.; took up a sorrel mare ae 3y
                    appraised at $25 by John Hamilton & James Price.               29 Nov 1831
                    McCullough, JP.
SOYE, Patrick - broke jail in St. Louis; age 35, under sentence for
                    manslaughter. R. Simpson, Sheriff, offers $200 reward.         26 Oct 1826
SPALDING, Agnes P. - Secretary of the Female Charitable Society, offers
                    for sale 25 yards of rag carpeting manufactured "by             7 Nov 1824
                    the poor" at Mme. Landreville's.
        Joseph - St. Charles Twp, St. Charles Co.; took up a sorrel mare
                    ae 6y appraised at $20 by Osbern Knott & Pierce                 8 Feb 1827
                    Atchison.  Ruloff Peck JP.
        Thomas - St. Charles Twp, St. Charles Co.; took up a strawberry
                    roan ae 2y appraised at $15 by Wallace Kirkpatrick &            2 Nov 1830
                    Roland Aubrey.  Robert G. Foster JP.
        Thomas & William - appraised a stray taken up by Moses Butcher.            28 Jul 1829
SPARKS, Abel - appraised a stray taken up by Palmer Breckenridge.                  13 Sep 1827
        Harris - Calumet Twp, Pike Co., "near Ramsey's Creek Meeting House;"
                    took up a brown bay mare ae 8y appraised at $40 by             17 Jun 1828
                    John J. Grimes & Wm. Bowles.  C. C. Eastin JP.
SPEARS, James - Fabius Twp, Marion Co.; JP, stray taken up by Sidney George. 29 Nov 1831
SPEED, Joseph M. - appraised a stray taken up by Silas Huskey.                      6 Apr 1830
SPENCE, Henry - candidate for Coroner, St. Louis.                                  26 Jun 1832
SPENCER, George S. - appraised a stray taken up by William Burns.                  15 Dec 1829
        James P. - found a pair of gold seals, asks owner to claim.                 6 Dec 1827
        Robert - St. Charles Co.; JP, strays taken up by Wm. Burns                 15 Dec 1829
                    and by Sebastian Willot.                                       14 Feb 1832
        Thomas - appraised a stray taken up by James Martin.                       29 Mar 1831
SPIRES, Greenberry - appraised a stray taken up by Norman Pringle.                  1 Nov 1831
SPRINGER, Charles - Harmony Twp, Washington Co.; JP, stray taken up by
                    Morton Fulbright (1 Aug 1825); by John Dean "on Indian
                    Creek" (18 Aug 1829); and, in Liberty Twp, by Josiah
                    Johnson.                                                        2 Oct 1832
SPRINGGATE, William - appraised a stray taken up by James C. Curry.                 2 Jun 1829

        MOR                          105

SPRY, Enoch - Lewiston Twp, Montgomery Co.; took up a sorrel horse ae 6y
appraised at $35 by John Carver & John Davis.                    3 Nov 1829
James W. Taylor JP.
STAM, George - appraised a stray taken up by Dr. Frederick Clarke.   10 Nov 1829
STANFORD, J. R. - offers "Knapp's Paste Blacking" and superior thick calf
brogans for men and boys, St. Louis.                             5 Jun 1832
STAPLES, Samuel - appraised a stray taken up by Peter Vinyard.       27 Dec 1831
STAPP, Andrew - appraised a stray taken up by James Brumfield.       31 May 1827
Elijah - Canton Twp, Marion Co.; JP, stray taken by Giles Sullivan.  3 Aug 1830
STARK, James - Prairie Twp, Montgomery Co.; took up a chestnut sorrel
horse ae 15-16y appraised at $12 by Thomas Hopkins &            17 Mar 1829
John B. Stark.
John - appraised a stray taken up by Henry Kissinger.            3 Jan 1832
STARKW,Joel Sr. - Gasconade Co.; offers $80 reward for the return of a
runaway slave and his two sisters.                              8 Aug 1825
STARR, William - dissolves partnership with R. T. McKenney, St. Louis.  13 Apr 1830
STEDMAN, J. D. - opens the new Missouri Lottery office.              28 Sep 1830
STEEL, Greenberry D. - appraised a stray taken up by John Crow.      29 Jun 1830
STEELE, Elizabeth - sues Robert Steele,. divorce, Pike Co., by next
friend Richard Kerr.                                            28 Oct 1828
STEPHENSON, T. D. - appraised a stray taken up by John Gill.         6 Aug 1823
- Dardenne Twp, St. Charles Co.; JP, stray taken up
by Fleming Miller.                                    3 May 1827
STERMAN, Thomas - Washington Co.; took up a bay mare ae 3y appraised at
$40 by Wm. Brown & Thos. Basket.  A. W. Hudspeth JP.           31 Jul 1832
STEVENS, Elijah - Perce Twp, Boone Co.; took up a bright bay mare ae 6y
appraised at $18 by Aquilla & James Barnes.                     6 Jul 1826
Joseph - appraised a stray taken up by Betsey Parry:  Anderson JP.  22 Mar 1831
Thomas B. - advertises his watch and clock business on Main St.,
St. Louis, opposite J. Warburton's store.                      26 Oct 1826
- offers a new supply of watches, jewelry, etc.              13 Jul 1830
STEVENSON, John - offers $10 reward for a bay horse strayed or stolen,
on the Missouri R. 28m west of St. Louis.                       2 Aug 1831
John G. - with John O'Rourke, sues Wetherill & Foster, St. Louis.  11 May 1830
STEWART, A. - appraised a stray taken up by Noah Beasley.            24 May 1831
Pleasant - Joachim Twp, Jefferson Co.; took up a dark bay horse
ae 3y appraised at $20 by Antoine Bird & Wm. Gray.             14 Jul 1829
Wm. McMillen JP.
Robert - with Jonathan Angevine, proposes to publish the
Missouri Courier in Palmyra.                                   3 Apr 1832
William R. - Merrimac Twp, Franklin Co.; took up a bright-colored
horse ae 6y appraised at $47 by Wm. W. Stewart &              18 May 1830
O. L. Wheeler & Samuel Thennon.  Samuel Conn JP.
STINE, J. R. - St. Louis Twp, St. Louis Co.; JP, stray taken up by
John Richardson.                                              18 Nov 1828
Jacob R. - with Thomas J. Miller, proposes to publish the
St. Louis Times.                                              17 Feb 1829
STOKES, William L. - found a gray horse with a saddle, no bridle, on his
plantation west of St. Louis.                                 13 Aug 1823
STONE, John B. - Dardenne Twp, St. Charles Co.; JP, stray taken by John Gill. 6 Aug 1823
STOTTLE, George Frederick - information wanted. He was said to be in
Potosi but was not found there.                               24 Jun 1828
STOUT, Aquilla G. - with Jacob S. Platt & Felix Ingoldsby sues William M.
Read for $2000, St. Louis.                                     2 Oct 1832
Jacob V. D. - dissolves tailoring partnership with Thomas Williams;
Stout will continue the business.                             6 Apr 1830
M. - T. J. Rickard took over his plane manufactory, St. Louis.   24 Jan 1832
STRICKLAND, John A. - appraised a stray taken up by Wm. W. Smith.    24 Jan 1832
STRODE, William - S. W. Foreman advertises for a gelding which was stolen
from Strode's home, 3m northwest of St. Louis.               29 Apr 1828
STRONG, Louis - appraised a stray taken up by Thomas H. Kelly.       16 Dec 1828
STROTHER, French - indicted for murder, broke jail in St. Louis; he was
24, his father lived in Scott Co. R. Simpson, Sheriff        26 Oct 1826
of St. Louis Co., offers $500 reward.
STUART, Alexander - offers "six likely Negro men" and "one likely Negro
woman" for sale, St. Louis.                                   8 Jan 1823
Charles - appraised a stray taken up by Joshua Herrington.       5 Oct 1826

MOR

106

STUART, John - Harmony Twp, Washington Co.; took up a sorrel mare ae 7-8y
    appraised at $15 by Wm. Atwood & Simon Frost. Hudspeth JP.    22 Dec 1825
   Robert - Monroe Twp, Lincoln Co.; took up a bay horse ae 15-16y
    appraised at $20 by Bracket & Wm. Daniel. Jn. Lindsey JP.    24 Jan 1832
   William - appraised a stray taken up by John Prather.    23 Dec 1828
STUDLEY, Nathaniel - licensed to sell groceries, St. Louis.    29 May 1832
SUGGS, William - appraised a stray taken up by William Eades.    9 Jun 1829
SULLENS, John - Boeuff Twp, Franklin Co.; took up three mares appraised
    at $38 by Allen & Enoch Greenstreet. McDonald JP.    31 May 1827
SULLIED, William - appraised a stray taken up by Uriah Hull.    8 Jun 1830
SULLINS, John Jr. - appraised a stray taken up by James Brown Jr.    6 May 1828
   Richard - appraised a stray taken up by Joseph Sullivan.    13 May 1828
SULLIVAN, Daniel - appraised a stray taken up by John Bray.    3 Jun 1828
   - St. Ferdinand Twp, St. Louis Co.; took up a sorrel mare
    ae 11y appraised at $15 by James Sullivan & Thomas    20 Oct 1829
    Heifner. Musick JP.
   Giles - Canton Twp, Marion Co.; took up a yellow dun mare ae 4y
    appraised at $30 by Wm. Duncan & James Armstrong.    3 Aug 1830
    Elijah Stapp JP.
   Joseph - Bonhomme Twp, St. Louis Co.; took up a sorrel mare
    ae 15y appraised at $18 by Richard Sullins & Samuel    13 May 1828
    Philips. A.P. Harris JP.
SUMMERS, Richard - appraised a stray taken up by John Dean.    18 Aug 1829
   - " by Josiah Johnson.    2 Oct 1832
SUMNER, Joseph - Portage des Sioux Twp, St. Charles Co.; JP, stray
    taken up by Asa Griffith.    1 Jun 1830
SUTTON, James - runaway apprentice of Richard Millagen (Millegan).    5 Jan 1826
   Robert D. - partner of Stephen Coleman, cabinet-makers in the
    shop formerly occupied by Wm. Reed.    3 Aug 1830
   - partnership dissolved.    20 Sep 1831
   William - appraised a stray taken up by Washington Edgar.    31 Jul 1832
SWAGER, Joseph - defendant in a suit for $1848.25 by John F. Kemper.    17 May 1831
SWEENY, James - offers grapevines, current sprouts, etc., St. Louis.    7 Mar 1825
   - bankrupt.    26 Oct 1826
SWERINGEN, J. T. - obtained a merchant's license, St. Louis.    29 May 1832
SYLVESTER, Joseph - runaway apprentice of Edward Charless; 1¢ reward.    25 Oct 1824
TABOR, Catton M. - obtained a grocer's license, St. Louis.    29 May 1832
   Joseph- partner of J. & W. Finney, miscellaneous goods, in the
    stone warehouse at the steamboat landing, St. Louis.    30 Mar 1830
   - announces the opening of the Methodist Burying Ground.    27 Nov 1832
TALBOT, Christopher & William J. - appraised a stray taken up by
    John Ferguson.    19 Jul 1827
   D. I. & William J. - appraised a stray taken up by John Best.    2 Jun 1829
   H. B. - has taken the house of Jesse Harrison in St. Charles and
    will open a House of Entertainment, the Virginia Hotel.    11 Dec 1832
   Thomas - advertises "Royal Charlie" at stud at his farm near
    Loutre Island.    6 Mar 1832
TALLY, John - Peno Twp, Pike Co.; took up a bay mare ae 3y appraised at $40    17 Jun 1828
    by George Mack & Wm. Onctatt. Samuel Lewallen JP.
TANNER, James - property of Stephen Jones and James Ravenscraft sold to
    satisfy a claim by Tanner.    6 Nov 1832
TAPLEY, Thomas - appraised a stray taken up by Anthony Wilkson.    30 Jun 1829
   - Valle's Mines; notifies of the death of a stranger from
    Virginia named Thomas Davis.    6 Nov 1832
TATEM, John - dissolves partnership with the John Perry Co.    12 Aug 1828
TAYLOR, James W. - Lewiston Twp, Montgomery Co.; JP, strays taken up by
    Cornelius Howard (7 Feb 1828), Enoch Spry (3 Nov 1829)
    and Shelton Ray.    22 Jun 1830
   John - sues Joseph McMullen for $600 damages.    16 Jul 1823
   Joseph - appraised a stray taken up by Cornelius Howard.    7 Feb 1828
TERRIL, Ebner - Bonhomme Twp, St. Louis Co.; took up a sorrel filly ae 2y
    appraised at $12 by Isaac Eoff & William Triplett.    2 Mar 1830
TERRY, William - Valle's Mines; is holding the property of Thomas Davis,
    a deceased stranger from Virginia, for relatives to claim.    6 Nov 1832
TETERS, Benjamin - Dardenne Twp, St. Charles Co.; took up a bright sorrel
    mare colt appraised at $10 by William Teters &    29 Dec 1829
    Christopher Wolf. Green Hutchings JP.

MOR

THEBO, Antoine - St. Charles Twp, St. Charles Co.; took up a bay horse
        ae 5y appraised at $13.50 by William Eckert, Solomon      22 Apr 1828
        Wettler, & Nathaniel W. Mace.
THENNON, Samuel B. - appraised a stray taken up by Wm. R. Stewart.     18 May 1830
THOMAS, Anthony - Joachim Twp, Jefferson Co.; took up a sorrel horse
        ae 8y appraised at $30 by Elisha Ellis & T. Findley.      24 Aug 1830
        Chauncey Smith JP.
    Berkly - advertises an auction of slaves and horses at the house   14 Oct 1828
        of Hubert Guion.
    James S. - asks his debtors to pay.                          29 Apr 1828
    Jonathan - advertises the St. Louis Cabinet Manufactory on       23 Oct 1832
        Market St. opposite the Catholic church.
    Martin - sues Neziah Bliss, mortgage foreclosure, St. Louis.    25 Aug 1829
        - candidate for the General Assembly, "Upper Steam Mills."  24 Jul 1832
    Moses - sues Wm. Elliott for $1000.                     2 Oct 1832
THOMPSON, Burwell J. - defendant, suit by Daniel Dunklin to foreclose   7 Nov 1824
        a mortgage, Washington Co.
THORPE, William - Albert Tison states that he has never employed Thorpe  9 Feb 1824
        as his agent in managing his steam mill and will not be
        responsible for Thorpe's debts.
THOURON, Nicholas - sues Thomas Townsend for $500, St. Louis.     10 May 1831
THROCKMORTON, Francis & Catherine - defendants, $500 damage suit by  12 Oct 1830
        Scott & Rule.
THURMAN, John - appraised a stray taken up by John Prather.      23 Dec 1828
TICE, John - Charrette Twp, Montgomery Co.; took up a bay mare, no   22 Jun 1830
        appraisal shown. James Hughes JP.
TIERNAN, Nicholas - apprentice of Edward Herrington who says he has run 27 May 1828
        away and advises the public not to harbor him.
        - responds that he is 21 and no longer bound.         3 Jun 1828
TIFFIN, Clayton - sues Johnston Gardner for $550.            30 Aug 1831
TIGHE, William - sues Isaac G. Gardner for $300.            6 Sep 1831
TILFORD, Andrew - Hurricane Twp, Lincoln Co.; took up two mares appraised 1 Jun 1830
        at $55 by Francis Allen & Wm. Daniel. John Lindsey JP.
TINDALL, Benjamin - offers $10 reward for runaway Negro John; he lived  5 Oct 1830
        two miles from Manchester.
TODD, Isaiah - St. John's Twp, Franklin Co.; took up a bay mare appraised 19 Feb 1828
        at $40 by Hartly Sappington & Matthew Caldwell. A. Hart JP.
TODSON, George P. - plaintiff, mortgage foreclosure suit against David  24 Jun 1828
        and Eleanor Delauny, Pike Co.
TOPPER, David V-sues Alexander Cunningham for $600, St. Louis.    24 Apr 1832
TORODE, John & Co. - "Missouri Clothing Store," #75 Main, St. Louis.  25 Jan 1831
TOWNE, Ephraim - buys the City Hotel from George Greene.        10 Mar 1829
TOWNSEND, Thomas - offers the "latest and most fashionable spring goods" 1 Apr 1828
        next door to McKenney's Saddlery, St. Louis. Also will
        sell a pair of carding machines, will buy hides & horns.
        - assigns his property to his creditors, asks debtors to pay. 5 Jan '30
        - defendant, suit for $500 by Nicholas Thouron.     10 May 1831
TRABUE, Anderson - obtained a grocer's license, St. Louis.       29 May 1832
TRANOR, Michael - appoints David Shepherd his agent while he is away.  28 Apr 1829
TRENT, Rosanna - by next friend William Drenan sues Wm. Trent for    29 Apr 1828
        divorce, St. Louis.
TRIMBLE, John - Union Twp, Washington Co.; JP, stray taken by Andrew Casey. 27 Jul 1830
TRIPLETT, Thomas - Calumet Twp, Pike Co.; took up a sorrel mare ae 5y  29 May 1832
        appraised at $20 by Christopher Kelly & James Estes.
        James W. Martin JP.
    William - appraised a stray taken up by Ebner Terril.        2 Mar 1830
        - took up a brown horse ae 3y appraised at $20 by Edward  6 Jan 1829
        Dobyns & Wm. Hanna. Thomas Mason JP.
TROTTER, Joseph - sues Judith Trotter for divorce, Marion Co.     1 Dec 1829
TRUESDELL, William - will not be responsible for transactions made by  28 Oct 1828
        George W. Himes, of Himes & Truesdell. (Himes made
        the same statement about Truesdell, same issue.)
        - Boon Twp? Bonhomme (St. Louis Co.?) JP, stray     13 Jul 1830
        taken up by Samuel King.
TRUSTEE, TRUSTY, T. C. - appraised a stray taken by Benj. Ellenwood.  27 Apr 1830
TULLOCK, Magness - Concord Twp, Washington Co.; took up a sorrel mare ae 3y 13 Apr 1826
        appraised at $10 by A. Fleming & Christopher Crider.
        - " a chestnut sorrel mare ae 6y, $15, Christopher &   17 May 1827
        Thomas Crider. O. A. Belknap JP, both strays.

TUNIS, Richard - with George Cromwell, sues John Burroughs for $900.       4 Sep 1832
            - assigns his property to his creditors.                       6 Nov 1832
TURNBOW, Allen - Dardenne Twp, St. Charles Co.; took up a bay mare ae 9y
            appraised at $30 by John Pittmann & Allen Farnsworth.          27 Aug 1823
                    Biel Farnsworth JP.
TURNBOUGH, Lewallen - appraised a stray taken up by William Burns.         15 Dec 1829
            - St. Charles Twp, St. Charles Co.; took up a yellow
            sorrel mare ae 4y appraised at $25 by Alonzo                   10 Apr 1832
            Robinson & Lewis Gurno.  Montgomery Perry JP.
TURNHAM, Joel - opens a warehouse at Liberty Landing, Clay Co.             22 Mar 1831
TURPIN, William R. - dissolves partnership with Joel Campbell in Louisiana, 13 Apr 1830
            Pike Co.; then takes John L. Williams as partner.
TWETTY, John - Liberty Twp, Crawford Co.; took up a chestnut sorrel horse
            ae 7y appraised at $50 by William Harrison & B.H. Hinkson.     31 Jul 1832
                    W. Hinkson JP.
        Russell - appraised a stray taken up by John Withinton.            22 Mar 1831
            - Bowles Twp, Franklin Co.; JP, stray taken by Henry Robust.   26 Jun 1832
TWITTY, William - appraised a stray taken up by John Jones.                 8 Jun 1826
TYLER, Zachariah - Bonhomme Twp, St. Louis Co.; took up a sorrel horse
            ae 4y appraised at $27.50 by Walter H. Dorsett &              13 Nov 1832
            John Hempstead.  H. Sappington JP.
UNDERHILL, Henry & Co. - "adjoining Mr. McCartan's," St. Louis, offer
            wines, groceries, soap, etc.                                   31 Aug 1830
            - adds clothing and dueling pistols.                           23 Nov 1830
            - sues Wm. C. Batchelor for $300.                               4 Oct 1831
            - assigns his property to his creditors.                       18 Dec 1832
VALENTINE, Eli - Boeuff Twp, Franklin Co.; took up a chestnut roan horse
            ae 13-14y appraised at $20 by John Doyel & George R.            1 Sep 1829
            Burros.  Jesse McDonald JP.
            - took up a dark bay mare ae 8y appraised at $20 by Caleb      17 Jan 1832
            Nix & Wm. Wyatt.  Thomas Baker JP.
        Ira - "on the Burbois," Franklin Co.; took up two horses           8 Jun 1830
            appraised at $60 by H. Estes & Wm. Renick.  W.G. Owens JP.
VANBERGEN, Martin - appraised a stray taken up by James Walton.            22 Feb 1827
VANGEYTE, Seraphinus - obtained a merchant's license, St. Louis.           29 May 1832
VAN LEER, A. W. & Co. - offer 50 barrels of apples.                        27 Jan 1829
            - dissolve partnership.                                        26 Jul 1831
VAN SCHOIACKE, Robert - appraised a stray taken up by Joshua Gentry.        1 Mar 1831
VAUGHN, Ennis - Bonhomme Twp, St. Louis Co.; took up a bright bay horse
            ae 8y appraised at $30 by Ephraim Young & John M. Link.        26 Jun 1832
                    H. Sappington JP.
VEACOCK, Samuel - dissolves partnership with Wm. Morrison.                 11 Dec 1832
VEEDER, Louis L. - advertises venison hams, cheese, pork, etc., at the     14 Apr 1829
            steamboat landing, St. Louis.
            - assigns his assets to creditors, asks debtors to pay.         5 Jan 1830
VINYARD, Peter - Jefferson Co.; took up a bright bay horse ae 9y appraised
            at $22.50 by Samuel Staples & Solomon Gilman.                  27 Dec 1831
                    Samuel McMullen JP.
VOTAW, Henry - his wife Jemima has left his bed and board.                 17 Sep 1823
            - appraised a stray taken up by Robert Kelso.                  18 Oct 1831
            - Bonhomme Twp, St. Louis Co.; took up an iron gray stud
            ae 3y appraised at $30 by James Votaw & Simeon Bittick.         3 Jul 1832
                    H. McCullough JP.
        James - appraised a stray taken up by Allen Link.                  26 Jul 1831
WADDELL, James - advertises "45 cases of clothing" via the steamboat       25 Nov 1828
            William Duncan, at St. Louis.
        Samuel - offers "cheap dry goods" on Main St., St. Louis,          29 Apr 1828
            opposite the Exchange Coffee House.
WAGONER,  Alexander - Peno Twp, Pike Co.; JP, strays taken up by James      29 Mar 1831
WAGGENER          Martin & John Hosteller.
            - " stray by James Keeney.                                     15 Feb 1831
WALKER, James - offers a 6-y-old Spanish jack for sale, on a large island  25 Oct 1824
            six miles above St. Louis.
            - wins a suit against James McKnight; McK's property attached. 28 Nov 1825
        Dr. John - "medicine and surgery," St. Louis; graduate of the       2 Aug 1831
            U. of Edinburgh; located at the Beacon office.
        Laken - St. Francois Twp, St. F'cois Co.; took up a mare mule ae 1y
            appraised at $25 by John Kennedy & John Samuel.                18 Dec 1832
                    Richard Murphy JP.
        MOR

WALKER, Neil - obtained a grocer's license, St. Louis.                                29 May 1832
WALL, Thomas - appraised a stray taken up by Robert Frazer.                           22 Jun 1826
WALLACE, William - "villains afloat." He says that Willis Boon & John
        Chapman on 19 June seduced his daughter Rosellick from                        25 Jul 1825
        his protection and house, and now have her in their
        possession, violating her chastity by villainous acts
        of seduction.
WALLS, Samuel - Joel Weatherford warns the public not to accept notes he
        gave Walls, "fraudulently obtained."                                          24 Aug 1830
WALSH, Edward - with John Cathcart, takes over the Union Steam Mill.                    4 Sep 1832
        J. & E. - advertise dry goods, sugar, tea, liquor, etc., opposite
        the ferry landing, St. Louis.                                                 19 Aug 1828
        John J. - wants to hire two or three journeyman segar makers.                 19 Oct 1830
        P. - with J. Servary, opens an Academy on Main St., St. Louis.                18 May 1826
        - opens a "conveyance and scrivener's office."                                18 Jan 1831
WALTON, James - JP, stray taken up by Archibald McDonald.                             22 Jan 1823
        - St. Louis Twp, St. Louis Co.; took up a gelding ae 7y
        appraised at $25 by J. H. Siddon, Martin Vanbergen, and                       22 Feb 1827
        Alex Willard. C. B. Penrose JP.
        Jonathan - sues John McCortney for $833.06 debt, St. Louis.                    16 Jul 1823
        Joseph - offers "a likely young Negro woman, about 25" for sale.              26 Aug 1828
        - dissolves partnership with Archibald Orme.                                  16 Feb 1830
        - appraised a stray taken up by Benjamin B. Ray.                              25 Sep 1832
        William - appraised a stray taken up by Archibald McDonald.                    2 Jan 1823
WARBURTON, J. - offers a "splendid assortment of English and domestic
        dry goods," St. Louis.                                                        13 May 1828
WARFIELD, Peter - bankrupt, St. Louis.                                                13 Sep 1824
WASH, George - appraised a stray taken up by Joshua Herrington.                        5 Oct 1826
WASSON, John W. - appraised a stray taken up by James Phillips.                       19 Jun 1832
WATSON, Henry - appraised a stray taken up by Solomon King.                            8 Jun 1830
        William - St. Charles Twp, St. Charles Co.; took up a chestnut
        sorrel ae 9y appraised at $40 by John Lilly Jr. & Osborn                       8 Jun 1826
        Knott. Ruloff Peck JP.
        William M. - appraised a stray taken up by Austin Willard.                    20 Mar 1832
WATT, James - appraised a stray taken up by James Brotherton.                         30 Nov 1826
        William - Calumet Twp, Pike Co.; took up a red roan mare ae 4y
        appraised at $35 by Ervin Guy & Samuel Smith. McQueen JP.                     31 May 1831
WATTS, Henry - Waverly Twp, Lincoln Co.; JP, stray taken by Wm. Wiley.                24 Jun 1828
        William - advertises his farm of 400 arpents for sale, on Big
        Ramsey's Creek near Clarksville.                                              30 Jun 1829
WATWOOD, A. L. - partner of Hiram Bascom, clocks and watches, St. Louis.              11 Jan 1831
WEATHERFORD, Joel - warns the public not to accept notes he gave Samuel
        Walls, "fraudulently obtained."                                               24 Aug 1830
WEAVER, Elijah - St. Ferdinand Twp, St. Louis Co.; took up a bright sorrel
        horse ae 5y appraised at $45 by Bernard McMinamy & John                       17 Jul 1832
        Barney. Fergus Ferguson JP.
        Jacob - Fabius Twp, Marion Co.; took up a bright bay horse ae 6-8y
        appraised at $52 by Squire Bozorth & Jacob West. Gash JP.                      7 Jul 1829
WEBB, John P. - Harmony Twp, Washington Co.; took up a bay mare ae 6-8y
        appraised at $30 by L. Huett & Wm. Black. Hudspeth JP.                        20 Jul 1830
        Statia - appraised a stray taken up by Elijah Marden.                         21 Feb 1832
WEBSTER, Jeb - appraised a stray taken up by James Wheeling.                          30 Jan 1828
WEED, Hampton - Louisiana, Pike Co., offers reward for lost leather trunk.            18 Nov 1828
        - dissolves partnership with Edwin Draper.                                    24 May 1831
WELBORN, Chapley - appraised a stray taken up by George Westover.                     19 Jun 1832
        James - Pendleton Twp, St. Francois Co.; JP, stray taken up by
        George Westover.                                                              19 Jun 1832
        Samuel - Pendleton Twp, St. Francois Co.; took up a chestnut
        sorrel mare ae 4y appraised at $25 by Thomas Welborn                           3 Aug 1830
        and E. G. Holbert. Sherrill JP.
WELCH, H. E. - Charrette Twp, Montgomery Co.; JP, stray taken up
        by Norman Pringle.                                                             1 Nov 1831
WELLS, Joshua - appraised a stray taken up by Daniel McCugh.                          27 Apr 1830
        - Calumet Twp, Pike Co.; took up a bay mare ae 3y appraised
        at $25 by Hiram Hansford & John Johnson. Eastin JP.                           27 Dec 1831
WEST, Jacob - appraised a stray taken up by Jacob Weaver.                              7 Jul 1829
        Washington - sues Daniel C. Ross & James Brown, St. Louis.                    10 Dec 1823

                                    MOR

WESTOVER, George - Pendleton Twp, St. Francois Co.; took up a black horse
          ae 4y appraised at $40 by Joseph Brown & Chapley              19 Jun 1832
          Welborn. James Welborn JP.
WETHERILL, John - in an auction & commission business with William Miles
          Foster, St. Louis.                                             3 Mar 1829
          - dissolves partnership.                                       4 Aug 1829
          - sheriff sale of whiskey, dry goods, etc., from the
          business, action of John O'Rourke & John G. Stevenson.        11 May 1830
WETTLER, Solomon - appraised a stray taken up by Antoine Thebo.          22 Apr 1828
WHEELER, Charles - Bedford Twp, Lincoln Co.; JP, stray taken up by
                              Jacob Presley.                             15 Nov 1831
          Daniel & S.B. - appraised a stray taken up by Ann Frasier.     19 Jul 1827
          E. P. - opens a provision store, St. Louis, Main below Mo. Hotel.  20 May 1828
          John B. - appraised a stray taken up by John Freeman.           5 Jan 1830
          Macom - appraised a stray taken up by Ferry Harrison.           8 Feb 1831
          O. L. - appraised a stray taken up by Wm. R. Stewart.          18 May 1830
WHEELING, James - Concord Twp, Washington Co.; took up a black mare, a bay
          mare ae 14, a brown mare ae 2, total appraisal $80 by          30 Jan 1828
          Jeb Webster & James Smith. Belknap JP.
WHISTLER, J. - of Bellefontaine, offers $4 reward for strayed sorrel horse.  12 Apr 1827
WHITE, Clement - appraised a stray taken up by Waddy Cobbs.              16 Dec 1828
          Frederick - bankrupt, St. Louis.                              24 May 1824
          Isaac - opens a wagon yard for the accommodation of market people  9 May 1825
          and travelers, St. Louis.
          J. M. - offers $50 reward for a runaway Negro, formerly belonging to  7 Jun 1827
          Bartlet Sims, from Mine Shibboleth.
          J. W. - selling a mare, colt and other items at Chouteau's orchard.  17 Jul 1832
          James - defendant in a suit by Absalom Carlile for $250, St. Louis.   3 Jan 1832
          James M. - sold his interest in Lane, Knox & Co. to Galena Mining Co.  8 Apr 1828
          - takes James Kennett as a partner at Selma.                  10 Aug 1830
          King - appraised a stray taken up by James Owens.             22 Dec 1829
WHITESIDE, A. J. - St. Ferdinand Twp, St. Louis Co.; JP, strays taken up by
          Abner Ball (14 Jun 1831) and by John Massey.                   7 Aug 1832
          John C. - appointed guardian of Francis Whiteside, "of unsound
          mind," Montgomery Co.                                         27 Apr 1830
WHITESIDES, Thomas - JP, stray taken up by Alexander Emerson.           15 Aug 1825
          William - appraised a stray taken up by Roger B. Pollard.     14 Dec 1830
WHITING, Charles - offers $100 reward for apprehension of a thief who
          stole tools and equipment from his steam mill on the          9 May 1825
          river bank above St. Louis.
WHITLEY, Samuel - appraised a stray taken up by Benjamin Ellenwood.     19 Jul 1831
          Solomon - Amos Kibby warns the public not to accept mortgages
          for "certain Negroes," given to him by Whitley.               1 Oct 1823
WHITWORTH, Samuel - Calvy Twp, Franklin Co.; took up a brown bay horse
          ae 15y appraised at $15 by Wn. King & Thomas Boyd.            23 Feb 1826
          Samuel Short JP.
WIATT, Isaac - Bonhomme Twp, St. Louis Co.; took up a dark chestnut sorrel
          mare ae 2y appraised at $12 by Cain J. Brown & David          13 Dec 1831
          Arnspigur. H. Sappington JP.
WICKERHAM, Jacob - Bonhomme Twp, St. Louis Co.; took up a roan mare ae 7y  10 Mar 1829
          appraised at $20 by George Sip & John McDonald;Bowles JP.
WIDDLE, Elias - appraised a stray taken up by Aaron Groom.               6 Jul 1830
WIGGINS, Samuel - Chestnut St., St. Louis, offers all of his household
          goods and furniture for sale.                                 20 Jul 1830
WILBORN, Thomas - appraised a stray taken up by Eleazer Clay.            6 Mar 1832
WILBURN, James - St. Francois Co.; JP, stray taken up by Eleazer Clay.   6 Mar 1832
WILEY, William - Waverly Twp, Lincoln Co.; took up a dark bay mare ae 9y
          appraised at $45 by Gabriel Reed, Samuel Baird, and           24 Jun 1828
          Quintin Moore. Henry Watts JP.
WILKINSON, J. J. - appointed inspector of flour, beef, and pork, St. Louis.  24 Jan 1832
WILKSON, Anthony - Platin Twp, Jefferson Co.; took up a brown mare and
          colt appraised at $35 by Thomas Tapley & James H. Moutry.     30 Jun 1829
          J. W. Garraty JP.
WILLARD, Alex - appraised a stray taken up by James Walton.             22 Feb 1827
          Austin J. - St. Ferdinand Twp, St. Louis Co.; took up a mare and
          colt appraised at $28 by Wm. M. Watson & Harvey               20 Mar 1832
          Clark. Fergus Ferguson JP.

                    MOR

                    111

WILLIAMS, Caleb - Elkhorn Twp, Montgomery Co.; JP, strays taken up by Thomas
            Chambers (15 Jul 1828) and William Skinner.            11 Jan 1831
      Hezekiah - appraised strays taken up by Abraham Eaton -    19 Mar 1823
            and by Robert B. Maxwell -                30 Aug 1824
      James H. - appraised a stray taken up by Francis Withinton.  29 Jun 1830
      John L. - partner of Wm. R. Turpin, Louisiana, Mo.        13 Apr 1830
      Lewis - appraised a stray taken up by James Criswell.     23 Mar 1830
      Phinehas - appraised a stray taken up by David Logan.    15 Nov 1824
      Thomas - merchant tailor, St. Louis, 1st house s. of Mechanics Row. 8 Jul 1828
         - dissolves partnership with Jacob Stout, who continues.   6 Apr 1830
WILLOT, Sebastian - Spencer's Creek, St. Charles Co.; took up a brown mare
         ae 5y appraised at $18 by Conrad Willot and Joseph    14 Feb 1832
         Berthelot. Robert Spencer JP.
WILSON, Aquilla - appraised a stray taken up by Jeremiah Brickey.    5 Apr 1827
      Avington K. - Little Rock Creek, Joachim Twp, Jefferson Co.; took
         up a black mare ae 7y appraised at $15 by Eli         5 Jul 1831
         Cadwallader & Alexander C. Wilson. Wm. McMillin JP.
      Jacob - appraised a stray taken up by Samuel Graham.      11 Apr 1825
      John - Bonhomme Twp, St. Louis Co.; took up a bay horse ae 7-8y
         appraised at $35 by Noah & Wm. Hickman. Henry Smith JP.  27 Nov 1832
         - appraised strays by Edmund Burgess (30 Jun 1829), Sampson
         Anderson (17 Nov 1829), and Uriah Burns.          13 Jul 1830
      Sydenham - runaway apprentice of W. R. Grimsley, cabinet-maker. 5 Oct 1830
         5'2 or 3", ae 17-8, "well made." 1¢ reward.
WIN(D)SHIP, Mrs. - a high school for young ladies, St. Louis; French, etc. 23 Oct 1832
WINSCOTT, Thornton - Prairie Twp, Montgomery Co.; took up a brown mare
         ae 9y appraised at $35 by George & Isaac Gray.       27 Dec 1831
                              John H. Dutton JP.
         - appraised a stray taken up by George Gray; signed "x."  27 Dec 1831
WINSTANLEY, Joseph & Catherine his wife, and Thomas Winstanley, former 6 Mar 1832
      owners of a lot bought by Pamela Hayden, St. Louis.
WISEMAN, Jonathan - appraised a stray taken up by Thomas Fitzgerald.  31 Jan 1832
WITHERTON,  Francis - Hurricane Twp, Lincoln Co.; took up a bay mare
WITHINTON      ae 12-13y appraised at $20 by David Hubbard and   24 Mar 1829
         David Highsmith. Benjamin Allen JP.
         - took up a black horse ae 11-12y appraised at $35 by  29 Jun 1830
         James Williams & John Gibson. Brice Hammack JP.
      James & Thomas - appraise a stray taken up by Samuel Bay.    30 Mar 1830
      John - Calvy Twp, Franklin Co.; took up a dark bay mare ae 11-12
         appraised at $35 by Russell Twetty & Robert Musick.    22 Mar 1831
         Jonathan Potts JP.
WOLF, Christopher - appraised a stray taken up by Benjamin Teters.   29 Dec 1829
WOODBRIDGE, Ardelia - sues Wm. Woodbridge for divorce, Lincoln Co., by
         next friend Martial Cottle.                    30 Jun 1829
      William W. - Bedford Twp, Lincoln Co.; JP, stray taken up by
         Edward Yates.                        22 Jun 1826
WOODLAND, Heath - appraised a stray taken up by Wm. Skinner.      11 Jan 1831
WOODS, Joseph - will conduct business of R. Millegan in his absence.  29 Jun 1826
      Joseph L., Jr. - "at the old stand of his father," a tailor.   7 Dec 1830
         - partner of George W. Caton; wants apprentices.      4 Oct 1831
WOODSON, Shedriot - appraised a stray taken up by Jacob Presley.   15 Nov 1831
WOOLFOLK, John A. - Hurricane Twp, Lincoln Co.; took up a gray horse
         ae 12-13y appraised at $30 by David Diggs and      11 May 1830
         J. A. L. McQueen.
WRIGHT, Hezekiah - appraised a stray taken up by Joshua Herrington.  29 Mar 1827
      John - St. Louis Twp, St. Louis Co.; took up a bright sorrel horse
         ae 4y appraised at $47.50 by Noah Revis & Anthony Kian. 5 Jan 1830
      Joseph - River des Peres, St. Louis Co.; took up a bay horse
         ae 6y appraised at $40. T. Sappington JP.         8 Aug 1825
WYATT, Dugal - Charrette Twp, Montgomery Co.; took up a yellow sorrel mare
         ae 12y appraised at $20, a brown mare ae 7, $20, appraisers 7 Feb 1828
         not shown. James Hughes JP.
         - took up a bay horse ae 5-6y appraised at $50 by James Bryan
         and Wm. James. Aaron Young JP.             12 Aug 1828
      William - appraised a stray taken up by Eli Valentine.     17 Jan 1832
YATES, Edward - Bedford Twp, Lincoln Co.; took up a sorrel horse ae 6y
         appraised by E. Collard & Edward Cottle. Woodbridge JP. 22 Jun 1826

        MOR

YETS, Charles - appraised a stray taken up by John Hearts.                14 Apr 1829
YOKUM, Jesse and Mary - divorce petition, stage legislature.               25 Jan 1831
YOUNG, Ephraim - appraised a stray taken up by Ennis Vaughn.               26 Jun 1832
    Aaron H. - Charrette Twp, Montgomery Co.; JP, stray taken up
                   by Dugal Wyatt.                12 Aug 1828
ZEIGLAR, Matthias - bankrupt, St. Louis.                                   25 Oct 1824
ZUMWALT, John - appraised a stray taken up by Archibald Gibson.            20 Jan 1829

omitted by error:

WOOLFOLK, Dr. J. - moved his office opposite the Post Office, Main St.,
                             St. Louis.                14 Aug 1832
    - dissolved partnership with Dr. C. Campbell.                      28 Aug 1832

WORTHINGTON, Samuel - candidate for constable, Bonhomme Twp, St. Louis.    31 Jul 1832

WOLFE, Henry M. - obtained a merchant's license, St. Louis.                20 May 1832
    - do not pay his accounts; his books have been
      "fraudulently obtained" from him.                            2 Oct 1832

WISER, John - advertises lime, flagstones, building and paving stones,
    other material, at his quarry. St. Louis.                       17 Jul 1832

WILLI, Samuel - St. Louis; wants two or three journeyman tailors, also
    a 12 or 13y-old apprentice.                                     17 Oct 1825

WILLETT, Samuel - dissolves partnership with W. R. Grimsely.              10 Jun 1828
    - advertises a cabinet furniture store on Church St.
    opposite the Green Tree Tavern, St. Louis.                      17 Jun 1828

## LIST OF LETTERS

REMAINING in the Post Office at Boonville, Missouri, on the first day of Oct. 1828, which if not taken out within three months, will be sent to the General Post Office as dead letters.

**A**

Anderson Wm
Allison Hugh
Anderson william

**B**

Bodin wm
Brayton James 2
Bone Azariah Rev
Boyd Robert
Bowles Philip
Burney james 2
Bingham john
Bryant Jordan

**C**

Circuit court clerk
Crawford George
Caton John
Cooper David
Campbell Benj H
Camplee James
Coner Starling
Calvert wm
Cropper Levin
Caffey Joel
Collins David
Campbell James
Committee Jackson
    corresponding

**E**

Estes Andrew
Edwards william

**F**

French Lewis
Fisher Abraham

**G**

Glazebrook john
Guyer Henry
Glover John
Gilmore Sarah
Greenbary

**H**

Heath John G
Hayden P R
Huff Harrison
Houx John 2
Howard Joseph
Howe John H
Harvey Washington
Hawpe Rudolph

**J**

Johnston Francis 2
Johnson Jesse

**K**

Kavanough Archibald
Kelly william J
Kirkpatrick Robert
Kimzey Benjamin

**L**

Lucas Samuel D
Laughlin John
Lilly David
Lewis Jesse
Lowry william C

**M**

Meredith Absalom
McMahan S W
Moore wm H maj
McCorkle Archibald Rev
Mullins Ahab
Miller John Esq
Mr Phaill Alexander
McLean James and Andrew
McCormack Rebecca
Moreland John 3
Miller John
Miller Samuel Esq

**P**

Parks Peyton
Pitman M

**R**

Read Anthony F 2
Russell Hiram
Rudolph Abraham
Ringo Peter
Ruby Mr
Rigg Thomas

**S**

Small Henry
Smith John
Sims James
Stephens joseph
Shockley Isom
Stewart Richard
Stone Barnet w
Stinson james jr
Self job, or David Trotter

**T**

Taylor Elijah

PEYTON THOMAS. A. P. M.

12 3w

116

118

Hervin 82
Hewitt 82
Hews 44
Hibbard 83
Hibler 83
Hickam 13
Hickey 83
Hicklin 13
Hickman 13, 441 83
Hicks 13, 34, 83
Hickson 34
Hieott 34
High 83
Highsmith 83
Hilderbrand 83
Hiler 44
Hill 13, 83
Himes 83
Hines 55
Hinesly 83
Hinkson 83
Hinkston 14
Hinson 14, 83
Hitchcock 14
Hixson 14
Hobbs 55
Hodges 83
Hoffa 50, 83
Hoffman 50, 83
Hogan 55
Hogeland 83
Hogh 44
Hogue 40
Holbert 83
Holden 14, 83
Holley 34
Hollman 83
Holloway 83
Holman 14
Holmes 44
Holt 40
Holton 83
Honey 83
Hood 14, 34, 84
Hook 14, 84
Hooper 84
Hoops 40, 84
Hoozer 14
Hope 14, 44, 50
Hopkins 55, 84
Hopper 14
Hopson 14
Hording 50
Horine 50, 55, 84
Hornbuckle 40
Horner 84
Horrell 44, 84
Horton 84
Hose 84
Hosteller 84
Hough 55, 84
Houghan 84
House 50, 55, 84
Houts 44
Houx 14
Howard 14, 34, 84
Howdeshell 84
Howe 14, 34
Howell 84
Hoxsey 14
Hoyle 84

Hubbard 14, 84
Hubble 44
Huddleston 14
Hudson 55, 84
Hudspeth 84
Huett 84
Huff 84
Huffman 40
Hufstetler 44
Hugh 84
Hughes 14, 34, 44, 55, 84
Hughs 14
Hull 84
Hum 34
Hume 14, 50, 85
Humphries 14
Hungerford 34
Hunt 14, 40, 50, 55, 85
Hunter 85
Hurls 85
Hurred 85
Hurt 34
Hurter 14
Huskey 85
Hutchings 85
Hutchinson 56
Hutchison 14
Hutson 14, 44
Hutton 56, 85
Hyatt 85
Imboden 56, 85
Inglish 14, 15, 40
Ingoldsby 85
Ingram 15, 85
Inks 85
Inman 56
Inskeep 85
Irvine 85
Isaacs 15
Ish 15
Isler 85
Ivers 56, 85
Ivey 15
Jackman 34
Jackson 15, 34, 35, 44, 85
Jacobs 15
Jacoby 50
James 15, 56, 85
Jameson 15, 85
Jamieson 85
Jamison 15, 56, 85
Janneret 85
Jaques 85
Jeanneret 15
Jeffries 86
Jenkins 15, 86
Job 15
Johns 50, 86
Johnson 15, 44, 56, 86
Johnston 15, 35, 86
Joiner 44
Jones 15, 16, 35, 40, 45, 50, 56, 86
Jordan 86
Journey 50
Judson 56
Jump 86

Kasson 86
Kavanaugh 16
Keady 86
Keathley 86
Keatley 86
Keen 16, 86
Keenan 16
Keeney 86
Keeny 87
Keer 87
Keesacker 87
Keil 45
Kelly 16, 35, 45, 87
Kelsay 16
Kelso 40, 57
Kemble 35
Kemper 16, 56, 87
Kennaday 16
Kenneda 87
Kennedy 50, 87
Kennel 87
Kennerly 56
Kennett 87
Kennon 87
Kenny 16
Kent 87
Kerly 16
Kerr 16, 87
Kertley 16
Keys 45
Keyte 87
Kian 87
Kibbe 16
Kidwell 40
Kilby 50, 87
Killgore 16
Kimball 56
Kimbrel 45
Kincaid 56
Kinds 50
Kinemont 87
King 16, 45, 56, 87
Kingsley 87
Kinkead 87
Kinne 87
Kinworthy 88
Kirby 87
Kirk 16
Kirkbride 35
Kirker 88
Kirkland 88
Kirkpatrick 16, 35, 88
Kirtley 16
Kirtly 35
Kissinger 88
Kitchings 16
Kizer 88
Klunk 88
Knolton 88
Knott 88
Knox 35, 88
Kopman 88
Kruper 16, 35
Kuykendall 16
Kyle 16, 88

La Beaume 88
Lacroze 50
Lacy 45
Laduke 88
Lamasters 56